The Boys from Rockville

THE BOYS FROM ROCKVILLE

Civil War Narratives of
Sgt. Benjamin Hirst,
Company D,
14th Connecticut Volunteers

Edited, with
Commentary, by
ROBERT L. BEE

Voices of the Civil War
Frank L. Byrne,
Series Editor

The University of Tennessee Press / Knoxville

The Voices of the Civil War series makes available a variety of primary source materials that illuminate issues on the battlefield, the homefront, and the western front, as well as other aspects of this historic era. The series contextualizes the personal accounts within the framework of the latest scholarship and expands established knowledge by offering new perspectives, new materials, and new voices.

Copyright © 1998 by The University of Tennessee Press / Knoxville.
All Rights Reserved. Manufactured in the United States of America.
First Edition.

A portion of this book was previously published as "Fredericksburg on the Other Leg" in *The Third Day at Gettysburg and Beyond,* edited by Gary Gallagher (Chapel Hill: University of North Carolina Press, 1994). It is used here with the permission of the University of North Carolina Press.

Frontispiece: Sgt. Benjamin Hirst. Photo probably taken at Falmouth, Virginia, on 13 March 1863. Charles D. Page, *History of the Fourteenth Regiment, Connecticut Vol. Infantry.* Meriden, Conn.: Horton, 1906, p. 193.

Figures 1 and 2 were previously published in *The Third Day at Gettysburg and Beyond,* edited by Gary Gallagher (Chapel Hill: University of North Carolina Press, 1994).

The paper in this book meets the minimum requirements of the American National Standard for Permanence of Paper for Printed Library Materials.
⊗ The binding materials have been chosen for strength and durability.
♻ Printed on recycled paper.

Library of Congress Cataloging-in-Publication Data

Hirst, Benjamin, 1828–1909.
The boys from Rockville : Civil War narratives of Sgt. Benjamin Hirst, Company D, 14th Connecticut Volunteers / edited, with commentary, by Robert L. Bee.—1st ed.
   p. cm.—(Voices of the Civil War)
Includes bibliographical references and index.
ISBN 1-57233-005-8 (cloth: alk. paper)
1. Hirst, Benjamin, 1828–1909—Correspondence. 2. United States. Army. Connecticut Infantry Regiment, 14th (1862-1865) 3. Connecticut—History—Civil War, 1861–1865—Personal narratives. 4. Soldiers—Connecticut—Correspondence. 5. United States—History—Civil War, 1861–1865—Personal narratives. 6. Connecticut—History—Civil War, 1861–1865—Regimental histories. 7. United States—History—Civil War, 1861–1865—Regimental histories.
I. Bee, Robert L. II. Title. III. Series: Voices of the Civil War series.
E499.5 14TH.H57 1998
973.7'446'092—dc21
[B]   97-33769

Contents

Illustrations

Figures

Maps

Foreword

~~~~~~~~~~

Benjamin Hirst, the writer of this series of letters, came from an immigrant family of English factory workers. After living in Pennsylvania, he settled in Connecticut where he worked in a mill. When the Civil War came, he joined the 14th Connecticut. His letters tell much about the history of a unit that became one of the Nutmeg State's outstanding fighting regiments. Thus, he was able to supply important information about Antietam, Fredericksburg, Chancellorsville, Gettysburg, and other battles of the Army of the Potomac in 1862–63. He also wrote well enough to furnish interesting accounts of camp life and marches. Moreover, he revealed much about his relationship with his wife, with whom he exchanged these letters and who visited him at camp in the field—unusual for an enlisted man's spouse.

This careful edition of Hirst's letters draws upon the works of the best contemporary Civil War historians to fit Hirst into the pattern of the nineteenth-century warrior. Editor Robert L. Bee also uses his subject's postwar writings to compare wartime views with those of the veteran. As an anthropologist, Bee is well qualified to show how the industrial discipline of the factory had at least partially prepared Hirst and the other "boys from Rockville" for the controlled life of the army. Hirst's voice of the Civil War is different from those of the rural men who made up the bulk of both armies. Bee also brings out the effects of Hirst's attitude on manliness and on marital relationships. He furthermore demonstrates Hirst's ties to his community and his views on several ethnic groups.

In addition to readers interested in military history, those who wish to study American society and to simply read letters of fine literary quality should enjoy these by this Connecticut Yankee.

Frank L. Byrne
Kent State University

Acknowledgments

I owe a special debt of gratitude to the members of the Alden Skinner Camp #45, Sons of Union Veterans of the Civil War, for granting me unlimited access to the originals of the Hirsts's letters in their remarkable collection of Civil War materials. Several years later, Nan Woodruff and Irene Silverblatt suggested to Gary Gallagher that my work may be of interest for part of a Pennsylvania State University summer workshop on the third day's battle of Gettysburg. That opportunity, and Gary's continuing support of my efforts, have been most deeply appreciated. My original manual typescript transcriptions were meticulously retyped on computer disk by Debbie Crary of the University of Connecticut Research Foundation. I am grateful to her and to her husband, Ken, for their efforts and friendship. The University of Connecticut Research Foundation also provided research funding for phases of this work. Reid Mitchell read and commented extensively on a ponderous early draft. Ardis Abbott, a doctoral candidate in history at the University of Connecticut and an avid student of Rockville's history, endured my many telephone calls and graciously provided me with important data. Guy Minor located the Hirst narratives in the *Rockville Journal*. William Keegan worked patiently and knowledgeably at producing the maps. I appreciate the continuing support of Jennifer Siler and the efforts of Stan Ivester of the University of Tennessee Press as well as the sensitive copyediting of Monica Phillips.

Others have made substantial contributions to my work. These include, alphabetically, the following: William O. Adams Jr.; Robert B. Angelovich and members of the Torrington, Connecticut, Civil War Round Table; Randy Bieler; Richard Brown of the history department, University of Connecticut; Allen Brownlee; Frank Byrne of the history department, Kent State University; Arthur F. Carter; Gerry Caughman; Frederick W. Chesson; Ross S. Dent of the Civil War/GAR Museum in Rockville, Connecticut; Charles C. Fennell Jr., an accomplished scholar and battlefield guide in Gettysburg; Edith Hoelle of the Gloucester County Historical Society (New Jersey); Bradford Keune, Alden Skinner camp historian and regional commander, Sons of Union Veterans; Myrtle Loftus of the Vernon Historical Society (Connecticut); David Matos; John W. Richardson; Thomas Riemer;

Florence Sankowicz of the Delaware County Historical Society (Pennsylvania); Bruce A. Trinque; Peter Wadsworth of the John Rylands University Library, University of Manchester, England; and David A. Ward of the Edsel Ford Memorial Library, The Hotchkiss School.

The shortcomings are entirely mine.

Introduction

The 14th Regiment of Connecticut Volunteer Infantry was created less than a month before the battle of Antietam. Its men fought there as part of the 2d Corps, Army of the Potomac. For the next thirty-one months they fought in every one of that army's other battles: Fredericksburg, Chancellorsville, Gettysburg, the Wilderness, Spotsylvania, Cold Harbor, and the Petersburg Campaign. And, they fought and died in the less well-known tragedy at Morton's Ford. They captured more enemy flags and suffered a higher combined total of combat casualties than any other Connecticut regiment in the war.

Sgt. Benjamin Hirst of the 14th Connecticut Volunteers fought along with them until mid-afternoon on 3 July 1863. He hoped to preserve and publish his wartime letters together with those of his brother John. As they stand in the original, Hirst's narratives constitute an effort to organize and communicate his versions of reality.[1]

This feature of the letters attracts anthropological attention. They offer clues to Hirst's world view, which was certainly shared to some extent with the other volunteers first mustered into Company D—they being mostly from the same small town. I'm interested in trying to characterize that world view.

And, because Ben was mightily interested in managing his home life as well as his military duties, the letters give us glimpses of the working-class culture of mid-nineteenth-century textile mill workers. When writing home to his wife, Sarah, he was bent on portraying one culture while trying to maintain an active participation in the other. He was a sergeant as well as a husband and fellow worker.

He served at times as a mediator between the company and the community, passing along bits of information about others and expressing the hopes and plans of a good number of men to an audience who knew most of them. Thus the truly heroic exploits of Frank Stoughton, Ben's shifty friendship with George Brigham, the reaction of Albert Towne's father to his son's death at Fredericksburg, and the Big Box Concern all had meaning for the cultures of both Rockville and Company D.[2]

Ben becomes the equivalent of the ethnographer's key informant in living cultures, with one important difference. I cannot ask him whether I've got it right. More crucially, I cannot be a participant-observer of life in Company D.

I am concerned with how Ben himself perceived and characterized what happened. I am interested in why he portrayed events, behavior, people and needs as he did. What did he emphasize? What did he ignore? What categories did he create? What was the structure of his and others' social behavior as he described it? The answers to these questions lie in his system of knowledge, beliefs, morals, values, and symbols that formed the basis of his constructions of reality.[3] But, by circular process, these answers must be sought by inference from the written constructions themselves.

Civil War soldiers' world views were of course not generally those of professional military men. Their widespread tendency to question authority, for example, has since been traced to prevailing civilian values of personal autonomy in mid-nineteenth-century American society or to specific civilian occupations such as farming.[4] But the precise nature of such linkage is not often explored: What *was* it about his particular prewar occupation that helped generate the soldier's behavior and beliefs?

Surely there would have been 110 different portrayals of the culture of Company D—one for each man mustered into its ranks in August of 1862. Each would have been shaped by its author's personality and life experience. The question of how "representative" or "typical" were Hirst's portrayals cannot be satisfactorily answered.[5] There is a lingering question of the extent to which Ben's childhood in England intruded into his constructions. Furthermore, historians insist that laborers in nineteenth-century American textile mills were different, not only from those in England but from each other. Yet for all the potential diversity, I believe it is possible to discern a generalized prewar ideal of "the respectable laborer." And I believe it is possible to trace the impact of this ideal on Ben's narratives.

This is certainly not to declare that Ben's prewar labor tells us all we need to know about his wartime expressions of, say, courage or patriotism. Surely he shared traits and perceptions with most Civil War soldiers, regardless of their prewar lives. Some of the similarity was due to a convergence of diversity; some of it was due to a prevailing "national" sense of manliness and right. Much of it was due to the shared experience of mass regimentation and mortal combat. My aim is not to suggest that Ben was somehow different from other common soldiers. It is rather to try to put his convictions and actions into a set of specific contexts in an effort to understand why he wrote what he wrote.

To ensure that my interpretation is not purely subjective, I offer a kind of triangulation of his accounts to better situate them and the events they describe. One vector of the triangulation is composed of published sources written by soldiers in Ben's regiment. One, *Mr. Dunn Browne's Experiences in the Army,* is a moving and articulate series of essays written just after—and sometimes even during—each of the events and battles described up to May 1864. The author, Samuel Fiske, was a captain in another company of the 14th Connecticut Volunteers. He was two months younger than Ben and also from a laboring class background; but, he worked his way through Amherst to become a minister and essayist on his world travels before the war. Ben and others in Company D read Fiske's essays, which originally appeared in installments in the Springfield, Massachusetts, *Republican* during the war.[6] Another source in this vector is the regimental history, including many recollections and excerpts from letters of men in Company D and other companies of the 14th.[7] Unlike the Hirst letters and Fiske's dispatches, the regimental history was written almost forty years after the war—more than ample time for some reconsideration and revision of the various realities of 1862–65.

A second vector is the literature on the culture of antebellum textile factory workers. Here I have sought features that fit—or undermine—the ideal of the respectable laborer, although this is necessarily a composite sketch rather than a fully developed controlled comparison of these sources.

The third vector of the triangulation is the voluminous literature on the common soldier in the Civil War. There are the published original sources such as Billings, McCarthy, and Watkins, and there are the comparative works of Wiley, Linderman, Mitchell, Robertson, and Barton.[8] I intend no lengthy systematic comparison of Ben's insights to those of others, but this literature provides a rich foundation that informs my efforts to see his world view. At this generalizing analytical level, one of Reid Mitchell's conclusions is particularly appropriate: "Combat, military discipline, ideology, and leadership have all been evaluated as determinants of soldiers' conduct during the war, but community values were equally important. In fact, they were crucial to the way in which Americans made war from 1861 to 1865. . . . During combat, could men think of their reputations? The answer is probably yes."[9] I wish to apply this and other general comparative insights to show how Hirst's behavior in army life and his portrayal of it for readers were both constrained by a wider prevailing world view. By so doing, we can come to know him better as a person—that is, as a product of his cultures.

Very close to where the three vectors meet lies a series of accounts Ben wrote for the local newspaper. These appeared in weekly installments between February 1887 and February 1888. Many of them are verbatim transcriptions of portions of his original letters and journal; they also offer valuable specifics about events and motivations missing from the originals. Yet they were written for a different audience, and under the influence of one-quarter century of energetic postwar veteranizing. In the epilogue, I will consider what a comparison between them and the originals can tell us about world view.

The Documents

In his first months of army life, Ben developed two types of portrayals of his perceived reality. His letters reflected his immediate and occasionally quite private reactions and were specially written for relatives and friends; but, he also kept a diary or journal, which was not so much a monologue opening up his innermost

Sgt. Benjamin Hirst. Photo probably taken at Falmouth, Virginia, on 13 March 1863. Charles D. Page, History of the Fourteenth Regiment, Connecticut Vol. Infantry. *Meriden, Conn.: Horton, 1906, p. 193.*

feelings and perceptions as it was an effort to portray important events in heroic style and content. His journal entries were for a readership beyond that of his letters; they were first drafts of newspaper columns published a generation later.

The original journal did not survive. Included here is Ben's recopied version, which he claimed was faithful to the original entries. He set to work on the copy in early February 1863 and finished it about six weeks later. It includes eleven sheets, each folded in half and written in ink on the four resulting panels. As each sheet was completed he sent it off to Sarah folded inside one of his routine letters. His copied version was not a verbatim transcript of his original entries. We cannot know exactly how much retrospective editorializing he performed as he whiled away monotonous hours in winter camp at Falmouth. In the copy, he summarized

John Hirst (right) with close friends David Whiting (center) and Elbert Hyde (left) in early September 1863. Hyde lost an eye in combat near Petersburg in June 1864; Whiting was killed at Reams's Station in August 1864. Charles D. Page, History of the Fourteenth Regiment, Connecticut Vol. Infantry. *Meriden, Conn.: Horton, 1906, p. 106.*

entire periods that he felt were uninteresting or otherwise peripheral to the important events he was bent on capturing.

The differences between his two types of portrayals are most readily seen by doing violence to the unity of the journal. I have broken it up into segments and inserted these at appropriate chronological intervals in the series of letters—much as he himself did in his newspaper columns.

The letters and journal preserve the original spelling and relative position of elements (date, location, salutation, main body, closing). The cross-outs and unbracketed insertions are his. Bracketed page numbers refer to pagination of the handwritten originals. Punctuation is less faithful to the originals: Ben's commas and periods look frustratingly alike; where there is doubt about which he intended to use I have transcribed what seems most appropriate in the context. Occasionally, I have inserted excerpts of his 1887–88 newspaper accounts to fill in important details of context surrounding his original narratives. These are set off by italics to avoid confusion with the original text.

On World View

World view refers to a culture's or an individual's conception of the universe and humans' role within it: what causes things to happen; how humans ideally ought to interact with each other versus how they probably actually will; the relationship of humans to things, to nature, and to the supernatural. It includes standards of good and bad, beauty and ugliness, proper and improper. It can be used as a basis for making judgments and as an incentive for behavior.[10] Individual world views typically begin to develop early in life and, once established, are generally persistent unless some crisis—war, for instance—sparks a fundamental reorientation.

For a culture to exist, there must be some general congruence among the world views of its constituents. But there is also world-view diversity or contradiction within a group and between groups in that culture, and even among the facets of an individual's world view. Here there was no smooth-fitting whole of harmoniously interacting ideas, values, and knowledge that some anthropologists once struggled to find in alien cultures. Ben's ambivalent attitudes about authority in a fundamentally authoritarian system are a recurrent instance in the letters. Some of the inconsistencies or contradictions between beliefs—and between beliefs and experience—generated changes in his world view and in behavior cued by it as the war continued.[11]

Ben's narratives were persistently guided by several key facets of his prewar world view. Manliness is the most pervasive—and the broadest. The others include respectability, authority, hierarchy, gender, and—far less apparently—religiosity and ethnicity. Each was linked by multiple bonds to the others, so that manliness, respectability, and gender all may have been at work in a given narrative segment. I am interested in exploring the probable origins and prewar development of these facets. Later, I will trace war's impact on them and relate them to the wider series of world views that prevailed at that time.

I also want to trace the striking similarity between the factory and the infantry regiment as sociocultural systems. Both, for example, were institutions that constrained behavior for virtually all of the individual's waking hours, and whose collective goals (profits or victories) could only be achieved by acting as a unit. I will explore the popular analogy drawn between both these institutions and the family: factory-as-family, regiment-as-family, thus factory-as-regiment.[12] I also want to stress the importance of the family itself to the operation of each of the other institutions. Whatever the alienating effects of factory labor or army service were on the individual at that time, in many cases individuals were not the fundamental adaptive units. Households were.

What follows is necessarily brief. It is not intended to be a study of the factory system. It is not a comprehensive look at all facets of Ben's world view. It is brief because of a tantalizing lack of specific information about Hirst and his family before the war. His war narratives say nothing of his life or his family before his emigration to America; they say precious little about his life after he arrived. The few clues must be used as keys to unlock a series of probabilistic generalizations found in the literature on early factory labor.[13]

Stockport and the Weaver's Trade

Ben's and his family's world view was rooted in the life of textile workers in one of the most extensive manufacturing areas of the young industrial revolution. In 1835, Ben was living with his parents, Joseph and Mary Whitehead Hirst, his older brother, Bill, and his younger brother, Joe, on Newbridge Lane in Stockport parish, Chester County (Cheshire), England. His father was a weaver in his early thirties at the time.[14] Ben's youngest brother, John, was born in October 1835 and baptized into the Church of England in the following year.[15]

Stockport parish and township then lay a few miles southeast of the factory city of Manchester. The entire region—Manchester, Stockport, and other Cheshire parishes, along with Lancashire and portions of Yorkshire—was at the epicenter of England's textile manufacturing district. Stockport township's ambiance was the epitome of sooty squalor. As a Cheshire saying went, "[W]hen the world was made, the rubbish was sent to Stockport." It was so appalling in 1845 that Friedrich Engels declared it was "notoriously one of the darkest and smokiest holes in the whole industrial area, and ... presents a truly revolting picture."[16] Brick tenements mushroomed between narrow streets and alleys and extended themselves like stairways up the sides of hills. Other parts of the parish were somewhat cleaner and more open than the sooty squalid tenement districts.[17]

When Ben was born in May 1828, his father most likely worked as a powerloom weaver in one of the textile mills in Stockport. If so, he had been at it for only a few years. Cotton textile factories using steam-driven powerlooms began a major expansion in the 1820s, with a particularly rapid spread from 1823 to 1825.[18] Before entering the factory, the senior Hirst and his wife may have been young handloom weavers in the same general area, part of the army of household producers who labored in the putting-out system.[19] The skills needed to weave basic cloth could be learned in three weeks' time. Once learned, the cotton weaving skills might be transferred fairly easily to woolen or silk weaving to take advantage of market fluctuations.[20] All members of such households cooperated in the work. The family was a unit of economic production as well as of reproduction and consumption.[21]

Ben's parents, his older brother, Bill, and eventually he, himself, were certainly aware of, and may have taken part in, the intermittent labor strife that pitted loom operatives against factory owners in the region. Stockport was a hotbed of workers' unrest.[22] In 1826–27, for example, fearful and frustrated handloom weavers launched widespread riots, burned factories, and smashed powerlooms.[23] The powerloom's economic threat was clear: it required even less skill to operate than the handloom, and a pair of powerlooms could produce as much cloth as seven handlooms in a given interval.[24] The senior Hirst may well have entered the factory as a last economic resort, armed with an abiding suspicion and hostility toward factory owners. Once in the factory, the rhetoric of organized labor soon would have become well known to him. The struggle was not merely over powerlooms and poor wages. It involved a rebellion against arrogant authority, to be sure. But also at issue was respectability for labor, manifested most powerfully in low-income laborers' anger at the lack of universal male suffrage.[25] At the beginning of the nineteenth century, weavers in the Stockport area faced a relatively bright future, with good wages and plenty of work. This left in them, according to one observer, "a spirit of freedom and independence, and . . . a consciousness of the value of character and of their own weight and importance," which fueled their agitation when economic conditions deteriorated in the early 1800s.[26]

The transition from household industry to factory did not destroy the family as a vital unit of economic production. Most of the family members could find at least part-time work in the factories, and their wages could be pooled to provide a relatively higher standard of living than if they had depended on the male head's pay alone.[27]

Ben's literacy offers circumstantial evidence that the Hirst household labored in one of the more "progressive" factory complexes that had sprung up in Stockport parish. By 1835, over 4,000 powerlooms were there, with an average of about 400 looms per mill.[28] One of these mills was built by Thomas Ashton in Hyde township, Stockport parish. His factory employed about 1,200 workers in 1832; about 400 of them were weavers—mostly women. Unlike the owners of the urban mills, Ashton lived close to his workers and built a school to offer reading, writing, and arithmetic to 640 pupils at night and on Sunday. There was a library for employees and an infant school during the week for 280.[29] Generally, children who worked in urban factories or in rural handloom households were not provided with such "opportunities"—if, indeed, after prolonged work in any setting they could endure sitting in school at night and during their only day off.[30] But clearly Ben learned to write relatively well—most likely in his childhood, when the demands on his labor time may have been somewhat less strident.

Probably, Ben and his brother Bill worked as children in some component of the weaving process; possibly, all four brothers were in the mills before the family emigrated to America in the spring of 1847.[31] Their father might have continued to work at home as a skilled handloom weaver of fancy goods while the children supplemented the household income with their factory work.[32]

The household was beset by labor and wage insecurity. Major recessions and expansive production followed each other about every two or three years. After the boom of 1823–25 came the depression of 1826–27, with riots and loom breakings. In 1829, there was another recession with some loom breakings in the Manchester area; 1832 brought a recession for handloom weavers, followed by a boom in powerloom labor in 1833–36. Another general recession hit in 1837 that lasted until 1842. Prosperity returned briefly in 1843–45, only to descend into a slump by 1847—the year the Hirsts emigrated to America. The economy and powerloom expansion picked up again in the late 1840s.[33]

In bad times, middlemen stopped buying textiles and factories stopped production and sent workers home. In good times, occasional labor shortages in the Manchester area were met by importing Irish workers. These immigrants likely were regarded by English weavers in much the same way as handloom weavers regarded the powerloom: they were threats to a decent wage; more, they were a drain on the public relief of the poor laws.[34] In 1852, after the Hirsts' emigration, anti-Irish sentiments erupted into open rioting in Stockport.[35] Although Ben's family lived near increasingly large pockets of Irish immigrants and may have felt economically threatened by them, he evidently did not grow up sharing the widespread anti-Irish sentiments of the time—as will be seen.

The Hirst family, like others, must have struggled during market slumps. In Stockport, they needed an alternative productive strategy, such as farm work.[36] Possibly, the family as a unit saved enough during the good times to help them live relatively well during the bad ones. This would be more likely if the senior Hirst held a better-paid supervisory position in the mill. Occasionally, they may have depended on poor laws compensation until the allotments were severely cut back in the late 1830s. Whatever the subsistence strategy, the future had to be uncertain.

Tension building from this uncertainty probably forced the Hirst family to consider emigration as the best option for a secure future. Hopes for income security may not have been the Hirsts' only motivation. Charlotte Erickson declares that often workers left England for other reasons: to have land of their own, to be with relatives already emigrated, or to improve the quality of their lives, which more money alone could not grant them in England. Still, a higher or more reliable household income tended to dominate these others.[37]

In his early years, Ben learned to think and behave as part of a team, both in the family and in the factory. He would have come to understand that the success of the team depended on each person doing her or his part. He would have been immersed in a male-dominant hierarchical situation—a powerless child worker subject to the demands of routine and of those higher-ups in charge of his time. He marked the conduct of overseers and determined what distinguished good ones from bad ones. Probably vigilance was there as well, learning how to skirt the rules without attracting the unwelcome attention of the overseer.[38] The organized labor rhetoric and actions could possibly have imbued his young consciousness with an ambivalence toward those in charge. The rhetoric and toil together may have instilled a developing will to get ahead, to someday leave the mills and enjoy a more fulfilling existence. The wage and employment instability may have helped him decide this. On the other hand, it may have accustomed him to uncertainty and given him a measure of resigned fatalism.[39] These patterns are all apparent in his war narratives.

The Factories of Delaware County

Not all textile factories and operatives were alike in America, any more than they were in England.[40] The mills of New England drew heavily on a rural native-born labor pool, while those of the mid-Atlantic region hired large numbers of immigrant Irish and English workers. Many of the latter were handloom weavers displaced by the English powerlooms. Factories in the Massachusetts towns of Lowell, Lynn, and Fall River attracted small armies of single-women operatives, while the mid-Atlantic mills worked a more evenly balanced gender ratio. Mid-Atlantic workers tended to move more frequently than New England workers. All, however, were affected by the same market and job insecurity that characterized textile labor in England.

Ben's family arrived in Philadelphia as a unit on 18 May 1847 and proceeded to the Chester area of Delaware County just to the south. There, the family split up. The father and mother, and probably some of the brothers, took up residence on Chester Island in the Delaware River, just east of Chester town. The parents evidently wished to try their hand at farming, possibly supplemented by occasional sojourns in the nearby mills of the Rockdale district. By 1849, Ben's brother Bill was living in the hamlet of Leiperville, about three miles west of Chester and eleven miles south of Philadelphia. He went to work as a textile operative in Callaghan's mill in the Rockdale district.[41] He married Anna Bowers, also of Leiperville, on Christmas day of 1849.[42] Ben, Joe, and John probably worked as weavers in the mills, possibly boarding with Bill and his wife, interspersed with farm work during slumps in the textile market—a subsistence pattern similar to that they followed in England. Chester-Rockdale was surrounded by fairly prosperous farms. Ben's wartime instructions to Sarah reveal at least some agricultural knowledge, and John's letters later in the war offered quick asides about when best to market crops and the varying quality of farm plots.

Ethnicity and kinship may well have influenced the family's initial decision about where to settle. There was already at least one enclave of English weavers close by in West Branch, one of seven mill hamlets in the Rockdale district.[43] Ben's father's brother, also named Benjamin Hirst, operated a blacksmith and machine shop in Chester for a time until the business folded in 1854.[44] Ben's narratives mention his chance wartime encounter with his cousin Benjamin Hirst Jr.[45]

Labor and Machines

The powerloom of the 1840s was a particularly noisy device. Many of them crowded into a large room created a constant banging din that made normal conversation impossible. The loom could also be dangerous. The heavy shuttle was driven laterally with great force across the warp threads.[46] Occasionally it would come loose and fly into neighboring looms or operatives unfortunate enough to be caught in its trajectory.[47] Then there were the belts that powered it and the other machines, occasionally crushing fingers or limbs and even dragging inattentive workers to their deaths.

The labor required a constant attentiveness to the machines, lest they launch a shuttle or otherwise break down, and to the cloth being woven, lest there be flaws from broken thread or other causes. Operatives had to be on their feet while the machines were operating. Until 1853, the typical workday in Rockdale was thirteen hours, six days a week. Leg circulation complaints were part of the trade.[48]

The labor also generated boredom; it was mentally and physically monotonous. The operatives were attendants to machines, not skilled craftspersons.[49] But always it was a watchful boredom, not unlike picket duty in combat; something could go wrong with the machines at any time, and very quickly.

Workers started and stopped their labor at the sound of the factory bell. The bell became a ubiquitous symbol of regimentation—like the army bugle. A schedule had to be followed rigidly if the mill was to make a profit. This was not simply an application of the Protestant work ethic; it was demanded by the technology of the mills themselves.

Unlike factories in England, most of the prewar mills in Delaware County were water-wheel driven rather than steam driven. This made for a cleaner atmosphere, freer of the sooty coal smoke pouring from smokestacks of steam-powered factories. The huge water wheel turned a central power shaft that ran through the factory; all machinery was powered by this central shaft through a series of gears, pulleys, and belts.[50] The entire mill was designed to be operated as a unit. The workers all had to be on their jobs while the central shaft was turning; none of them could work when it was not. A few tardy or absent operatives could cause a slowdown of the whole unit.[51]

The factory workday typically began with the bell at 5 A.M. and ended with the bell at 7 P.M. Workers were given thirty minutes for breakfast and forty-five minutes for dinner (i.e., lunch), all signaled by the bell. In winter, the workday ran from 6:30 A.M. to 8:30 P.M.[52]

The Factory as a Sociocultural System

The Rockdale district was home to just over 2,000 people in 1850. Nine percent of them were English, 15 percent were Irish.

Like Thomas Ashton of Stockport parish, the mill owners of Delaware County tended to live near their factories and workers. Many of them were immigrants from England or Ireland; many had been textile factory laborers who had managed to save capital on their own and create business partnerships with wealthy elites. They became role models for others seeking a better life, exemplifying that it was indeed possible for a man of humble working-class origins to make something of himself. They believed firmly in hierarchy and actively sought power. Yet, they and their families also felt some obligation to guide the moral, intellectual, and spiritual development of their workers.[53] They sought a relationship of friendly trust with their operatives. Although wealth separated them, managers and operatives knew each other quite well. They went to the same church on Sundays, knew each other's gossip, watched each other's children grow. Mill owners were the fathers of the factory family—as long as benevolent paternalism did not get in the way of profits.

In their social and business relations, the owners hewed to their ideal of manhood. Among the foremost of manly qualities was what Wallace labels "fidelity-to-contract," meaning "a real man keeps his promises." Manhood in this view was a "state of social responsibility, and . . . to be a man was not just to be a virile adult male but a male credited by a community of other males with being honest in their ceaseless mutual business dealings. Thus the contract principle was at once an ego ideal and a theory of society."[54]

Mill owners were often on the lookout for managerial potential among their operatives, while upwardly mobile male operatives often sought the attention of owners that could blossom into rewarding patron-client relations. An ambitious male operative could rise through the intermediate ranks of boss weaver and loom fixer to become an overseer.

The overseer was himself an experienced weaver responsible for supervising the setting up of the looms (the specific duty of the loom fixers), disbursing the weaving jobs and yarns to individual weavers (specifically handled by the boss weavers), for keeping a record of the yards of cloth woven by each loom, and for maintaining the standards of quality of the final product. He was also responsible for keeping a close watch on the behavior of each of the operatives in the weaving operation. Simply put, he was there to enforce the factory rules and maximize productivity. Typically his wages were based on the output of the operatives under his supervision—the infamous "premium" system that opposed his own best interests to those of the operatives.[55]

He had power. A word from him to higher authorities could get employees fired and possibly blacklisted for any other employment in the region. Yet, if he were consistently harsh and overbearing to subordinates, he would not only build unproductive resentment, but also find himself possibly being hauled into court.

Therefore, a good overseer was a good manager and a shrewd judge of character. "The skills of management were skills in social relationships: being able to command when necessary, to persuade, to mollify, to cajole; to mediate between the human needs of the operatives below him and the economic demands of the directors and owners above him; to coordinate his schedule and organization with that of the overseers adjacent to him in the process."[56] Ideally, his eternal sharp-eyed vigilance of the operatives' conduct was tempered by an elder-brotherly concern for their welfare. In this and other respects, overseers were much like army sergeants. Their best interests were served by maintaining the hierarchy of authority. Generally, they supervised thirty-five to fifty-five men, women, and children in the weaving rooms—about the size of an average infantry company during the Civil War.[57]

From the workers' perspective, the overseer's tremendous power had to be wielded properly. Given workers' prevailing sensitivity to their own respectability, overseers specifically had to avoid arrogant pretension and be careful not to abuse their power. A New England weaver's poem aptly characterizes the workers' view:

> The overseers need not think,
> Because they higher stand,
> That they are better than the girls
> That work at their command.[58]

Not all overseers were fair or unpretentious, and not all workers were predisposed to see them as well-intentioned elder brothers. The literature of antebellum organized labor movements is rife with anecdotes of overseers' groveling allegiance to mill owners and deliberate misuses of power for personal gain.[59] Aggrieved workers vented their feelings against an unpopular overseer by drawing caricatures of him on factory machinery or walls, or calling him names like "Old Bird" or "Old Cock" behind his back; he might even be hanged in effigy. (Late in the war, John Hirst concluded that "some Old blue fogey" would likely be hired to fill an open superintendent's position in a Rockville mill.) Yet formal complaints against overseers risked retaliation. Formal court action was also risky and expensive.

As Ben matured in the Delaware County weavers' trade, he continued to develop convictions about manliness, authority, and power. These grew from his accumulating experience with owners and overseers, and probably from his own movement up through the ranks in weaving rooms before the war.

Like soldiers in the army, mill workers were obliged to follow a series of formal and informal factory rules. Some of these rules were clearly for safety, such as no smoking and no inebriation on the job. Some of them, such as the schedule, were dictated by the literal and figurative linkages to the power shaft and wheel. Other rules went well beyond the demands of the factory technology to reinforce prevailing views on morality. Women were expected to behave in a chaste manner, and "undue familiarity" between men and women was forbidden. Fighting, swearing, and obscene language were also prohibited. Workers were not to visit with one another or sit down on the job. The overseer could dismiss operatives for being "disorderly, disobedient, refractory, indolent, incompetent, or a reputed bad character."[60]

Among themselves in the weaving room, workers sought social relief from the monotony and the rules by intermittent hijinks, and by whatever casual conversation could be snatched over the bashing cacophony of the machinery. During these interludes they were careful to leave some of their number on watch, monitoring the machines and keeping a lookout for the overseer.[61]

A strong theme of respectable equality informed workers' views of their positions in the factory hierarchy. One female operative later recalled: "[M]ill people were on the same ground with the clergyman, the lawyer, the merchant, the landlord, and the artisan. . . . we were understood and respected; thus we respected ourselves. . . . We met our agent, superintendent, and overseers at church, in the Bible-class, in society, and everywhere. They were considerate and kind, like brothers."[62] But there was also a strong interplay of ambition and egalitarianism among the workers themselves. A popular variant of the poem about overseers emphasized the egalitarianism:

> The best of weavers do not think,
> Because the higher they go,
> That they are better than their friends
> That work in the rooms below.[63]

Ambition was not condemned as long as it was free of arrogant pretense and manifested in skill, wisdom, and honest toil. Cultivating "clientship" with factory owners or overseers could help one move up. Yet, in the minds of one's fellow workers, there must have been a very thin line between honorable ambition and dishonorable currying of favor. Workers developed a savoir-faire about how to accommodate their behavior to the hierarchy and rules while still maintaining a vital personal advantage and identity.[64] Ben would work at this strategy throughout his military service.

The informal means of social control in the weaving room were the same as in every other small community in the world: gossip. "[I]n no place is an evil report more quickly circulated, and apparently believed, than in a factory."[65] Furthermore, these particular factories were situated in small towns, giving weaving-room gossip a fertile matrix for spreading well outside the factory walls. Persons conscious of their public image—as Ben was—carefully controlled their behavior so as to steer clear of gossip.

The Respectability of Labor

Immigrant workers in the Mid-Atlantic region came from a heritage of emerging labor organization and radical ideology. In bad times, some districts were persistently more conflict-ridden than others. Manayunk, a few miles to the northwest of Rockdale, was a center of labor unrest during much of the antebellum period; Rockdale, by comparison, was intermittently more calm.[66] Compared to England, the competition between powerlooms and handlooms was not a major labor issue. What turned out the workers in America was largely wage and job insecurity.

A prolonged and bitter strike in 1836 generated mutual hostility between owners and operatives that effectively put an end to whatever benevolent paternalism had emerged earlier. The hostility lasted for several years, through a minor depression of 1837 and another major strike by Rockdale workers in 1842.

By 1844, the Rockdale mills had rebounded from strikes and a devastating flood to ease into a decade of "calm prosperity."[67] Ben's family arrived during the calm. By 1854, however, the Rockdale-Chester area was into another major recession that lasted until 1860. Weavers and overseers alike lost their jobs. Factories went belly-up, as did Ben's uncle's blacksmith and machine shop in Chester.

In 1853, near the end of the prosperous decade, many of the Delaware County factory owners at last decided to observe the state's ten-hour workday law. But the Callaghans, owners of the mill where Bill Hirst worked, remained steadfastly opposed. On 6 June, 1855, the *Media Advertiser* of nearby Media, Pennsylvania, reported a strike of operatives in Rockdale: "The workmen employed at the establishment of Mr. Callaghan, at Rockdale, made a strike, about two weeks since, in consequence of Mr. C. refusing to agree with the provisions of the Ten Hour Law. . . . On Monday evening of last week quite a large and enthusiastic meeting of the operatives took place, when Reuben Crowther was called to the chair, John Robuck nominated Vice President, and William Hirst, Secretary."

Laborers' agitation would often take the form of mass rallies and harangues from glib organizers or of fife-and-drum-led processions through the villages. Their agitation escalated into intimidation of nonstriking workers ("nobs," or "nobheads") by jeering, ridiculing, and occasional beatings. At its violent worst, it infused torch and hammer-wielding rioters bent on arson and loom breaking.

Insofar as fidelity-to-contract was a facet of the manly world view held by managers and respectable workers alike, the strikes were a manifestation of its betrayal. The managers felt betrayed by those employees whom they had paternalistically sustained. The operatives felt betrayed by the fatherly managers whose only real interest was profits. The hostility and the sense of betrayal remained as suspicion by both sides even during Rockdale's decade of calm prosperity. Although Ben never mentioned his role in any of the labor action, he must have been affected by the prevailing sense of betrayal and suspicion—if jaded cynicism had not already set in.

Although wages were often at the heart of labor agitation, basic views about respectability and value of life were being contested as well. Workers' public statements in troubled times repeatedly stressed their concern about becoming "mere machines" mindlessly repeating simple movements, to be cast out or shut down in hard times. Another widespread analogy was "slavery," drawn because of lowered wages but also because of endless hours of work with no chance to develop one's mind to its full human potential. (Civil War soldiers would later characterize themselves as machines or slaves.) Elaborations of these and other analogies helped win a system of free public schooling for Pennsylvanians in 1836, if working children could have taken advantage of it. It also won them a reduction of the workday to ten hours in 1848, if the Delaware County owners would have accepted it then. Human dignity and respectability were fine as long as their cultivation did not cut into profits.[68]

The strike rhetoric of the local worker-oriented newspaper, the *Upland Union,* was similar to that later used by Ben to describe the conduct of some officers and pretentious "leading citizens": "Under this gross violation of promises and professions the present strike has been produced, and the sympathy of the whole community is on the side of the workmen, who have been deluded by political knavery and humbug."[69] So was this published excerpt from a labor organizer's oration: "The lordly manufacturer, speculator and adventurer dispise [*sic*] the people and believe themselves born to reign over them and drive them to and fro over the land as beasts of the field."[70] The *Union* was unswervingly Democrat in its politics. Hirst and his family voted Democratic. But despite their strongly pro-labor platform, Democrats were locally outnumbered.[71]

Rockdale's evangelical Protestant clergy persistently urged workers' docile acceptance of the factory system. In labor confrontations, they favored a change in workers' attitudes rather than an overhaul of the factory system itself.[72] In the major confrontation of 1842, factory managers declared the strike was distinctly un-Christian. The clergy viewed it as a falling away from grace. Church and Sunday school attendance abruptly fell off, "no doubt because strikers did not like to be told that they were morally wrong in striking."[73] Possibly, Ben's subdued religiosity stemmed from the ideological residue of these troubled times.

But *could* a family make a decent living on mill wages in Rockdale? Wallace declares that they could—during good times, at least. Many of the laborers aimed at acquiring enough cash to purchase farmland in the West. Between 1840 and 1842, however, piecework wages for weavers effectively dropped by 50 percent.[74] In some cases, families actually did manage to save enough to buy modest farms in the West, or to stay put in Rockdale to buy into operations and become owners themselves. But it must have been very difficult to do either of these things in the midst of the market turbulence of the 1840s and 1850s. Indeed, that turbulence was sparked partly by some owners' insistence on paying workers with credit chits for the company store rather than cash. Workers in nearby Manayunk had difficulty merely meeting their survival needs, to say nothing of buying land.[75] Bill Hirst finally did buy a small farm in early spring of 1864, trying to put an end to the constant worry about factory closings.[76]

As in England, workers' families were the basic economic unit. The family typically emigrated and resettled as a unit, often with adult brothers as its kinship core—as two generations of the Hirsts did.[77] Once in Rockdale, a family generally rented housing from the factory owner at reasonable rates for as long as its members worked in his mill. All family members contributed to the household's maintenance. The adult males and the children worked in the mill and pooled their wages in a household budget. This effectively kept many of the children out of school. In the 1850 census, only about half of Rockdale's eligible working-class children had attended school during the previous year. The family also sought to take in boarders to supplement their wage income.[78] Typically, the wife/mother cooked, maintained the household, and managed the household budget. She also may have cultivated a small garden to help keep food costs down and possibly keep alive a familiar pattern of laboring families in the English or Irish countryside. Her labor and skills were absolutely critical to the economic survival of the family, and she was treated accordingly, despite the prevailing male dominance in the wider social sphere. Her family role in this regard was very different from that of wives/mothers among the elite owners, where the male household head handled all matters pertaining to business. Bill Hirst's wife, Anna, and Ben's wife both probably took up the household role of laborer's wife.

Whether or not motivated by dreams of farms in the West, Rockdale workers tended to view their factory work as temporary—a view they shared with operatives in New England. This, along with wage instability, may help explain another workers' trait: frequent moving. Wallace calculated that a working family had only about a 10 percent chance of remaining in the Rockdale district for more than a decade.[79]

Despite the ethnic clustering in hamlets in the district, there seemed to be no anti-Irish agitation of the severity reported in Manchester—or in southern New England after the Irish influx of the 1840s. To be sure, management blamed English and Irish trade unionism for agitation among Rockdale laborers, and some of the labor organizers were Irish or English. But this never was transformed into the deep ethnic cleavage reported elsewhere, despite the fact that many of the Rockdale owners and operatives had grown up in hotbeds of ethnocentrism.[80] Ben provided a kind of litmus test of this: On 10 June 1852, near the end of the "calm prosperity," he married Sarah Quinn in the Catholic church in Chester.[81]

Rockdale's tolerance did not extend to African Americans. Although Black laborers were not a significant presence in the district or county, their presence in southeastern Pennsylvania was increasingly seen as a social problem in the 1830s. They, rather than the Irish or other white immigrants, were seen as a threat to unskilled labor and as a drain on the resources for relief of the poor. In 1837, Pennsylvania's new constitution revoked the voting right of free African Americans.[82]

In Wallace's analysis, the Delaware County manufacturing culture that the Hirst family entered was split by two competing world views. The cleavage set apart the "evangelicals"—essentially promanagement, conservative, politically Whig, spiritually Protestant, and oriented toward immutable rules and hierarchies of power—from the "humanists" who took their ideological cues from the Enlightenment. The contradiction between them was particularly sharp on the issues of authority and power: "Where the Enlightenment taught that all men were equal, the evangelicals taught that there were mutually dependent social classes. Where the Enlightenment taught that social life is based on negotiable contract, the evangelicals taught that it is based on government and law."[83] After 1838, the "infidel" Enlightenment ideology was shouted down in Rockdale's various public forums; but some laborers simply sequestered their thinking and bided their time until the next strike reopened the rift. Many individuals subscribed to some facets of both ideal-typical views. Ben seemed to be one of these. He was indifferent to the ecclesiastical enthusiasm of the evangelicals, yet not willing to submit all issues of hierarchy to negotiated contract. In fact, even outspoken labor organizers did not condemn the clergy or attack the institutions of society or the existence of the factory system; instead, they bore down on those who exploited that system unfairly.[84]

Ben and his wife and brothers remained in Delaware County through 1856, the year John Hirst first voted in a presidential election. (He voted Democratic, for James Buchanan, but wryly swore in a pension affidavit after the war that "he has seen his Error since.")[85] By then, another major recession had spread into the county, and Ben, Sarah, and his brothers Joe and John moved to New England to seek economic security once again. Meanwhile the Hirst brothers' parents both died while still in their fifties. Mary died in Chester in 1855; Joseph Sr. on Chester Island in 1858.[86] The oldest Hirst brother, Bill, and his wife stayed in Leiperville when the others moved north.

They first settled briefly in Dedham, Massachusetts, where they remained long enough to make new friends (or rekindle a prior friendship) with the Bottomly family that would carry over into the war years. Apparently the continuing economic slump soon pushed them out of Dedham and toward Rockville in northeastern Connecticut.

Rockville and the Weaver's Trade

Rockville in the late 1850s was very similar to the Rockdale district. Its population was 1,900 in 1850 (compared to Rockdale's 2,006); its several textile mills were situated along the Hockanum River, which bisected the town. They were closer to each other than Rockdale's, but Rockville still fit the description of "factory village."[87]

By 1860, Ben and Sarah had saved enough money to buy a modest house with enough land for a small garden and some hogs.[88] Joe and John lived with them, as did a girl named Margaret Penfield—"Maggie"—who was then thirteen years old. Maggie was probably a relative of Sarah's or Ben's. She may also have worked in one of Rockville's mills. In 1862, she was just learning to write. There were no other youngsters in the home. There was a pet dog named Curly and another domesticated animal of unknown species named Dick.

Ben and his two brothers took weaving jobs at the American Mill, which specialized in weaving a medium-grade woolen cloth then known as cassimere.[89] Whether they had earlier shifted back and forth between cotton and woolen weaving is not known, but it is likely. At any rate, the three men settled in as woolen weavers. The market was probably glutted with unemployed cotton weavers at that time. Woolen weaving required more strength because the cloth was heavier; thus the weaving operatives in this and other Rockville woolen mills were overwhelmingly male. The middle brother, Joe, was a loom fixer in the mill. Ben, older and more experienced, probably was at that or a higher level in the factory hierarchy.[90]

*Civil War Narratives of Sgt. Benjamin Hirst,
Company D, 14th Connecticut Volunteers*

Part I

ANTIETAM AND
TEDIOUS SERVICE
30 AUGUST TO 6 DECEMBER 1862

Chapter 1

The Context

Ben, Joe, and John Hirst joined Company D of the 14th, raised by Capt. Thomas F. Burpee in July 1862. Ben and Joe signed up on 16 July; John signed up four days later. Ben was thirty-four years old, Joe was thirty-two, and John was twenty-six. Seventy-five of the 110 men in Company D, including Captain Burpee and the Hirst brothers, were from Rockville.[1] In the first years of the Civil War, brothers, cousins, in-laws, and friends from a single town or county joined up together and stayed together in a company or regiment for the duration. At the outset, before disease and combat took their toll, most of Company D's enlisted men knew each other and shared experiences and concerns over and above those that would develop in the months at the front.

The 14th Regiment was authorized by Gov. William Buckingham on 22 May 1862, but enlistments were sluggish at first. Why bother to enlist for three years? The army and navy were scoring victories and the state's original quota of 13,037 men had already been filled.[2] Besides, the 14th was initially slated to become part of a 50,000-man contingent at a camp of instruction at Annapolis, Maryland—hardly a glamorous future for prospective recruits.[3] Only about 250 men had volunteered by mid-July. They languished in the dusty doldrums of Camp Foote just south of Hartford, waiting for another 750 to fill the ranks. Then the early summer combat reverses of the Union army inspired more emphatic pleas for volunteers from both the governor and President Lincoln. These were followed by a rousing series of patriotic enlistment meetings throughout the state. By late July, the pace of recruitment quickened; there was no more talk of the 14th becoming a garrison regiment.

Company D was the first company to be raised in this period of renewed resolve. Soon afterward, Company B marched into camp as a unit "with band playing and flags flying" and an escort of firemen from Middletown.[4] By 22 August, the regiment had reached its full strength of 1,015 men who represented towns throughout the state. On 23 August, they were mustered into Federal service. Ben was mustered in as a sergeant; he was appointed to that rank by the regimental commander, Col. Dwight Morris, about a week earlier. Joe and John mustered in as privates. On 25 August, with more music playing and flags flying and crowds of people to see them off, they boarded the steamers *City of Hartford* and *Dudley Buck* bound to the South and to war.

The three-day journey featured a mixture of modes of transportation, including a larger, more crowded steamer, railroad, and shanks' mare. Officers and men recalled the filth and crowding on steamers and cars, interludes of crowds of patriotic well-wishers along the route, and longer periods of short rations, sleeplessness, and dusty marching to their destination. The regiment was reportedly the first to march into Washington after Lincoln's call for an additional 300,000 men. It marched in review past the president, Secretary of War Edwin M. Stanton, and Gen. Winfield Scott. Lincoln seemed distracted as Company B approached the stand. Already experts at grand entries, the company got his attention by spontaneously breaking into song ("We are Coming, Father Abraham"). Lincoln doffed his stovepipe hat and bowed, and allegedly pronounced the 14th the "finest looking body of men that had passed through Washington."[5]

The regiment went into bivouac the night of 28 August on Virginia soil, near Arlington Heights. The next morning, they were jarred awake by the long roll of drums and eight of the companies were speedily issued rifle-muskets for the first time. (Two companies, A and B, had been designated "flank companies" according to the tactics of the time, and had received Sharps breechloading rifles the night before.) The weapons had been brought in crates with the regiment from Hartford.

The men left all their personal baggage, formed up in light marching order, and were marched swiftly northward some ten miles to Fort Ethan Allen near Chain Bridge and Rockville, Maryland. The alarm turned out to be false. There they remained until 7 September, when they again set off on a series of marches that culminated in the battle of Antietam. The 14th Connecticut was joined with two other new regiments, the 130th Pennsylvania and the 108th New York, into the 2d Brigade, 3d Division, 2d Corps of the Army of the Potomac.

There was some hard drilling at Fort Ethan Allen, probably consisting of maneuvering into the various military formations used in closing with the enemy.[6] It is unlikely the men received marksmanship training with their new rifles or rifle-muskets. Whatever it consisted of, the intensive training had to be crammed into about seven days, along with guard and other camp details as well as formations and inspections.

The regiment moved into the Antietam area via Rockville, Clarksburg, Hyattstown, Frederick, and South Mountain. It narrowly missed the battle at South Mountain on 14 September, but spent the night on that battlefield amid the carnage and faced a sobering view of the effects of combat at first light on the fifteenth. The men resumed the march through Boonsboro and Keedysville, bivouacking on the fifteenth and sixteenth about a mile beyond Keedysville toward Sharpsburg.[7]

They were awakened at 2 A.M. on Wednesday, 17 September, and issued ammunition. They entered the Antietam fight through the East Woods, where they formed into a line of battle with enemy shells raining shrapnel and heavy tree limbs down upon them. They followed the 3d Brigade into a low marshy area between the Mumma and Roulette farm buildings, Company A on the right pausing under fire to pilfer apples from Mumma's orchard, Company B on the left snaring a group of Confederate sharpshooters in Roulette's spring house. The line crashed southwestwardly through a tall corn field, staying mostly out of sight of Confederate infantry until it came to a fence at the edge of the corn. Across the fence before them was a large open field. Eighty to a hundred yards across the field were the Confederates hunkered down in the sunken farm road soon to be renamed Bloody Lane. As the brigades clambered over the fence and out into the meadow, they were blasted by Confederate musketry and fell back to the relative concealment of the corn. There they remained over an hour in position before falling back to the vicinity of the Roulette house.[8]

From the Roulette house, the 14th was ordered to support Kimball's brigade, now to its front, in its attack against the sunken road. The 14th moved to its left to occupy a stone wall along a lane leading southwest from the Roulette farm to the sunken road. After a brief interval, its orders were changed and it moved out into the Roulette lane to support yet another brigade, Brooke's, of the 1st Division, which was by then under heavy fire in its assault on the sunken road. While in the Roulette lane, a shell burst over the Hirsts and Company D, killing three men and wounding four.[9] Just after General Richardson's mortal wounding, Gen. Winfield S. Hancock ordered the 14th to its left front out of Roulette lane to plug a gap between Meagher's Irish Brigade and Caldwell's Brigade. The new position was in a freshly plowed field at the crest of a small hill overlooking the sunken road. The greenhorns of the 14th marched upright into position, sending out guides to orient the regimental front, all according to the manual of tactics. A battle-hardened officer on the 3d Division staff saw what was about to happen and hastily ordered the 14th's lieutenant colonel to get his regiment down flat on the ground—immediately. But the Rebel artillery already had the range and began to lob shells that burst directly over the 14th's position.

The men of the 14th groveled in the soft earth of the field for the rest of the late afternoon, taking occasional fire from Rebel batteries. There they spent the rainy night, and the next day and night. By dawn on Friday, they realized that even the Confederates' rear guard of sharpshooters had pulled out to the south. By midmorning that day, they were relieved and went into bivouac in the East Woods to their rear. They had lost a total of 137 men.

They were spared the burial details because of their active combat on the front lines and were praised for their fighting tenacity in the official reports submitted after the battle.[10] There was an army-wide inspection on Saturday afternoon and an impressive religious ceremony and fresh beef ration on Sunday. The regiment moved out on Monday, 22 September, to Bolivar Heights overlooking Harpers Ferry.

In the Bolivar Heights camp, the men of the regiment were appropriated for various details: guard and picket mostly. Many of them also became very ill with

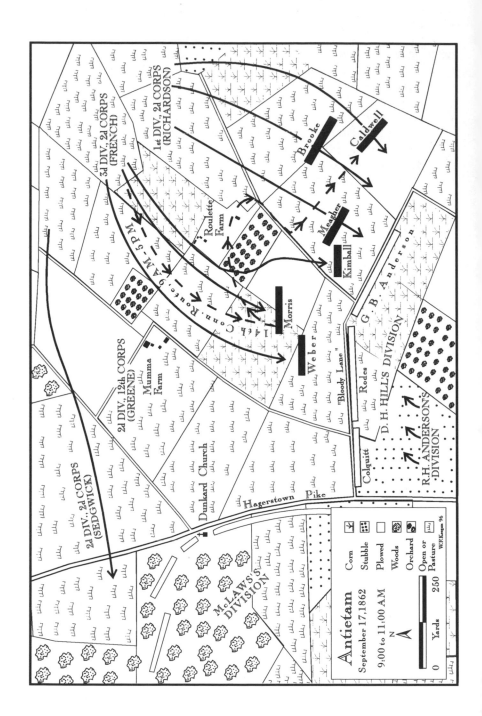

Antietam
September 17, 1862
9:00 to 11:00 AM

Corn
Stubble
Plowed
Woods
Orchard
Open or
Pasture

W.F.Kn{'a'}pe 96

N

Yards
0   250

diarrhea, brought on, they believed, by the "bad water" at the camp. There they remained until 30 October.

The regimental history recalls the camp routine: The drummers rolled reveille at 5:30 A.M., and the men had to be present in ranks before the drum roll ceased four or five minutes later or face punishment. After roll call they fixed their own breakfasts, having to walk some distance for wood and water. At 7:30 came sick call, with guard mount at 8 A.M. for about thirty men detailed for the duty from the regiment each twenty-four hours. At 8:30, the men began two hours of either company or battalion drill. From about 11 A.M. to 3 P.M., they made their dinners and lounged or did various housekeeping chores. From 3 P.M. to 5:30 P.M., they were put through more drill, followed by a dress parade. Then came supper and a retreat call at sundown. The regiment had a fine band, and often the retreat ceremony featured a concert. There was a final roll call at 8 P.M.; lights out sounded at 9 P.M.[11]

On 30 October, the 14th left the "bad-water camp" to march south through Upperville and Warrenton, Virginia. At that time it totaled about 450 men.[12] It marched in the review staged when command of the Army of the Potomac was taken from General McClellan and handed over to General Burnside. On 19 November, it went into another wretched camp at Belle Plain; the discomfort and illness this time were caused by poor drainage and a weeklong rain. Companies of the regiment were detached here and there for various details, including the particularly loathsome one of unloading supply barges. The men camped in the marshy spot until 6 December, when they made an unpleasant march to join the army along the north bank of the Rappahannock River at Falmouth. Cold rain, sleet, and hail all contributed to the muck along the route. The men bedded down that night as best they could in a foot of new snow.[13]

Chapter 2

The Letters and Journal

The italicized passages in the following chapters of Ben's narratives are those written in his newspaper accounts of 1887–88. They are inserted to add relevant details to clarify or elaborate on points in the originals without destroying or altering the original text itself.

In the spring of 1861, when President Lincoln issued his first call for men to suppress the rebellion, the old militia company located in Rockville and known as Company C, 1st Connecticut State Militia immediately went to work filling up its ranks with new men and drilling nightly for the purpose of tendering their services to the governor. But owing to the larger towns and cities first getting recognition from the governor, Connecticut's quota was filled without the company being called upon to leave Rockville, although it was allowed 11 days' pay per man, while waiting orders. Upon the first call for 3 years men, a large number of the company enlisted and formed a company for the regiment forming in Hartford under the name of Colts's Rifle Regiment, but owing to the absurd standard adopted as regards "hight and weight"[1] the men became disgusted and a large number came home and rejoined the old militia company with the idea of perfecting themselves in drill and discipline, for future exigencies, while others stayed in Hartford and formed the nucleus of Co. F, 5th C.V., the three company officers and twenty-seven enlisted men being from Vernon. During the winter of 1861 and 1862 the militia company had semi-weekly drills under the instruction of Gen. E. W. Smith, Capts Maro Thompson, Thos F. Burpee and other officers well known to the old state militia, both officers and men fully believing it was but a question of time when they would be called upon for active service. In the spring of 1862 in a conversation with Capt Burpee, he stated to me, he thought the time had nearly come, and that if our army upon the Peninsula met with any serious reversals, he should feel called upon to volunteer and wanted myself and others to be ready to go too. So when the call was made for 300,000 men to serve three years or during the war it created great excitement in Rockville as everybody seemed to feel that the crisis had come and that nearly 100 men would soon leave our little community, to go to that great drama of war then being enacted all over our land. Men of all political parties put their shoulder to the wheel for the purpose of forming a full company for the first regiment under the new call. Many patriotic citizens made speeches and promises of various kinds to the men who felt able and willing to go. Amongst the many who urged a prompt response to the call of the government was the Hon Dwight Loomis, Geo Maxwell, Dea Kellog, Dea Talcott, the elder Capt Hammond and Thos Barrows, Esq, agent of the American Mills company, who pledged the company to pay the wages of every married man in his employ who enlisted, while in the service, and that every man should be re-employed upon his return home. This promise was faithfully kept by the company although Mr Barrows did not live to see it, as he was killed by an accident at the depot in Hartford in the fall of 1863. But while he did live he took especial care and interest in the families of all his absent employees. July 12, 1862, Thos F. Burpee enlisted for the war and called upon his old comrades of the militia to join him in forming a full company at once for the field. Among those of the old company who responded were Sergt. (afterwards Capt) Brigham, Serg. (afterwards Capt) Stoughton, Lieut Vinton, Lieut Emery, Sgt Otis Waite, Sergt Ben Hirst, John Hirst

Lt. Col. Thomas Burpee, who raised Company D in Rockville before transferring to the 21st Connecticut Volunteers. Photo courtesy of Alden Skinner Camp #45, Sons of Union Veterans of the Civil War.

(afterward Col. Sergt), Chas. E. Dart, (afterwards Col. Sergt.) and nearly every member of the company either enlisted or sent a friend to fill his place. At a meeting of the company Thos F. Burpee was unanimously elected captain and took us with full ranks to Hartford where we were assigned to the 14th C.V. and had the honor of serving with it until the end of the war. Before the regiment left Hartford, Company D met with serious loss in the promotion of Capt Burpee to be Major of the 21st regiment then forming. The old members of the militia felt it to be a personal loss, as the captain had become endeared to them by long personal association, and even now in this year of our Lord, 1887, it would be true to say that no other officer of the company ever filled the place made vacant by his promotion. . . . Perhaps no company of the 14th regiment had so many nationalities in it as had Company D,[2] and yet it was a very harmonious company, all of its members being more or less acquainted with each other before enlisting, and when we left Hartford for the seat of war, August 25, 1862, our last good byes were given in almost every language spoken in Europe. Our march through Hartford to the boat was a day long to be remembered, loaded as we were with all kinds of useless articles that kind friends thought were necessary to our health and comfort. The day was hot and the streets were lined with our friends and neighbors vieing with each other in cheers and congratulations that we were off at last.

I have often wondered what our ideas of soldiering were at the time we left Hartford, and can just imagine how I must have looked as I clambered up the companion ladder to the boat's deck with a Sergeant's sword dangling between my legs, my haversack and pockets filled with a miscellaneous assortment of literature, grub, patent medicine, fluid extracts, etc., a knapsack on my back filled with shirts, drawers, stockings, collars, cuffs, combs, and brushes, with a pious book or two to read when we got settled down in camp, and snugly stowed about the middle of all, a beautiful silver plated flask of w—— with my name, company and regiment engraved thereon, so I could not lose it; and outside of all a big pair of cow hide boots to keep my feet dry during the coming winter, and a canteen filled by an admiring friend with something to keep my stomach warm. Besides all this, was an assortment of patent army knives, army spoons and condiments to put in my victuals if by any chance the company cook should forget to season them to suit. That is the way I, a fair specimen of the regiment, must have looked upon that occasion. Cheers and tears from friends on shore, cheers and tears from the boys on board, and we are fairly on the way at last.[3]

Letter File #1

Arlington Heights Aug. 30. 62

Dear Sarah. I write you these few lines to let you know that we arrived here all well after a most fatiguing journey. You saw us leave Hartford. We got to New York the next morning but was not allowed to go on shore. We then whent on board cars at Elizabethport N. Jersey. From their we whent to Harrisburg Pa. traveling all night we staid on the cars and were sent from their to Baltimore arriving their in the Afternoon. We got the best Welcome in Baltimore that we got any where. We were then put on board freight cars and arrived [here via Washington, pitched] [p. 2] ... our tents and turned in glad enough to sleep on the ground. At 3 o'clock next morning we were turned out to get our guns and 40 rounds of Amunition in consequence of the near approach of the Rebels. We were then sent to guard the chain Bridge above Washington. We crossed the Bridge last night and are now at fort Ethan Allen. We can hear heavy firing all morning but do not fear as Gen Sumners Corps has just arrived and we have 50,000 men arround here.[4] I saw Anthony [Quinn of the 72d Pennsylvania] and [P]Rice Kelly just now both first rate. They marched from below Alexandria since last night. We expect their will be some fun around here every hour.[5]

⌒〜〜⌒

Letter File #2

Sunday Aug 31st
Heights near Chain Bridge Va.

Dear Sarah, I wrote you a few lines yesterday, while a Tremendous Battle was raging almost within sight of us.[6] We are stationed with a Rifle pit to take care of which runs parralel with one side of Fort Ethan Allen. It was thought that if the Rebels were able to Break through our lines they would attempt to Reach Washington by the way of the Chain Bridge, to defeat which all the troops near Washington were sent here, us amongst the rest. We left our Knapsacks, Woolen Blanket, and over coat in Camp near Fort Richardson, and marched with our new Rifles, 40 rounds of Amunition and 2 hard Crackers for a days rations. This was on Friday. We could hear Firing occasionally all day. We Past several smal works in [p. 2] our March, the guards of which cheered us as we whent past. I did not sleep much that night you may be sure. Early in the morning Gen Sumners Famous advanc Brigades began to arrive. I had the pleasure to see the old Veterans of McCllennans [Mc-Clellan's] Army arrive having made a Forced march from below Alexandria during Friday night.[7] Amongst them were the 69, 71st, 72nd, 100th Pensylvanians, first Minisota, 15th, 19th, 20th Mass, Rickets Famous Battery of 12 guns, and others that I cant remember, having no paper to make notes. Brother Anthony heard that there was a green Conn Regiment here and in less than 5 minuets from his Arrival he was shaking my hand. He looks first rate, and as tough as a [p. 3] young Bear. I Also saw Price Kelly and Joe Taylor from Chester [Pennsylvania] besides a many other ones that I used to know. It certainly looked like war to see this Body of 10,000 Warriors marching along in Rags and Tatters some of them without shoes, all in there dirt not having washed their Faces for 6 days, but all cheerful and hopeful and with increased confidence in their Gallant Leader Mc Cllennan. They staid here but a few hours when they took up their march for ~~Fairfacks~~ Fairfax Court House to (if possible) have a hand in the Battle then raging. All the morning of Saturday we could here the Booming of Canon, but about 10 oclock it became Tremendous. It was one continued Boom Boom until sunset. Sometimes it would [p. 4] seem to get nearer at others die away in the distance. We think we have gained a great Victory as we have not heard a gun fired to day, and it is now 12 oclock at noon. But we cant hear any thing from Washington until to morrow. All our Boys from Rockville are well and in good spirits but it is raining like Blazes and they are all trying to find some way to keep themselves dry. This will account for the Blured apperance of this letter as I cant keep my paper dry while I am writing. Give my love to Mr Morse and my respects to the folkes in the mill. I cant tel you where to direct for me, but think if you direct 14 Conn, Co. D, Washington it wil find me. Love to you. B.H.

⌁⌁⌁

Letter File #3

September 4th 62
Heights Above Chain Bridge Va.

Dear Sarah, I take this oppertunity to write you a few more lines to let you know that we are all wel at the present moment. Altho we have had a pretty hard time for green troops, we stand it first rate. If you could make out to read my last letter you would perceive that I thought we had gained a Victory, but such was not the case. Altho we had the Rebels in a trap, through the incompetancy of Gen Mc-Dowel[8] they were allowed to get out and to inflict serious damage to our troops. Those brave men that whent from here friday last arrived at Centreville too late to be engaged in the Battle, but in time to cover our retreat. They were all Loud in their Denunciation of McDowel whom they call a Traitor, and if what they [say] [p. 2] is true he ought to be shot. Yesterday the whole of the Armies of Banks and Sigel, Pope and part of McCllennans whent past here to take a new position in Maryland and form a new front out here.[9] You must not be discouraged at the news you here from out here, because through all the Blundering, our troops inflicted as heavy losses on the Enemy as they inflicted on us, and the men are not discouraged in the least, but they do not want any more of Gen Popes Strategy. Brother Anthony came to see us again yesterday. He was pretty wel used up as they had been marching and counter marching ever since we saw him and he said he was pretty near played out. But he thought a few days rest would make him all right. He saw Tom the day before, and he was [p. 3] all right. Tom McGee of the Conn 5th was here on Tuesday. He was first rate. I have just shook hands with Mr. Bugbees son Servestor [?]. He is in good health and spirits and looks first rate. Mention this to Mr. Bugbee and give him My Respects. There was several others

here that I did not see as I was in charge of a party of 60 men cutting down Woods in our front, to impede the Rebels, if they should attempt to come this way. Consequently, I did not see half the men that were here yesterday. We have not yet received our knapsacks or tents, that we left at Camp Chase last Friday, so you see that we are roughing it. To begin with, I went on Guard on ~~thursday~~ Monday morning and in the Afternoon there came up a tremendous storm which wet me through [p. 4] in about 2 minuets. It lasted all night but I stood it out until 10 oclock the next morning when the new guard came on for the day. I am glad to say that [at] the present moment I am in as good health as I ever enjoyed. I hope you are all in as good health. You must write me as soon as you get this as I want to hear how you are all getting along. You must tell me how all the folks are at the mill, and I should like to have a Newspaper once in a while. Give my respects to all the folks, and send Word by Mr. Morse to Bridge that his time has come to offer something for his Country besides paying taxes. I must now conclude. I remain your Affectionate Husband, B. Hirst.
Direct to Sergt Benjamin Hirst Co D.
14 Conn Vol. Washington, D.C. Tell Bridget that I heard that William was well on Monday last when my informant says he saw him. B. Hirst.

～～～

Letter File #4

Chain Bridge Va.
Sept 6.th

Dear Sarah, I have just received your letter and feel very glad that I got it as we were just on the point of leaving here for some point unknown to us, we have 2 days provisions in our Haversacks and were drawn up in line, when the order was countermanded for an hour or 2. So you see I am going to be prompt in writing to you when I have the chance. you must not be alarmed at what you hear from the seat of war as 2 thirds of what is sent to the news papers are lies. the Army [p. 2] was never in better spirits than now, and it is the universal opinion out here that Jackson was whipt but for the incompetency of McDowel. but that is past Genl G B McCllenan is again Commander in Chief out here and if he is properly sopported in Washington all will yet be wel. we received our knapsacks and overcoats again yesterday, but they had been overhauld by some scamps and all our loose things stolen. I lost my Tobaco and part of my medicen but the worst of all they stole your Daughereotype. there will be a big score to be settled if they are found out, as it was done by some of our own men left to guard the baggage. but thank god I am [p. 3] well and dont need any medicen for the present. we have pretty good health out here, but there was more sick today when we got the order to march, then there has been since we left Hartford, but I am glad to say that no Foreigner was of the

Party. tel Luther [Morse] I will write him very soon, and I hope he will try to take things cool and not worry himself as he is sure to come out right in the end. Joe, John, Tom [Butterworth], [Thomas] Wilkie and myself have one smal tent for the 5 of us and we are all well and get along nicely together. all the men that you are aquainted with are well. a man at my elbow is just saying that Hary Owen is [p. 4] very sick at Allexandria he says he saw him on Wednesday.[10] if you see David McIntoshes Wife tell her he is wel, altho he has been in the Hospital for a couple of days. he came out in good health so he says. Albert Towne says he wrote home yesterday and he wil write again soon. You had better fatten the Pigs and sel them as soon as you can. it wont pay you to keep them long. I am afraid we must fall in any minuet so you must excuse this hasty scrawl. I remain your affectionate Husband Ben Hirst

Try and spel a little better whe you write B H.

⌒〜〜⌒

Journal Excerpt #1

Where We have been, in
Virginia and Maryland

Dear Sarah

My old Diary being about worn out, I propose to send you a copy of what I noted in our Tramp through Maryland and Virginia. I shal just copy as I wrote at the time. before leaving Hartford wrote, I Benjamin Hirst was mustered into the United States Service on the 20th day of August 1862. [Details of marches and camp at Fort Ethan Allen, as already described in letters.] . . . [p. 3] All still until the 7 day of Sept when we were ordered to be ready to March at a moments notice, we were to leave our knapsacks behind and at noon were marched into Maryland to join the Army under Gen McCllennan, then marching to meet the Rebels at any point they might choose. Arrived at Clarksburg on Thursday the 11th and took our position in Line, being placed in Sumners Corps, Frenches Division, were Brigaded with the 108 N.Y. and 130 Pa. all new troops like ourselves. on the 12th arrived at Hyatsville and Encamped at White Oat [Oak?] Springs, on ground that the Rebels occupied a day or two before, saw Sugar Loaf Mt around which we seemed to be marching. Saturday the 13th heard heavy firing in the Mountains, and took up our line of march for Fredrick City, the Boys singing John Brown and other such stuff.

2d sheet [of?] 5

As we approached Fredric city we saw the first desolating effects of War. the Railroad Bridge and Depot was burnt down by the rebels previous to their falling back, and along the road were several caracases of Catle that they had killed, but had not time to dress. saw something covered up with a Blanket, unwrapt it and saw the first dead Rebel, *his body swollen and black.*[11] he had been shot through the side with a bullet and fell in his own tracks. About noon entered the City and the Welcom we received from the Citizens soon banished the gloomy feelings, that some of the men got, when viewing the Ruined Bridge in the City. everything was lovely our Flag Floated from every conspicious Place while man, Woman and child, seemed to vie with each [p. 2] other in their greeting to us.

We passed through the main st which was thronged with Thousands of happy People, who hoped we should soon overtake the rebels and Pay them for their insolence in Invading Maryland. as we passed along noticed a large yard, in which was a lot of Rebel Prisoners. one of them was in a great passion, and shook his fist at us in a very threatning manner. we laughed at him which made him worse. in a Engine house was a lot more one of who asked what Regiment. 14th Wooden nutmegs was the reply. then you will soon get your heads grated says he with a grin that made us all laugh. We encamped just outside the City and it was here that I got the first good look at Mc Clennan and Burnside.[12] both were cheered lustily, but little [p. 3] Mac had the preferance.

<hr>

Letter File #5

Sunday Sep^t 14. 62.
On the Hills near Midleton [Middleton] Md

Dear Sarah. I write you these few lines to let you know that we are now in front of the Rebels having had a march through a great part of Maryland.

Monday Sept. 15th
I had to close my writing as when I had got so far we had to fall in to sopport some movement then going on in our front. after a Forced march of 3 miles we came to what was the Battlefield (on a smal Scale) of yesterday. this morning I saw the first effects of shot and shell on men. but it would make you *sick* [p. 2] to describe it to you. to day is the 9th day that we have been on the march and I am happy to say that we have had first rate health during our journey. by we I mean all those that you are aquainted with. our Company left 7 men at Fort Ethan Allen, and I believe that 4 more have given out on the march. the rest are first rate. We have been Placed in Genral Sumners Corps, Frenchs ~~Brigade~~ Division. and Morrises[13] Brigade. it is composed of old and new Regiments and I believe it is composed of good fighting material. you must keep up as good courage as we [p. 3] do, believe nothing has happened to us until you know for certain. for myself I have no fear for the result. I sent a letter to Luther [Morse] a few days ago. I hope he shows it you. after I closed his letter we were sent on Picket duty and had the luck to get a couple

of Chickens and some sweet potatoes and had a good feed, that is Wilkie, Tom [Butterworth], Joe, John, and myself. we are now getting plenty of Crackers and Coffee, which does very well to keep soul and body to gether. it would make you laugh to see the messes that we cook. a piece of fat [p. 4] Pork and a ear of corn with a couple of Crackers broke in it makes a first rate soup. if you dont believe it try it. I think when I come home I shal set up a cook shop in the old Country style. Cat^n Hammond came up with us last Friday [12 September] and took charge of his Company. his Man *Holt* said he saw you but could not tell what you said to him. Write me as soon as you can. Love to you all.

I remain your
Affectionate Husband
Benj Hirst

Journal Excerpt #2

Sunday September 14th, heard heavy firing in the mountains, and understood that the Rebels were disputing our passage through them.[14] We soon started for the Scene of Battle and as we gained the sumit of a hill about noon, could see our Artillery at work, and the Flash of the Rebel Guns; we were halted within sopporting distance and got our dinner, about sunset were pushed rapidly forward for a mile or two and rested again, after crossing a creek twice, that each time wet me up to the midle; after another march we encamped on the Blood Stained Fields of South Mountain. this days march was the most Fatigueing that we had yet had, and I was very soon lost in sleep and slept until daylight.

Monday September 15th, 1862 [year written in pencil]

Awoke on the Battle field of yesterday, and after getting some Coffee, began to look around. soon saw War without romance, there was dead men lying around everywhere some with their heads shattered to Pieces, others with their bowels protruding while others had lost their legs and Arms. what my feelings were, I cannot describe, but I hoped to God never to see such another sight again. about 10 oclock we were drawn up in line on the road side and had the pleasure of seeing Gens McCllenan and Burnside ride past us. we then marched in the Direction of Keedysville. about 3 P.M. passed through Boonsbrough and saw a lot of Reb Prisoners brought in. we passed severl lots coming in during the day.

2 Page.

after Dusk we passed thousands of our men, who were encamped on both sides of the road. they told us to go in and that it would be our turn tomorrow. we passed through Keedysville about 9 oclock P.M. and about 10 encamped in the imediate front of the rebels. Tuesday Sep 16th about 8 oclock A.M. firing comenced, and severl shot and shell came flying over us. the sound was far from agreeable, and the Boys were in a great ferment. some of them got sick (and have not yet recovered Feb 63) and a many cheeks were blanched. [I?] soon got used to it, and I saw one Lieut have his foot shot off, without feeling alarmed for my own safety. in about an hour the firing ceased, the Rebs changed their position, and did not annoy us again that day; but we began to suffer for some thing to eat

(3 page) as we had been on short commons [?] during our whole march, every haversack in our Company was empty. but some of us got some crackers from another regiment, and one of our Boys shot a Pig in the Woods. we skined it and brought it in without detection. whent to sleep early, fully expecting to be engaged in the morning, were called up during the night to get rations, and were each served 80 rounds of Amunition at the same time. could sleep no more that night, but did not forget to prepare something to eat, and eat it as though it was going to be the last meal in this World.

Letter File #6

Saturday Sept 20. 1862.
Batle Field near Sharpsburg
Md.

Friend Luther [Morse],

I propose in this letter to give you some faint idea of our trials and tribulations in getting here, so that you for one will know that we done our share in this great Batle (even if we should not happen to get in the newspapers). We left Fort Ethan Allan on the 7th of Sept and arrived at Clarksburg on the 11th. having nothing with us but our overcoats and a ruber Blanket. . . . on the 12th marched through Hyatsville. on the 13th heard heavy firing in the mountains and took up our line of march for Fredric City . . . . in crossing the Monocacy River saw the first sighns of active war. the Depot and Railroad was a heap of ruins, and the stench of dead horses and men [p. 2] was very disagreeable. arrived at Fredric City about noon time, and were received with the waving of Flags and Handkerchiefs, and they gave us plenty water, but what we wanted the most (something to eat) we could not get the Rebels having cleaned out every thing in the way of Grub (and here i might as well say that in our 13 days tramp uncle sam, found us 3 Rations of Pork and one of Beef, but i have made out to have plenty of Coffee and have always had one cracker left in my haversack). Sunday morning heavy firing was heard on the Heights opposite to us, we got 3 days rations of Coffee and Crackers, and then whent to see what it meant, about noon came in seeing distance of the rebel and our own Batterys, the Rebs were away up in the mountain, and it is said disputed our passage with 40000 men. but they had to leave, and when they whent it was with a run. about 6 oclock PM we were ordered to the front and whent with a run across fields and through 2 creeks when we came to [p. 3] Halt, the Road in front being jamed up with killed and wounded. about 1 oclock in the morning we were moved further to the front. when we were encamped in the midst of the Batle field of Maryland Heights, i walked around about one hundred yard and saw enough to ever make me step out of my tracks to see dead men, they were killed in every conceivable way. some with a Buckshot, and others Blown to pieces. there were hundreds of Rebel Guns and equipments in our track during this days march. Tuesday waked up and found that the Rebels were in Force in our front, as they sent us their Compliments in the shape of a few shells, which dropt in our midst killing and wounding several of our division (the green horns soon learnt to fall on the ground when they heard the peculiar sound of a shell hissing through the air). our Artilary soon returned the compliment and made Secesh shut up until evening, when the same program was gone through. . . . [p. 4] at daylight of Wednesday morning commenced the greatest Batle ever fought on this Continent, and i believe it will take 3 or 4 days more to know how many were killed and wounded on each side, the Batle extended 14 or 15 miles in length and the Union troop held the Field every where within a circuit of a quarter of a mile from where i am now sitting there is over 2000 dead Rebels yet unburied. but to return to our own Regiment we were marched at the head of our Brigade until we came to Antietam creek, which we forded [then we entered?] a piece of woods in which the Rebels were posted. they gave us a voley and skedadled to draw us on towards their Batteries. we formed line of Batle and whent after them without damage until we came to a piece of Corn field. here most of us threw away our overcoats and Ruber Blanket (since which time we have not seen them and never will again) and whent in. on coming in front or rather near the front a voley tore through our ranks killing and wounding quite a number. the Regiment was thrown in some confusion and most of the

5th Page

Boys fell on their Bellies, firing indiscrimately and i am sorry to think wounding some of our own men on the left of our line of Batle. i saw the whole of this at a glance and roard like a mad Bull for our men to cease firing until they could see the rebs. they finally crawled back a few yard and staid ther a few minuets very still during which time i carried Wilkie from the front to the rear. i then came back to the front, and got a splendid view of the Rebels in a piece of corn opposite to ours. there was just 4 of our own Company and a few men of a Delaware Regiment [probably the 1st Delaware] giving them fits and i was just in the humour to join in, until i fired 13 rounds into their midst. (tell old Mrs Burrows that her son Sam, stood up to the work along side of me like a man, and like myself came out unhurt) seeing our colours falling further back we backed out to our Company, who were all lying on their faces expecting the Rebels were going to charge on us. i am not going to charge any one with cowardice, but there were always too many wanting to go to the hospital with any one that [p. 6] was wounded and they never by any means came back again until yesterday (a few got back the morning after the Big Fight). the Regiment was again formed in good order outside of the corn field just as a rebel Battery got our range and sent several shells over our heads. we were then moved further to the left on front to sopport one of our own Batterys, in getting to which position, we as a Regiment were complimented for the coolness displayed in marching under fire. we were then Faced behind a stone wall just as the Rebels broke through the place lately occupied by us, but the 2d line of Batle soon settled them, and we were again moved further to the front, during which a shell dropt in our midst killing 3 and wounding 4 more of our Company. I had just told the men to close up, and had got a couple of files ahead when it came to us with a whiz and the job was done, (Sam Burrows, and Gross were covered with blood, and Albert Towne had his Haversack shot away without hurting him. he is as sound as a nut at present.) we closed up like Veterans and moved on as if [p. 7] nothing had happened. we came under the shelter of a hill behind which the 81st Pa were lying, in their front was one of our Batterys with every horse killed. they stood up and gave us 3 cheers as we took position along side of them. while lying here 2 more of our Company were wounded, it was here that Gen Richardson was wounded, i saw him carried off the field. after a while us were moved further to the front during which move i counted our Company, and found we had out of 84 that moved with us in the morning, just 24 men [plus] 2 Sergeants (myself and Frank Stoughton) and our 3 company officers, in all 29 men. *Sergt Brigham came up soon afterwards, having been sent to the rear with a wounded friend.*[15] all our field officers were dismounted, our Flags well Ridled with shot and shell, and the Regiment all told numbered 345 men. we took our position in Face of a Rebel Battery who soon paid us their compliment in the shape of shot and shell, but did us no damage altho every shell Burst directly over our heads. i could see the men at the [p. 8] Guns and watched the course of every shell and i can assure you it was with no pleasant feeling, as we were not permitted to fire a shot. the sun now began to set and the Batle so far as we were concerned was over. we were again moved a little to the front so that we could see over the hill, and laid here all night. we maintained the same position all day on Thursday, while they were fighting away off to the right and Left (this Position was 1 1/2 miles inside of the Rebel front line) but were not allowed to fire only keep their Scouts at a respectable distance. about 3 oclock yesterday morning i heard the Rebels leaving their position and at daylight there was not one to be seen in our front. I believe they have got enough of the devil this week. I must now close with a list of our company Loss known to be killed. . . . write me soon and tel Sarah to do the same. Love to you all. Direct to me the same as the first. Benjamin Hirst.

** P.S. I send you a feather from a Southern Plume. give the thickest one to my Wife. and keep the other for yourself. B Hirst

Rock wall along Roulette Lane at Antietam, probably photographed in September 1891. The 14th occupied this position for about two hours on 17 September 1862. Charles D. Page, History of the Fourteenth Regiment, Connecticut Vol. Infantry. *Meriden, Conn.: Horton, 1906, p. 193.*

Journal Excerpt #3

Sept 17th 1862, turned [out?] this morning about 3 oclock, and began to make final preperations, for the business before us. just at early dawn

4 sheet. Diary part 1
    commenced that gigantic conflict known as the Battle of Antietam, what our position in line of Battle was I did not know, all I know is that we were marched back a litle ways, then turned to the Left, in decending a Hill had a pretty good View of a portion of the Rebel line, saw several of our shels drop in the midst of a corn field and soon saw a lot of Rebs leaving at Double quick. we crossed Antietam Creek, where I had the presence of mind to fill my Canteen with water. *[S]ome of the boys wanted to take off their shoes and stockings to keep their feet dry, and here two or three left us not to be seen again that day.* Filed Left again, in the direction of some woods that were in the rear of where I before saw the rebels, we were pushed along at a rapid Pace for about 20 minuets; when we gained the woods, I got a glance at some Rebel skirmishers that were being driven [p. 2] in by the first Deleware Reg belonging to our Division; here we were ordered to march by the Left Flank through the Woods, and the shels began to fly over our heads, and Boys began to waver, when Gen French road up to us saying: forward there; forward.

for Gods Sake Forward. I'll ride over you, Etc., We got steady in a moment. and pushed along as fast as we could, through the Woods we whent, over the Fields, and right into a large Corn field where the Rebels lay concealed. they gave us a destructive Voley as we entered, which was the first intimation that we had of their prescence.... we maintained our position during the varied changes [p. 3] of the Day, and at night the 14 *Conn* Vol with their Decimated ranks still held a very advanced position of the Field.... Thursday 18th were ready at an early hour to renew the Conflict, having got more Amunition served to us, but no Grub was forth coming, and the rebels kept out of sight, but once in a while we got a bullet flying over our heads if we sat up. Friday 19th, it was early perceived that the Rebels had left during the night, ... leaving their thousands of dead on our hands. these with our own, made a horrible stench in a short time as the weather was so warm. we were moved to the rear during the day, and in consideration of the long time we had been in Front, were spared the disagreeable Duty of helping to bury the Dead. Saturday endeavored to find poor Wilkie who I had left wounded along side a Fence on Wednesday, but could find no trace of him. *Thomas Wilkie was a native of England, aged about 40 years. He had been a soldier in the British army during the Crimean war and often used to tell us about his army life. To his particular chum, Thomas Butterworth he would say, "Na Tom, when we get a feighting, tha mun load, and I'll doe't firing." He fell by my side in the cornfield....* [16] saw several hundred Dead Rebels they were laid in rows, and were being buried in long Trenches. Sunday We devoted to cleaning our Arms and persons, and trying to find Blankets and Haversacks on the Battle Field, our own having been stolen from where we were ordered to leave them. had Religious services this afternoon and every one wore a More Sober Face than I had before observed. for myself, I devoted my time in writing that account of the Battle [p. 2] you so much admired.

～✦～

Letter File #7

Camp Antietam
14 Reg't, C., D CV
September 21st 1862

Dear Sarah,

I write you these few lines to let you know that we are all well at present. our Corps (Sumners) yet occupy the Batle field of Wednesday and have not yet buried all the Secesh dead, altho men have been digging graves ever since. I think we shal have to burn some of them. all the rest of the Army has left here in chase of the rebels, most of them on their heels. I think they must have given them the Devil for the past week, as what Prisoners I have seen saw that they made a great mistake when [p. 2] came here, and I think the rebel skeedadlers will be of the same oppinion before they again see Richmond. I have just heard from John Abby. he is yet alive, but he can't recover as the ball whent through his arm into his body and is lodged in his liver. when he was shot he was doing his duty nobly, he was in the front, and when i first saw him he was he told me some indistinct words about his Wife. *John Abby, born in Wiclow, Ireland, in the year 1827 or 1828, came to this country in 1851. . . . On the morning of Sept 17, just after we crossed the Antietam creek, Abby made the remark to me that he did not think he should come out alive. He left a wife and two children.*[17] I got Martin McGwin [McGuane], and another to carry him of, and they will be able to give his Wife all the particulars. I have also heard from Wilkie. he is in Hospital and in a fair way to soon rejoin us. there is also one of the Talcots that cant recover. the corrected list of yesterday gives our Company loss at 3 killed, and 17 wounded. our Regiment at 108 killed and wounded. a pretty fair begining for the Louzy fourteenth. we dont know how soon we may leave here, but hold [p. 3] ourselves in readiness to go at the word. I want you to send me some postage stamps as we are giving 5 cents for a 3 cent stamp. you might also send me some of the new postage Currency, as chang is scarce. you must not think by this that I am hard up because I aint having yet 15 dollars in my possesion. as soon as we get settled in some place you must send me some handkerchiefs and Towels, as all that I had have skidadled to parts unknown, besides my Ruber Blanket and overcoat. however I am part owner in one Rebel Blanket which is very useful of nights. I have had but one letter since we left Hartford. it is 15 days since our Regiment got a Mail, and the Greenest Regiment in regard to getting letters and Grub that there is in the Service. but I reckon the Boys will learn in time [p. 4] give my respect to all enquiring friends and tell them they would learn more in one month soldiering, then most of them are aware of. tell Morse to give my respects to M Strong and tell him I have yet got his Pipe and have smoked it on 2 Batle fields and in one Batle. I hope you are getting along as well as usual. you must get the hatch way finished. and get a barrell of Cider in the cellar as soon as you can get some that will keep, as the Army mean to finish up this business in less than a year

I must now conclude as I must go on guard to night. I wrote Morse a letter yesterday it is as near correct as I can make it. tell him the Dead around here was over 2000

I remain your Affectionate
Husband Benjamin Hirst.

⌐～～～⌐

Journal Excerpt #4

Monday 22 September, 22d 62 [last 5 characters in pencil]
We arose early this morning and commenced our march for Harpers Ferry, distant about 17 miles. we started about 7 oclock and had a Tremendous har[d] task

to keep up. it was close up close up all the time, the officers and men were falling out every mile, and our Capt Park Hammond, after wasting his breath all the time, to get the men along, fell out himself, and that was the last of him, as he soon after whent home in Cityzens Clothes. his commission had not got here, or he would have been reported for a Deserter. Lieut Emery also Fell out, and it came near finishing him; about 2 oclock we arrived opposite Harpers Ferry. the Bridges across the Shenandoah river were burnt, and it was a Glorious [p. 3] sight to see our Troops fording the river and climbing the opposite Heights. We crossed the river up to our waists in water, our fine Band playing Yankee doodle and Away Down South to Dixie all the time they were crossing. We marched straight through Harpers Ferry and Bolivar until we gained Bollivar heights, where we encamped, (and a more miserable Crew you never beheld, we had no tents and one half of us were without overcoats and blankets, our knapsacks with all our litle notions in them were in Washington.) I then began to look around for some kind of shelter and saw some men digging in a Rifle pit in Front of us. I saw them take out a tent that had been hid there the week before when our troops surrendered the place

[The ink and stationery of the following are different from the preceding, indicating it was written at a different time.]

to the rebels,[18] me and a few more soon pitched in, and were fortunate enough to secure one for ourselves. Next day we devoted our time to making ourselves as comfortable as circumstances would permit, and we soon found out we were in no enviable place. twas cold and Dreary the whole time we staid here, and over one half were down with the Dysentery in a very short time.

～～～

Letter File #8

Camp Harpers Ferry
October 1st 1862

Dear Sarah,

I received 2 letters and Newspapers from you last night and was very happy to get them as we had not heard a word from Home since I last wrote you at Fort Ethan Allen. the latest letter I got was posted on the 24 Sept, and the other on the 8th. I think there is a letter or 2 due me yet. ~~after we left Fort Ethan Allen~~ I sent you a letter every few days after we left Fort Ethan Allan, and I hope you got them all as I tried to have them read continuously like the N York Ledger.

We do not know how long we may be here, we have no convenience for Staying here, and have less for a further March into dixie. the things we lost at the Batle have not been replaced [p. 2] and the other things we left at Fort Ethan Allan have been sent to Washington and there remain to our detriment. the consequence of this neglect, has already produced its natural results, about one half of the Regiment have got the Dysentery, and a many of the other half would (so they say) sooner shoot at our own Field Officers (Regimental Field Officers) than the minions of Jeff Davis. They are not the men they pretended to be, they can say go, but have forgotten how to say come. Their own comfort is all that they look too, and they care not how they use better men than themselves. I do not write this in any Factious Spirit, but because I know that we might be made more comfortable if our line officers would be Gentle men (a few instances: at inspection of the men on the 21st every man who had cut his body belt, to suit his notion, was charged with the Price of a new Belt. [p. 3] (so ordered Col Perkins) a few days ago another man wore his body belt passing through the loops of his cartridge box (as all the old soldiers wear them) Col Perkins ordered him to be fined 4 dollars. as I saw for myself on Frank Stoughtens Book. this same man done more real service to his country at the Batle of Antietam than all Col Perkins done since he joined this Regiment. again all the Rations that we have received since we occupied this place (a week ago last monday) has been our rations of hard Bread and Coffee, Sugar, and pork. we have had Fresh meat once, rice once, and Beans once. there is now a plentiful supply of goods in stores at Harpers Ferry. but Col perkins will not pass a man off this camp. (our Camp is on Bolivar Heights) so that those of us who have got a little money are compeled to get things of the Sutlers at their own Prices. you must not think that I am [p. 4] discouraged by my writing to you thus because I am not. as long as I have health and the means to get what I can eat, I shall do so, when my means fail and the present system is carried out in our Regiment, there will be one less Soldier and one more theif around (friend Morse can make notes of this letter as it is for him especially that I am entering into our grievences. he wants the truth and I write nothing but what I know to be true SS B Hirst.) again at the Batle of Antietam we were ordered to throw away our Ruber Blankets and overcoats, now they say we must pay for them, (no one but the skidadlers, had a chance to see about them until Friday Evening of the 19inst when there was not a rag left worth carrying away). now for a Brighter side we yesterday got our letters, and also 3 visitors from Rockville, namely Messrs Tracy, Corbin and Prescott. it done most of us [p. 5] good to see them, especially those who got letters by them. I did not get any until just now when I got one from Mrs Morse, which seems to flatter me very much. if I had thought my letter [about the Antietam battle] would have been so extensively read I would have wrote it a litle more inteligibly. the Boys are now getting their parcels brought by our visitors and I guess it will cure a many of our Company of the Blues, a disease that has not yet reached my litle squad of Tom [Butterworth], Joe, John, a Boy named Tom Stafford and myself. Tom has just got a parcel which pleases him Hugely. you say you would like to send me something good to eat, but I dont think it advisable to do so at present as we dont know but what we may leave every day. you might get us some good stockings and a comforter knit and send me word when they are ready, and I might be able to tell you where to send them too when they are ready to be sent [p. 6] if we dont get our knapsacks in the course of a few days I shal also want another shirt and 2 pairs of Cotten drawers, the drawers you had better get ready, the shirt you can buy at any time if i should want it. you might also send me a cigar box or a small Box of Liquor packed with care so as not to get broken. Luther will know how to do it. we can get plenty of cheese at 20 cents per pound tobaco 1 dollar loaf Sugar at 20 cents dried beef at 25 cents Bologna 25 Scotch Ale 40 cents per Botle and Porter [?] the same. give my respects to Dr Bailey and Family and tel him I should like to have his Pills and Diarahea medicine and another Box of that Salve [?] and a vial of Lavender, as all the things that I had of the kind has skidadled. I will write him as soon as i get a chance. give my respect to all enquiring Friends I remain your Affectionate Husband

Benjamin Hirst.

Lt. Col. Sanford H. Perkins, commanding the 14th at Fredericksburg. Box 1, Vol. 1, PG 85, #S1436, Edward B. Eaton Collection, Connecticut State Archives, Connecticut State Library.

Letter File #9

Camp Harpers Ferry.
Oct 13.th 1862.

Dear Sarah,

I have just received the good things you sent me and it has put new life into me. I had slowly began to recover from my sickness, and when we got the things you sent it has completed the cure, especially your Likeness which I value more than all. Carroll is waiting for me to finish these few lines, and we must go on Picket Duty in an hour so I cant write you but a few lines. John sends Maggie [Penfield] a Testament. it is his Birth Day to day.[19] give them our love (that is Mother [i.e., Sarah's mother] and Maggie, I will write you again tomorrow. I send you a looking glass that John Picked up on the Battle Field of Antietam. when you look at yourself in it remember me always. Carroll [p. 2] says he must go, and they are calling for me on the line. Love to all your Affectionate Husband until Death reunites us

Benjamin Hirst
to His Beloved Wife

Letter File #10

Camp Harpers Ferry
October 15.th 1862

Dear Sarah,

I write you these few lines this morning, thinking you will probably get them before you get the one i sent by Mr Carroll. you must know that we did not get the things you sent us until Monday forenoon, altho Carroll got here on Friday, but the longer we had to wait for them, the more acceptable they were when we got them. every thing was in good order but that Bottle of Bitters which got Broke and spoiled Toms Loaf of Bread. tell the folks not to send plain Bread out here as we can now get a pretty decent Loaf for 10 cents, and Ginger Cakes at 1 cent each. every old house and shanty in Bollivar has been made in[to] a store and it Beats all the Fairs that I ever saw [p. 2] for Jews and Cheap Johns.

They think nothing of charging 9.50 for a pair of Boots. you need not make me those Cotten drawers I spoke of, but let me have another under shirt like the last, and a good pair of Mitts with a high wrist band. also a good heavy pair of Cow hide boots. these with the things in my knapsack will make a pretty heavy Kitt.

I supose before you get this that Capt Hammond will have arrived Home. he tried to get away before, and that was what he wrote to his Father about, he has never been mustered in to the United States Service, and they cant make him serve outside of Conn. he never bid us good Bye or let us know that he was going home. We did not know until he was some miles on his way. the Boys hope he will never regret it, if he does not come back again. *He did his duty like a man while with us, but the march from Antietam to this place was too much for him.*[20]

[p. 3] I am a great deal better since I got your Likeness, and the good things that we have been Feasting upon the Past 2 days. John is a little sick yet, but hopes to get over it in a day or two, Tom is first rate, and Joe dito. I am sorry to say that Poor Wilkie has had his Leg took off. I last night saw a letter from the Hospital in which this fact is mentioned, also that another of our Hartford Tent mates, has lost his Life. his name is James Henderson and he was shot in the hand at the Battle. he died with Lock Jaw. there was 2 letters came for Wilkie on monday evening. I shal write him to day, and send them to him. if you see his Wife tell her his Address is, Mount Pleasant Hospital (Ward No 4) Washington D.C. the rest of the wounded are doing well. Gross and Hospotsky have joined us and are doing duty. I forgot to tell you that Crombie skidaddled to Parts unknown. he is a C———d to the Back Bone

[p. 4] I must now conclude for the Present. give my Love to all.

your Affectionate Husband
till Death Ben Hirst

❧

Letter File #11

Charlston Road. on Picket.
Sunday October. 19.th 1862

Dear Sarah,

I write you these few lines to let you know that I am well at the present moment, and hope that this will find you all the same. I thought I should have heard from you last night, but sopose that Mr Carroll did not get home as soon as he intended. I sent you a few lines by him and also wrote you last Tuesday Evening. tell Dr. Bailey that his Diareaha Medicine has done me a great Deal of good, the other Botle i have not had any occasion to use yet. that sweet Bread you sent kept first rate, and it lasted us until last Evening. the Pears that you sent were the Best that I ever eat. that is judging by the one I eat myself. the rest I gave away. Joe is well, and he last night got a letter from Old Stearh who says he has sent us a box of Bologna, with a litle fixings. John is not as well as ought to be, he has had a bad cold and it has pulld him down considerable but he hopes to soon be fit for duty. Tom keeps first rate, and Sam Barrows dito, most of the other Boys are but indifferently well. the past week has been a trying one with us, the nights are very cold, and we have not yet got our knapsacks or Blankets. *In camp it is cough, cough, cough all night long, from one end of the line to the other.*[21] I have got an old overcoat that I x x x. it helps me considerable at night, especially when on Picket ([as] we were [p. 3] 4 times the past week.) I sopose you would like to know what Picket duty is. it is nothing but a chain of Sentinals all along our Front, sometimes 3 or 4 miles in advance of our lines. we have several Regiments doing this duty each day. they are to be on the Alert at all times, to stop all persons attempting to pass them without the proper authority and to give warning of the approach of the Enemy, besides keeping them at Bay as long as posible. sometimes we go in one direction and the next a different one. last Thursday we were at Weverton, Maryland, and in the night it rained like the Devil. after standing it as long as posible I and Tom dug for a large house which was filled with troops. every window in it was broken, and Tom and myself [p. 4] thought ourselves very fortunate in getting possession of the 3 top steps of the Garret stairs for a bunk. it would make you laugh to see what ideas we are getting of Luxuries. the Boys in our tent (when in Camp) think we are a litle Aristocratic because we have an old door to lay on, and a piece of board for a Pillow. we often Plan what we will do when we get home. my idea is to rent the house and move into the Wood shed. that is if it would suit you. joking aside Dear Sarah when we do come Home, we shal know how to appreciate the Blessings of Home, and I think it will make us Wiser and better men. give my respects to all. and the next time you write tell me if you killed the pigs yet. and how Curly gets along. John asked me how much money he left in your hands can you tell. Love to Mother and Maggie and yourself. I remain your Affectionate Husband Always. B. Hirst.

Journal Excerpt #5

We staid at Harpers Ferry, or Rather on Bollivar Heights for 5 or 6 weeks during which time nothing very interesting happened. it was Drill one day and Picket the next until we got tired of it, especialy Picket as we did not have Blankets enough for the men notwithstanding the Newspapers to the Contrary. one time while on the Reserve [p. 2] Picket, our outposts were attacted by some Rebel Cavalry and were pierced. our Company and one other were ordered out to reestablish them. we started at Double quick, and passed the 10th N. York. 72. [?] and away we whent on the Road to Halltown, until we passed outside our Videttes. we got stiff joints for our trouble, and that was all, for Devil a Rebel could we find. While here I devoted one day to looking around Harpers Ferry, and it must have been a busy place before the Rebellion, some of the houses, were good substantial houses, and the Government Works, had been built in the best manner but all was now in ruins, they having been burnt at the breaking out of the rebellion, by our own men rather than let them fall in the hands of the rebels. I also [p. 3] saw the engine house in which the Traitor John Brown was captured, and saw some marks of the conflict the Chivalry had with him. I afterwards visited his cave but had not time to explore it. About the midle of October a Strong Colum was sent in the direction of Winchester to reconoiter, and our Regiment was sent into Maryland to Guard a Ford, and Rail Road Depot at Weaverton; no Rebels made their appearance and we were marched back the next day;

We also about this time sent in requisitions for Shoes and Clothing, and sent to Washington for our knapsacks. but we were destined to never see them again. There has been so much said about McCllenan, having everything sent to him, that the Army required, that it has since disgusted me with the Lying statements made in the Party Newspapers. We had never yet got what belonged to us, our Requisitions for Clothing were unheeded because the Quartermaster had them not, and he could not get transportation for our knapsacks until it was too late for us to get them. (a many of us had a Blanket and underclothing in them.) it was sheer Humbug at this time, to say the Army had everything they wanted. When we started from here on our Virginia Campaghn my whole Kit was the Shoes, Pants, Vest, Blouse and Cap I had in Hartford. I had 2 shirts on my back, a Stolen Overcoat, and was a share holder in a rebel Blanket, a fine assortment for a Winter Campaghn, but there were other ones worse of than me, as they were without overcoats and Blankets both. all we had at night was a flimsy shelter tent, and one Regiment in our [p. 2] brigade did not have them even (130 Pa).

Letter File #12

on Picket again near
Harpers Ferry Va.
October 24th 1862

Dear Sarah

I received yours of the 17th and was very happy to hear that you are all well, and to be able to say that I am well too. you must be somewhat mistaken with regard to my not writing as I have certainly wrote at the least once in every week, and would write oftener if I had the time, which I have not, sometimes when I feel like it. I cant lay off duty like some of the rest, sick or Well i have never been excused from Duty one day as yet. so you must not think I am neglectful if you do not get as many letters as you would like. I shal write you as often as I can, and am much pleased with your improvement in writing and spelling, as shown in your last [p. 2] letter. I hope you will continue to improve. Gustav Winnans [Winans] has not yet got his Box, but he last night got his money from Adams Express. there was 5 dollars for Sam Barrows that he got, there is no prospect of our getting any money as yet. I shal want some pretty soon as I am getting run ashore. Anthony Quin owes me 4 dollars, but I have not seen him this 6 weeks, so I shant get that in a hurry. the kind of shirts I want is light blue Flanell undershirts, to come up pretty well around the neck, and to have long sleeves. The boots to be No 8 large Cow hides, with the Pegs well cleaned inside. a good pair of mittens for myself and one for John. I have not said any thing to John in regard to Krempien [?] as I know that she has not sent him any Wine or any thing else. John Watslong sent a small botle of Whyskey [p. 3] and some Tobaco, in the box you sent. that is all that he has received. I have seen some of Watslongs letters to John, and think the Wedding if any, will be with him, as his letters seem to imply.[22] We have not yet heard when Carroll got home. I hope you like your litle present. it was all I could get worth sending. When you write me again tell all about Poor Abbys Funeral, and how the Folks on the hill take it. how did Morse like his hard Tack and Bacon, I hope he enjoyed it as well as I have at times. we are getting some fresh meat just now and it seems a great Luxury. I think we shall soon move further into Virginia and may have another fight if the Rebels dont leave Winchester, as we want it for our own use. i think the sooner it comes of[f] the better. Sam Barrows [p. 4] has just asked me to ask his mother to send him a pair of Buckskin driving Gloves. you tell her. if you think it best, send us the[m?] in place of the mittens. Dear Sarah i had just got so far in my letter when our outside Pickets came running in, saying the Rebel Cavalry were after them. Co D and B were sent to receive them and away we whent at Double quick for about 1 1/2 miles, but could see nothing but a niggar cutting Corn stalks. had to stay there until Dark, so that will delay this one day later. give my respects to all my Friends, and Love to Mother and Maggie. I remain your Affectionate Husband Benjamin Hirst

Direct according to the first Direction. namely Washington D.C.

Letter File #13

October 27.th 1862.
Near Bolivar Heights.
On Picket again

Dear Sarah,

I write you these few lines to inform you that Mike Tiernan Died last night, he had been sick ever since we came here, and was near dead when they moved him to the Hospital. his disorder turned to lung Fever, and he Died at 10 oclock last night. the Boys Telegraphed to Rockville this morning. Gustav Winans has not yet got his Box, owing to the way it was sent to him. there is nothing brought to Harpers Ferry but what is addressed to Soldiers. so when you send me those things have them Directed thus.

Benjamin Hirst
Co D, 14.th Conn Vol.
Harpers Ferry, Vir.

if not they will be detained at Sandy Hook 2 miles on the other side the River, and we cant get a pass to go [p. 2] over there, and it may be a week or two yet before Gus Winans gets his Box. I had some Boys from old Chester to see me yesterday and paid them a visit. they belong to the 124 Pensy Vol and while I was with them I was introduced to Mr. Benjamin Hirst Junr, Cousin Ben. his Mother (Aunt Molly) is Head Nurse in the Mt Pleasant Hospital, Washington D.C. Ben showed me a letter from his Mother in which she says she has a man in her Ward who lost his leg at Antietam, and that he belonged to the same Co and Regt. as his (Ben's) Cousins Joe John and Ben, so I guess that Poor Wilkie is in good hands, if she takes to him. Emma Fields husband is soldiering and a good many seem to know me that I cant remember. It is thought that we shal Winter here and the Colonal has gone to Washington to see about our knapsacks and Blankets. we have been furnished with [p. 3] new overcoats and Pants, besides Shoes and Stockings, so we are a litle better off than we were, but the nights are colder here than in Rockville. we have Frosts quite often at night, so you must hurry those Boots and Gloves along. I am in good health at present and have arrived at the stage that old soldiers consider Vetran, namely regular in my Bowels, and Lousy. and most of the other boys have the later if not the former. Tom [Butterworth] says he is a older soldier than me, as he got them a week ahead of me. however we have a good hunt every day and soon hope to get rid of the cusses. *Perhaps you may recollect that among other gimcracks sent out here were some nice little bags filled with a highly perfumed insect powder, warranted to kill. Well some of the boys swear that these bags are headquarters for new tribes. The bags are at a discount now.*[23] why dont Morse write me about the Grub i sent him, and how he is getting along. how does Holgate get along, and tell me if his Wife has come home. give my respects to him and tell him tom would like, first rate, if he could go to Heusers and get his beer. it is harder for him to go to sleep now, than it used to be for him to keep awake. [p. 4] I wish all the Rest of the Boys were as well as myself, and hope that you are all better. if so you are doing well. I should like to have some Cayene Pepper sent to us, same as what Mrs. Butterworth sends to Tom. I must cut this short as we are ordered to Camp again so give my Love to all. I remain your Affectionate Husband Ever. Benjamin Hirst Co. D, 14 Conn Vol.

Harpers Ferry, Vir.

Letter File #14

October 30.th 1862
Camp near Harpers Ferry

Dear Sarah

I write you these few lines in a hurry, not knowing if I shal have time to finish this as we have been under Arms since day light this morning, and there is a great movement of troops going on. what it is we dont know.[24] I received a letter from you last night and am glad to hear you are well, but I dont want you to dig Potatoes. it will be the best for you to hire some one to do it. I am sorry to inform you that i received a letter from my Aunt Mary [Hirst] informing me of Poor Wilkies Death and sending me a lock of his hair. I have sent the hair to his Wife. enclosed in this you will find my Aunts letter. that 25 cent bill was not [p. 2] out here. John is getting better and Joe is doing duty again. I also recieved a letter from Kate [Smiley] cramed full of Politics. they are all well at present. we have not had any letters from Washington for 9 days before last night. I got the letter with the postage stamps in it. you had better kill the hogs as soon as you can, and be sure to keep enough of Pork to last you one year. about your coming here to see me you must not think of such a thing at present, as you would never be satisfied with yourself if you did. it is enough for a man to do, let alone a woman. as long as I am in health I shal do. when anything happens to me I will send for you. I must now conclude for the present. I remain your Affectionate husband Benjamin Hirst. P.S. send me 10 dollars in your next letter, if you have it and I will pay you to suit when I see you B.H.

While at Harper's Ferry a call was made upon Co. D for a color Sergeant. Stoughton, Brigham, [Charles E.] Dart and myself talked the matter over, when Dart solved the question by saying, "Here goes for color sergeant in the next fight."[25]

Letter File #15

November 1, 1862
On the Road in Louden, co. Vir.
But the Devil take me if I know Where.

Dear Sarah

I take this oppertunity of writing you a few lines, while we are resting on the Road side. I think the Grand Movement has comenced and that we shal have a hand in it. if we do so I hope you will hear a good account of us. our Regiment dont look so big this morning, as we have but about 300 Muskets with us. you can judge the Regiment by our Company, we have just 31 Muskets. on our leaving Bollivar Heights we had about 40 but some of them have got sick and we have 4 or 5 in the Rear Guard. [Lt. Chelsea] Vinton is the only Company officer we have with us, and and I am the only Sergeant with the Company, as Frank Stoughten fell out sick this morning. I hope the whole Regiment wont get sick before we get to our journeys end. enclosed in this you will find a letter from Brother William [Hirst]. it seems [p. 2] he thinks, some of us "may" kick the Bucket, and as he wants to know where we would like to be burried if it should happen. I will answer for Myself by saying at Old Chester, by all means, unless you should happen to go before me in which case I should want to be with you. enough to that, I shant go that road at present so you must keep up your courage as I do mine. John altho getting slowly better, was left at harpers Ferry. Joe and T.B. [Tom Butterworth] is with us lively as ever. you had better send your letters to me Directed to Washington D.C. as we shal be able to get them sooner that way than any other. you did not tell me what you sent in Gus Winnans Box. he had not got it when we left Harpers Ferry so I might as well give it good by. I must now conclude, give my love to All my Friends, to Mother and Maggie and keep a big Lot for yourself. your Affectionate Husband Benjamin Hirst

Journal Excerpt #6

October 30th, 62 Were under marching orders early in the morning and about noon started, very glad to leave bollivar, as we had lost 19 good men there by sickness. after going about 5 miles we encamped for the night. Oct 31, made but a few miles more, on account of the trouble in getting so large a Force in order.

Nov 1 and 2d, came onto the Rebel Pickets each day and drove them in without much trouble, passed through Grove Ville, a small pretty Place, [and camped there] this night. a final disposition was made of our Knapsacks; it appears that they were started in a Team the Day after us, and the quarter master in charge, despairing of getting up to us, had them unloaded in an old Barn and left them there. they were Pillaged by our own Troops, and afterward [p. 3] were carried off by the Rebels, who were allowed to hang on our Rear.

November 3d Passed through Crab Ville [?] and had had a Artillery Skirmish with the Enemys Cavalry at Snickers Gap, and Encamped near Upperville for a day or two. this Valley (Louden) is the Richest I have ever seen, it was abounding in Grain and Cattle, and we crossed several beautiful streams of water in our March.

Letter File #16

Camp near Uperville [Upperville] Vir
November 6.th 1862

My Dear Sarah

I avail myself of the present oppertunity to write you a few lines. you will perceive by my last letters that we left Bollivar Heights last Thursday. I sent you a letter in the morning, not expecting to move so soon, but as soon as the mail had gone we received the orders to be ready to move at one minuets notice. I then wrote you a few lines in Pencil, advising you of it. we marched that day about 6 miles, and then camped for the night. the next day marched again, and then pitched our tents expecting to stay ther 5 or 6 days, but the next morning, were on the move again. I then wrote you a few lines on the road side. we have made another march since, and have been encamped here for 2 days but are in readiness to move at every [p. 2] minuet, so you can see what are our present prospects of settling down for the Winter. I am happy to say that I stand it so far as well as the best of our men. I have had plenty to do since we left Bollivar. the first day I had charge of the rear Guard, another day served in Guarding our Amunition train, another was the only Sergeant with the company. but am now glad to say that Sergeant Stoughten is with us again and in better health, and quite a number of our Regiment have come up, making our present number about 460 men. I think i told you we left John at Harpers Ferry. he was getting better but we all thought he had not better march with us until he got stronger. we have no present means of knowing how to write to him as letters come to the Regiment (that is when they come at all). I think some of our Rockville Friends would change [p. 3] their minds about all the south being in a starving condition if they could see this Beautiful Valley. with all the grain and Cattle yet left here, everything looks Lovely around, and it is a pity it will look so differant after we are gone. as this Section [is] strongly Secesh every house and barn has to be guarded from our own Depredators. they will not take our money, but take Secesh money at sight, and in that they are wrong as I think we shal at least hold this Valley until a settlement is made, of which there is no sighns at present. I did not get that Box from Winans and dont know that I ever shal. We came near getting our knapsacks but our officers with their usual Ability defeated us out of them after getting them within 4 miles of the Regiment. they left them in an old Barn on our line of march here, pretending they wanted the teams to go [to] [p. 4] the Ferry for stores. we have since learned they have been Rifled of their contents by the other men that came after us. some of our men saw them and there was no guard over them and that any one could help themselves to what they wanted, so I think we can bid good by to them. we have got to our old Diet again, that is Pork Crackers Coffee and Sugar, and are very glad to get that. you must send me some money as soon as you can put it in a letter and I shal probably get it in a week or two. I must now conclude as the mail is closing. give my respects to all.

I remain your Affectionate
Husband Benj Hirst.

Journal Excerpt #7

Nov 7th resumed our march, and were visited with the first snow storm of the season. Nov 8 passed through Rectortown and Salem, (both Deserted places) and encamped about 8 miles from Warrenton. November 9th, resumed our march and arrived at Warrenton about noon. this must have been a very Fine city before the

Rebellion, but every thing now seemed desolate. of inhabitants I saw none but a few, Ladies, Peering at us through the half opened Blinds and most of them were Weeping as they looked upon us. as we marched up the main street our Band played Yankee Doodle which did not seem to console them a bit. we finally encamped on the Allexandria road. We staid here 3 or 4 days, and it was here we heard that the Gallant McCllenan was superseded,[26] and it was here he passed in Review of us for the Last (but not his Final one) time. I saw Warriors Weep as he rode bye, while hats and Caps were thrown high in the Air by the men and officers. Saturday 15 We started on a Forced march towards Fredricksburg. Sunday marched 17 miles. once during the day I fell out for the first time, being completly exausted. during this days march [p. 2] I was very glad to pick up Tur[n]ip Peel (that some more fortunate devil had thrown away) and eat it to stay the cravings of my appetite for something differant to crackers and Pork. next day we marched about 10 miles arriving about 2 miles in the rear of Falmouth, early in the afternoon. here we encamped.

... *I had a talk with a native Butternut. He told me there were not over 300 rebels over the river at Fredricksburg and there was a good ford just below the dam. Our division of the 2d Corps was in the advance and we fully expected to be ordered across and secure the city. Gen. Sumner and his staff had a talk at the head of the column, which resulted in our encamping where we were.*[27]

Letter File #17

Sunday Nov. 16.th
in Camp a few miles from
Fredricksburg.

My Dear Sarah,

I received your letter dated the 8 inst. yesterday morning just as we were on the point of marching again. you must not be suprised at not hearing from us, as they only send us letters when it suits the Government. some of our letters are 2 weeks on the way. enclosed in this you will find a letter from Washington. it was received by me yesterday morning or I should have sent it to you sooner. I want you should show it to Mrs Wilkie. Last Sunday we marched into Warrenton having had a tough march through Louden Valley, being in sight [p. 2] of the Rebels every night but found them gone in the morning. I saw Tom Quinn last Sunday, he was looking for us as we entered Warrenton. he was in good health and spirits. The Old Woman [Tom Quinn's wife?] was out to see him and Anthony she tried to get him home, but did not suceed. We encamped near Warrenton 4 or 5 days during which time the Soldiers General [McClellan] took Farewell of us. but he will arise again. yesterday we marched about 10 miles and to day we made 16 miles. but it has gone very hard with a many. you would see sick men at every Rod, notwithstanding that

(Damnable Lie) we are the Best Fed and the Best Clothed Army in the World. I received a letter some time ago with 5 dollars in it and some Postage Stamps. yesterday I received the same amount in your other letter [p. 3] you are not more sorry than myself at not getting thos Dough nuts, as I thought about them every day. and what is worse we have not seen Mr. Hunt, since the day after we left Harpers Ferry, and we have not received a thing through his hands as yet. it was Humbug to send him out at all. the sooner he goes home the better. I hope we shal get the things soon, but we see no prospect of it yet. dont send any thing again until I write you, for it may be a month yet before we get setled for the Winter, as the Boots and Mittens would be very useful.

Monday 17.th 1862 I had to stop writing last night as it got too dark to see and we have no candles. on the march to day we marched 9 miles and are encamped about 1 mile from Fredricksburg. Vir. the Rebels are on the other side of the Rhaphanock, [p. 4] so you may look out for Deviltry in a few days. I am glad to hear that you are in good health and I hope you keep up your spirits, as I try to keep up mine. if the women of Rockville could see the Desolation that reighns here, they would indeed wish the War at an end. not that I wish you to understand that I repent of my coming here, but that I have become disgusted with the Knavery and Humbug as shown by our Leaders in regard to our Comfort. but every dog will have his day. and some of these will have a short one. I am happy to say that my health is pretty good but I am Devilish tired in my legs, as Cracker and Pork for a week together is but poor Grub to march on. I have not heard a word from John since we left the Ferry. I have got 2 letters for him, but dont [know] where [to] send them. Sam Barrows wants his mother to send him 5 dollars. I guess Mr. Morse has trouble of his own, and that is the reason he does not come to see you. his Brother Lewis is about Enlisting and he does not know what to do with his things. I must stop writing at present. Love to Mother and Maggie not forgeting your own Dear Self. I remain your Affectionate Husband Benjamin Hirst.

Journal Excerpt #8

on the 17th were ordered with our Brigade, to Belle Plains near the mouth of Potomac Creek. when we started (it being about 4 P.M.) Old French rode up to us and said he would not part with us without showing us what he thought of us. he rode at our head right through Falmouth where he stood uncovered until we had filed past him. from Falmouth to Belle Plains is but about 8 or 9 miles, but owing to the late hour when we started, it was resolved by our Col. (Acting Brigadier Gen) [Dwight Morris] [p. 3] to encamp for the night, soon after Gen French left us. Resumed our March early next morning, and had gone about a mile when it became apparent to all of us, that Col. Morris was lost. it was in Vain he examined his Chart; he could not tell the East from the West, so he marched and Counter-marched us until I wished the Devil had him where he belongs time and again. we finally fell in with one of our Cavalry Pickets, who furnished him with a guide. we arrived at Belle Plains about 4 P.M. having been marched about 22 miles to make about 6. we were very glad to ~~through~~ throw ourselves on the Wet ground, and in our wet clothes try to sleep until morning. this was the first time Morris had had a separate command, and it was here he proved himself not fit for a Corporals Guard. one of his orders [was] to Bunch Em up (meaning to form Divisions,) and another was Straighten Em Out (meaning Left Dress.) He has been Named old Bunch Em ever since and he justly deserves the Title.

Gen. William H. French, commanding the 3d Division, 2d Corps at Antietam, Fredericksburg, and Chancellorsville. Box 5, PG 85, #L7578, Edward B. Eaton Collection, Connecticut State Archives, Connecticut State Library.

Col. Dwight Morris, first commander of the 14th. Charles D. Page, History of the Fourteenth Regiment, Connecticut Vol. Infantry. *Meriden, Conn.: Horton, 1906, facing title page.*

Letter File #18

Camp on Belle Plains. V
Friday November 21, 62

Dear Sarah,

I write you these lines, to let you know that we have changed our location again, and may posibly stay here for a week as our Brigade is on Detached Service. we have just gone through the severest trial, that we have had since enlisting. I had rather go through another Antietam every few days, than what we have had to endure the past 3 days, at the same time I stand it as well as the best of them. 3 days ago our brigade was detached on special duty to this place which is called Belle Plains. it is situated about 45 miles from Washington and near Potomac Creek just above Bull Point on the Potomac river. it is a perfect level plain and about 3 miles long and one wide. our duties are to guard the Government [p. 2] Depot here, and guard Bagage Wagons repair roads and help unload Vesels. when our troops capture Fredricksburg, we shal probably go to the Depot at Acquia Creek. if we do so it will be several weeks job. by that time Mr Hunt may be here with the things entrusted to his care. if he should not get along in time for Thanksgiving, it will be a slim affair for us. if I could have had 10 dollars to spare i would have given it for those Boots, that you sent to his care. I was going to tell you of our march here, from Front of Fredricksburg. all day on the 18th, we were kept under arms as the Rebels were in Force. we had Roll Call every hour, until 4 oclock P.M. when We were ordered to this Place. our Brigade Genral (Col Morris) was instructed to march us about 5 miles that evening thus making a nice easy march of about 10 miles for us next day. he done so, but when [the] Damd Nicompoop waked up [p. 3] he was lost, and he floundered us all over the Country until Evening, this in a cold drizly rain until each man was wet through was no joke. when we got here we had to lay in our wet Cloths until morning when he moved us again a litle nearer to the river. this compeld us to pack up again and leave the litle wood we had got together. we had just our shelter tent up (a shelter tent is 2 or more pieces of cloth about 5 ½ feet square with Buttons and Button holes on 3 sides of each piece, these when buttoned togather, you can crawl under, but can not sit upright in them) when it began to rain like the Devil again, the ground which is clay was soon flooded, and those of the men who were too tired to stand, were soon Stuck in the Mud, and all were well Soaked all night. it rained all day to day but our Teams brought us plenty of Wood and we made out to get our cloths dry, besides Tom and Joe and myself bought some boards to lay on tonight. I reckon we shal do [p. 4] pretty well tonight, besides the Weather looks like clearing up. I have not heard from John yet, or the other boys that we left at the Ferry. We have a very slim Company at present owing to the Shirks we have. the disease seems to be infectious, as some of the stoutest men in the Company get it. of effective men we have about 30. and the New Capt appointed over us, has been in Hospital since his promotion. in the list of Promotions they gave nothing to our Company, owing to Lieut Emerys sickness, and Capt Hammonds Skidadling home. it is rumourd that Lieut Vinton has sent in his resignation, so they go. Saturday morning Nov. 22.d Slept good last night and feel a litle more like myself again, and begin to think i can stand anything, especialy if I could get a Glass of Rum when I feel like it. you will have to send me a few more dollars until Uncle Samuel pays me what he ows me, when I will return it, and some fine day I will return myself. and i think a litle Wiser if not better man. I hope you keep well, and keep up your courage as becomes the Wife of a Soldier, because nothing will please me better than to hear that you are doing so. Tom [Butterworth] wants to know why his Wife dont write. he is not in the best health. neither is Joe. some of the Irish boys are down in the mouth so that taking all things together you have one of the toughest men of the lot. give my Love to mother and Maggie and accept the same yourself. your Affectionate Husband Benjn Hirst.

Direct to Washington as before. B Hirst

Letter File #19

Camp Belle Plains Vir
Thursday, Thanksgiving day. 62

Dear Sarah,

I write you these few lines to let you know that we are still staying here, and that there is no sighn of Mr Hunt coming here, or the big boxes either so that I must depend on something else to keep Warm, and in order to do that i must have some money. all that I have at this moment is five cents, and Tom is as bad off as myself. Joe is but litle better off, as he yesterday gave six dollars for a Pair of Boots. I think you had better send me about 20 dollars, so that I can get what I want, and if those things should happen to get here before the money, i should have no need to spend it all. I must have one or the other very soon or I shal be a bad Egg before long. wet feet day and night are not the best things in the world for long life, and I have no present desire to visit Kingdom come, so write as soon as you get [p. 2] this, and relieve the sorrows of your Poor Old Man whose trembling limbs bear testimony to Republican neglect. I received the other day a letter from John he is in the Convalecent Camp at Alexandria and is getting along first rate. Tom Butterworth is around yet but he cant sleep at nights owing to the pains in his back. I am better than I was when i last wrote you and but for a Night Cough, should be in good health. I think a quart of good Brandy would Cure it, in short order. Lieut Vinton has resighned and expects to go home in a week or two (sooner if he can get) so you see we chose a bully set of Officers in Hartford, and the men who elected them are not worth their Salt to the Country or the cause. I presume if we get Winter Quarters somewhere they will be with us in short time, but they cant Lie to us whatever yarns they might write home about things they know nothing about. I think you Women in Rockville ought to pitch in to those men who got up that Big Box Concern, it was a foolish [p. 3] expenditure of the Peoples money and has done more harm than good. get him home, get him home, as soon as you can; and hear his account how one days march played him out, and see how many of us he Conversed with, and if he can tell one of us from Tom the Devil. every thing in the fighting line seems to have come to a stand still. at the very point where we ought to have had one, when our division arrived opposite Fredricksburg we might have walked in the City without much trouble but to day it would be a big job for our whole Army to do it, and in my humble opinion the longer it is put off, the more difficult it will be. I must now go on duty so you must excuse me for cutting this short. give my respects to all enquiring friends and Love to mother and Maggie I remain as Ever

your Affectionate
Husband
Benjn Hirst.

Letter File #20

Camp Belle Plains Virginia
December 1st, 1862

Dear Sarah,

I received your letter Dated the 25 Nov, and was very glad to hear from you, and that you are all well. I am also glad that Leonora Sloan is boarding with you as i think she will be good Company for you. I think the men here are recruiting their health a litle, as in addition to Crackers and Pork we are getting a litle rice and a few beans, and to day we made a litle Tea. to us this is high living. I reckon when i come home and you ask me what i want for dinner I shall be able to tell you ([if?] icod i would like to tell you now). how is it you dont get more of my letters, I write you about every 4 or 5 days, and get an answer about every 2 weeks, and i look for one from you at least once a week. [p. 2] I certainly enclosed a washington letter to you in one of mine, and in this you will find another one from Aunt Molly [i.e., Mary Hirst], which one i thought I sent from Warenton, as I received it there. Every thing seems to be at a stand still for some thing or other. i reckon that Mc Cllenan was not the slowest Gen in the service, but this will probably be one of the finishing touches of the War, so i for one am content to wait and see. What does that old fogy Hunt, have to say for himself. when I saw him at Bollivar I thought, he was going to do big things for us, as he said he Represented the Town of Vernon, and was authorised to get us any thing we wanted. in Place of that some of us have been deprived of getting things we wanted, just by trusting unto him. the whole Dam'd business is humbug and the Town was Humbug'd when it sent out Hunt, we are Humbug'd out [p. 3] of our Boxes, and you the Soldiers Wifes of Rockville were Humbuged out of your dollars. this is the general opinion in the Company, expressed in a hundred different terms every day. when you send me anything again, let Town Agents go to the devil. I want you to send me the money i wrote you for, last week and I will soon make out to furnish myself with what I want. just put it in a letter and drop it in the Post Office as you would any other letter, and I shal probably get it before Winter is over. I yesterday got a very kind letter from Mr Bottomly, he wishes to send me some Spice Bread and fixins for Christmas. I wrote him back thanking him for his kindness, and told him how, your spice bread came, (to the Devil), and left it to his own judgment if it was best to send any thing to a soldier of Uncle Samuels well fed Army. [p. 4] I am in better health today than I have been since we came here, and I am glad to say that Tom is getting first rate again. none of our sick have come from Alexandria yet, but we expect Brigham and another or two every day. we wish that some of them would come as it is hard work for the few healthy men we have, to do all the Business that is required of us. but i have big faith that i shal "surwive" as Sam Weller says. I must now conclude give my respects to all those Friend who enquire after me. Love to Mother and Maggie, send me the New York Mercury steady, and dont forget that my pockets are as empty as Uncle Samuals Treasury. I remain your

Affectionate Husband as Ever,

Benjamin Hirst.

———⁓———

Letter File #21

Camp Belle Plains, Virginia
Friday Night. 9 oclock Dec 5.th 1862

Dear Sarah,

I have just received your letter of the 28, inst and hasten to answer it as it may be a few days before I get a chance to write you again. Tomorrow morning at 6 oclock we break up our Camp here, and march, I believe, to join our Division at Falmouth. Uncle Sam has no further use for this place at present, and it seems to us as though he had won the Elephant and did not know what to do with it. We have thousands on thousands of men around here, and not [one] of them, as much protected from the inclemancy of the Season, as i used to think necessary for my Hogs. It may be a Military necessity, but it is a very uncomfortable one for us and Cripples our Armies far more [p. 2] than does Gen Lee or Stonewall Jackson. for myself i stand it far better than I had any idea of. what would you think to see us sleeping in our garden, on the ground, with nothing over us but a sheet, pined to the ground on the sides, and raised up in the midle by a stick, with another stick at each end of it, to keep it up; this would be a Shelter Tent as used in the Army. I was very glad you sent me the 8 dollars in your letter. I sopose before I got yours, you got mine, in which i told you what I wanted, am still of the opinion you had better send me the rest of the money and not depend on that box for any thing. every one of us give it up for a bad job. I got your letter with the Pills in it, and also the 5 dollars for Sam Barrows, which I gave to him, and the Poor Devil wanted it bad enough. I to night also got the mittens and Cayenn Pepper you sent me. the mitts [p. 3] could not have come at a better time as it is Storming all day. Snow and rain about equal. the 9 miles march in the morning will be a hard one, as there is hardly a pair of Boots in the Brigade. but i trust to the Grit, that never yet faild me, to carry me through all right. I also got the pepper in the mittens. it will warm us up once in a while. you mention Lieut Emerys coming next monday. hope it is so. I guess when he gets here, that Vinton will go home. you say Fred Cohoon has got home I guess it is on Furlough from the Regulars. he is a poor, mean, Shirking Cuss wherever he is, but he cant Dodge quite so much in the Regulars.[28] I have not heard from John since i last wrote you, hope he will soon join us again. I must now conclude for the present, hoping this will find you all in the enjoyment of good health I remain your Affectionate Husband Benjn Hirst.

P.S. if i cant post you this in the morning I will add a line or two at Falmouth Sunday Dec 7. 1862. I could not mail this until to day, and I am glad of it as I have just received your letter of the 3ᵈ enclosing 15 dollars. I am glad you sent it along so quick. we had a tough march yesterday Mud and Slush 4 inches deep. got through it but we had to leave Tom at Belle Plains owing to Rhuematism. when we got here, John, and Brigham and Irwin Stoughten were here looking for us. John is looking first rate. he did not yet get the letter with the 5 dollars he sent for. how did you direct it. in this is an order from Joe for 10 dols. get the money at the Bank for him and send it to me in your next letter. let Hunt go to the Devil. when I see him again, he will know my mind. you must not judge all our Yankees by such men as come back to Rockville, we have good and true men here, such as David Whiting, Albert Towne, J[ohn]. Williams, *Metcalfe, Goodell, Dart* and a many others that I could mention.[29]

of such I am glad to be with. I will write again soon. your Affectionate Husband. Benjamin Hirst.

Journal Excerpt #9

We staid Encamped at Belle Plains until December 5th, and had no easy time of it, as we were incessantly engaged in unloading boats; the Railroad Bridge over Potomac Creek being burnt down, all our suplies were for a time brought this way, and it was curious to me how the Hundreds of Teams kept each in its own train, and got loaded each day, only to make room for Hundreds of others. We had details made from our Reg night and day for unloading, Sundays not excepted. one Sunday there came an order from Washington for the Contrabands to cease work until [p. 2] sunset, and we had to make an extra detail of White men to fill their Places, as the Army could not get Rations fast enough, if the Boats were not unloaded as fast as they arrived here. during our stay here saw Burnside several times attending to his duties. and it was here that our Pontoon Trains were landed, and some of them were detained here several days, because they could not get Horses enough to take them away. altogether our stay here was an unpleasant one, and we were not sorry to be relieved on the 5th of December when we were ordered to report to Gen French in Front of Fredericksburg.

. . . *Charlie Dart received a box from Rockville a few days ago and seven or eight of us met in Charlie's tent to finish up the box and discuss the probable outcome of the next movement. Charlie, half seriously and half jokingly said he would give something handsome if one of us would take his place [as color sergeant] for the next few days, that he did not want to take much with him in the next fight and we had better finish up all the good things now.*[30]

Chapter 3

The Narratives and World View

Ben constructed his letters to be read by others besides his wife. These others included his mother-in-law, his coworker and friend Luther Morse and Morse's family, the families of soldiers he mentioned, and "all enquiring friends" who might read them. Thus he took pains not only to make the letters read properly, with attention to spelling and grammar, but also to make them look presentable. He used pen and ink for most of them and a line guide that left parallel rows of small perforations down both margins of the page. He was very concerned about his image among his audience back home.

The style of the letters is vintage mid-nineteenth-century literate working class, complete with formal salutations and closings that strike modern readers as overdone.[1] In his reflections about what to write, he lingered on behavior and events, chronology and geography, not feelings or emotions. Ben's letters were constructed on a framework of several basic and recurrent topics: health; the flow of goods, letters and money between him and Sarah; the army experience; and strategies of the absentee household head. His commentary was fundamentally guided by his adult prewar experience. It was shaped by basic premises about manliness and his understanding of the proper husband-wife interaction, about health and illness, and about his growing familiarity with the principles constituting his army social identity. Many of these last were virtually identical to those of respectable prewar factory workers, except for the new emphasis on courage. Courage became the dominant criterion of manly respectability and grew to permeate thoroughly what he wrote.

Health

"I am in good health and hope you are too" was not only an obligatory opening, it was a fundamental preoccupation strengthened by the absence of nurturing loved ones. More soldiers were dying from sickness than from combat. The amount of space devoted to discussing it was an indication of its importance to Ben and other men. Good health was a treasured but precarious condition. Who was sick was important information partly because one never knew when a cold might become fatal pneumonia. The friends and relatives at home were anxious to know; they did not want a sudden, tragic shock. Ben's and others' tallies of the sick and infirm must have caused some consternation as well: often they failed to describe the symptoms. Others' sickness was noteworthy also because it meant extra responsibility and work for Ben. At times, he was the only sergeant present for duty in Company D.

Good health, in Ben's mind, was logically linked to proper shelter from the weather and to good food. Ensuring that the men had proper food and shelter were the responsibilities of officers, giving him an important basis for his tirades against them.[2]

Like many soldiers, Ben preferred to doctor himself, using medication sent by a physician in Rockville rather than that doled out by the regiment's surgeon. The regimental surgeon's panacea was the much-dreaded "Pill Number Nine," whose effects were said to be worse than the affliction.[3] Ben used his Rockville doctor's remedy for his diarrhea in the Bolivar Heights camp and would have self-prescribed rum (if only he had some) for his cough. Sarah sent him cayenne pepper to use in a warming drink on cold days as well as a seasoning. What he treated with the doctor's salve is not known.

Although he was obviously concerned about health, he was affected by the manly ideal of not complaining about his own. The same ideal led him to boast that he did not shirk his duty by going on sick call. When he declared that "we all thought he [John Hirst] had not better march with us until he got stronger," he was relieving John of the onus of shirking: others had insisted John stay behind. When Ben was apparently quite sick, he simply did not write (1–13 October 1862). He probably wished to spare Sarah needless anxiety, but whether his two-week silence had that effect is debatable.

Surely the men of Company D also fretted about the health of loved ones at home. Ben worried about Sarah's physical and mental well-being, urging her not to become depressed and not to ruin her physical health by digging potatoes.

For these reasons, at least, he wrote about health. It was also a subject that was fairly easy to write about. Somebody in the reading audience was sure to be concerned or relieved by the information, the description was fairly straightforward without requiring much concentration on grammar or style, and it could fill space when the writer had temporarily run out of things to say about the monotony of camp life. (There was, in Ben's and others' view, a conception of an appropriate length for routine letters to loved ones.)[4]

Constructing the Army Experience

Ben wanted to stay healthy, but he also wanted to appear manly in the eyes of his army comrades and the folks at home. Some of the manifestations of these manly ideals were specific to army culture and social organization, but most were adaptations of the broader set of ideals of conduct that were shared by respectable mid-nineteenth-century factory workers.[5] This factory culture incorporated some of the even broader set of Victorian ideals. Ben tended to portray these ideals by constructing juxtapositions or contradictions: the ideal quality compared to its opposite—"manliness" versus "womanliness"—for example.[6]

Good and True Men vs. Shirks

For a sergeant in the army, conducting one's self in a manly manner was the fundamental behavioral guideline. Several distinct but related qualities made up Ben's and others' composite ideal of manliness.

One of them was courage.[7] Taking high combat casualties without skedaddling was a manifestation of a unit's courage. A courageous unit was honored in official reports and respected by fellow units. The better the unit performed in combat, the more frequently it deserved to be exposed to danger; it was an honor to lead dangerous attacks. The callow 14th was meant to be inspired when a general reviewing them in Baltimore dubbed them, "A splendid regiment, not one drunken man in the ranks; too good a regiment to be sent anywhere but to the front!"[8] The men in courageous units thereby disappeared more quickly, but standing up to the sharpened and repeated danger was a source of individual manly pride—ideally.

Courage was cool aggressiveness in combat: At Antietam, there was Ben commanding the men to close up under rebel shelling—an approved but tragically wrongheaded action; Ben roaring like a mad bull at his panicked greenhorns to stop their shooting at friendly troops; Ben out in advance of the line of battle, firing exactly thirteen rounds at the Rebels; Ben fitfully enduring Rebel shelling while lying exposed in a freshly plowed field. In his portrayal it was a sharp binary contrast: manly courage versus shirking, skulking cowardice. At one point he could not even bring himself to write out the word "coward." It was an expletive.

Surely, as a sergeant with responsibility for the conduct of his men, he had to know each of them. There was a vital reason for marking the shirks, for their flight could endanger the others. The knowing process was ongoing. Some were written off as shirks immediately; others were being closely watched by him and other courageous ones. Ben wanted the folks at home to know this. Eternal vigilance against shirks and cowards was one of his major preoccupations, just as in less mortal circumstances overseers marked the behavior of those in the weaving room.

For many men under fire, the instinct to skedaddle was overridden by the even more powerful need for social approval from one's comrades. Men spoke and wrote of preserving the union and being instruments of God's vengeance, but their private precombat rumination worked at not letting their fellow soldiers down when the bullets were flying. Ben's recurrent mention of shirks may have helped strengthen his own unspoken resolve (although, at the time, he seemed not to be troubled with self-doubt). We can assume that he mostly practiced what he preached. That is, his expressed concern in letters was manifested in his calculated public behavior among the men of Company D. His openly measuring scrutiny would add to the social pressure on himself and them to act with courage under fire.

His focus on the theme of courage in his narratives also reveals how important it was to maintain an image of courageous manliness among the readers at home.[9]

Steadfastness—dependability, the faith-to-contract—was a related but broader quality of manliness that applied not only to combat behavior but to other contexts as well. Once an obligation was made, it had to be fulfilled. In adversity, duty must be done—ideally without complaint. A week after Antietam, it was his men's display of manly steadfastness that inspired Capt. Samuel Fiske to exclaim, "I glory in our common soldiers!"[10] But steadfastness without complaining quickly became impossible. Fiske in his very public grumbling realized he was deviating from the

Capt. Samuel Fiske, 14th Connecticut Volunteers. His "Dunn Browne" dispatches were widely read in the regiment. Photo courtesy of Thomas Riemer.

ideal, but the conditions were sufficiently wretched to warrant it.[11] Ben gave ample lip service to the steadfastness while coping with his versions of adversity. He had to set an example, of course, for his men and for the others at home. But he was hardly uncomplaining about much of it. His "soldierly grumblings" (to use Fiske's term) centered on those who were not fulfilling their part of the obligation, from "Uncle Samuel" to his company officers. In fact, both Ben and Fiske implied that the ideal of steadfastness without complaint was specially amended for soldiers. Complaining at times was not only allowed, but expected.

Patriotism was a manly quality Ben often invoked but never articulated. Evidently patriotism prompted him and many others among the Rockville boys to join the militia earlier and then volunteer for three years. Nowhere did he mention hefty bounties as motivation (these were to come to others later in the war, when the enthusiasm for volunteering had played out). For him, if not for all in Company D, there was a modest supply of money at home to help him and his brothers weather the fickleness of the army's pay schedules. When manifestly down in the mouth about the state of military affairs, his early enthusiasm was replaced by steadfast vows to see his obligation through. There was never a question about ultimate victory for the Union.

In this first group of letters, the patriotism and steadfastness were bolstered by the naive conviction that the war could not last much longer. In his view, the rebels had skedaddled at Antietam, and Sarah had better get some good cider put away because the army meant to "finish up this business in less than a year." This conviction also eased the adversity of army life for him and members of his company that late autumn. It was bad, but it couldn't last long. They could stand it.

It was also manly to be forthright, honest, without affectation. For example, in the funeral sermon for Captain Fiske, Amherst professor W. S. Tyler declared: "He was a *genuine* man; free from affectation and art; incapable of disguise or concealment; a mortal enemy to shams and all mere seeming; as natural, simple, open, and ingenuous as a child."[12] This ideal prompted Ben's quick detection and condemnation of those whom he felt were putting on airs (some officers, for example) or were deceitful. The Mr. Hunt who was to arrange the Big Box Concern was a particularly deserving target of Ben's righteous wrath and that of other Company D men who were bilked by the same apparent scam. Ben likewise grappled with the truth—to get it right, even if it meant crossing out a written passage and inserting a correction here and there.

And it was manly to withhold expression of certain kinds of emotions.[13] Expressing anger was acceptable as long as it was righteous and controlled. Expressing fear and homesickness was not. Avoiding admissions of fear went along with behaving according to the ideal of courage. Confessing homesickness was more specific to the individual. For Ben, there was duty to be done. There was no use going on about how desperately he wanted to be home. Evidently, he also wanted to keep Sarah from deeper depression. Certainly his duties required his entire attention at times, but there were long periods of idleness—picket and guard duty, for example—when he must have yearned for her and home. Ben never mentioned music in his letters, and only fleetingly in his journal; but it is possible that some Civil War songs were popular with the troops precisely because they allowed expression of emotions that would in other genres be considered embarrassingly unmanly. "Home, Sweet Home" along with some verses of "All Quiet along the Potomac Tonight" and "Weeping, Sad and Lonely" are well-known examples.

Death—particularly one's own—was another topic best left publicly unexamined. Ben wrote that he didn't want to dwell on the subject of his own death in letters. His answer was almost offhanded to the question of where he would like to be buried if he died. Yet he was concerned with displaying proper behavior following the death of a friend or acquaintance, sending home a lock of Wilkie's hair and asking for details of poor Abby's funeral back in Rockville. Later, his brother John would manifest the same preoccupation.[14] After the war, Ben wrote an anecdote about his experience at Antietam for the regimental history. Its premonition scenario was familiar to Civil War soldiers:

> While we were lying in the rear of the stone wall [on Roulette's lane leading to the sunken road], Sergeants Brigham, Stoughten and myself were talking over the events we had passed through in the morning, and W[illiam]. P. Ramsdell quietly remarked that if he was going to be hit, he would prefer to have the top of his head blown off. When midway between the wall and the position assigned to us, I was about the center of the company, urging the boys to close up, when a rebel shell came whizzing by and struck about two files in my rear. As soon as I could turn I saw about a dozen men lying in a heap and the first man I recognized was W. P. Ramsdell with the top of his head blown off.[15]

Here is a perspective on death that he may have been reluctant to spell out during the war: a man who declared that he would die in the coming battle, or who described how he hoped to die, was increasing the chance that death might take special interest in accommodating him. Perhaps Ramsdell by his utterance invoked his own death. Death was as capricious as it was ever-present.

Authority vs. Equality

Ben's portrayals of those above him in the company and regimental hierarchies were abundantly negative. Officers were sketched as bumbling, arrogant shirks—the embodied contradiction of the manly qualities he strove to emulate. Unlike others in the 14th, he was conspicuously silent in his letters about marching past Abraham Lincoln on two different occasions (when passing through Washington on the way to the front and at a review of the Army of the Potomac after Antietam). McClellan received a complimentary adjective now and then.

This is in keeping with the prevailing "American" ideal of questioning authority. It is also a perspective familiar to Ben from his prior experience in the mills.[16] Unlike yeoman farm work, factory labor was hierarchical. Unless one was a mill owner, one toiled under the critical eyes of others who controlled him or her by manipulating wages. One's superiors in the system had to be closely watched, perhaps envied; played up to, yet kept at sufficient social distance to permit occasional surreptitious slacking off, criticism, and mockery. A good overseer or superintendent could make one's life tolerable; a poor one brought disaster. So it was with the army system. Ben had been socialized to it before he joined up.

Officers' arrogance chafed Ben—aggravating his conviction that they were no better men than those in the enlisted ranks. Ben got to know his company officers while they were all in the militia under very different social and military conditions. The militia officers were elected to commissions once Company D had been recruited. Later in the war, this procedure was abandoned for the excesses it produced in preelection politicking and postelection insubordination.[17]

Captain Fiske, too, grumbled about the army hierarchy. October 1862 was a particularly active time of criticism. Fiske diplomatically spared his fellow officers in the regiment. He recklessly fired at loftier targets. He had little use for the army high command in general, but his favorite target was the bombastic McClellan. He clearly did not share Ben Hirst's admiration of the man: "The grand Army of the Potomac, I am happy to inform you, . . . is safe (and so are its enemies)."[18]

Still, Ben might not have gone to such lengths of criticism if the regimental officers had been better qualified. In those early months, Company D and the 14th as a whole were not being well served by their officers. Just as it was being mustered into Federal service, its primary recruiter, Capt. Thomas F. Burpee, left Company D to become a major in the 21st Connecticut Volunteers. His replacement, A. Park Hammond, reported late and was indisposed with sunstroke after Antietam. He went home when it was determined he had not been properly mustered into Federal service. Hammond's replacement could not immediately take over the company because he was ill. Col. Dwight Morris, the regimental commander, was boosted to brigade command before Antietam. His replacement, Lt. Col. Sanford H. Perkins, was in Ben's portrayal a narrow-minded martinet, more concerned with proper wearing of belts than with his men's food and shelter.

As in the factory, Ben's attitude toward superiors was ambivalent in the army. He was disgusted by their lack of manliness, but he and his men in Company D were dependent upon them to make army life bearable, if not always to keep them alive. He gave no clues about how he may have resolved this ambivalence in direct interaction with officers. We cannot know if his public behavior somehow conveyed his contempt to them. It seems unlikely. Probably he did his duty, almost certainly kept his social distance, and tried to avoid unfavorable notice of those wearing shoulder straps. Nonetheless it was daring to write home about them as he did, given the way news evidently traveled to Rockville and thence back to the front.

Initiated vs. Uninitiated

In Ben's and other soldiers' view there was a distinct behavioral and conceptual difference between those who had been in combat and those who had not. Ben admired veterans of the peninsular campaign and described them as "fit" and "tough." To be sure, they were also dirty, tattered, and lice infested. After Antietam, when the 14th's men had been initiated, at least one of them wanted to wear his cartridge box on his waist belt "like the old soldiers." Veterans had demonstrated their courage, their patriotism, their manliness. The cartridge-box display was one symbol of having passed the test. And it meant one less belt to blacken and brass plate to polish for inspections if it had been allowed.

For Ben, and certainly for others, becoming a veteran involved acquiring a body of wisdom.[19] He mentioned this new wisdom often, but did not clearly or systematically describe it. We can infer that it entailed a sharper awareness of the limits of one's own endurance and bravery. He mentioned as well a kind of savoir-faire that came from being in the army. There was a way to get good grub in camp, or regular mail, or have a little something to eat on the march when others (less cunning) had nothing. It would take some time, but Ben felt he could figure out the system—just as he had that of the mills.

Like Ben, Samuel Fiske was at first struck by veterans' unkempt appearance: "[A] regiment of veterans appears to one uninitiated like a regiment of ragamuffins." But Fiske's construction of veteranness added even less flattering dimensions to Ben's portrayal: "[T]he older the regiment, the more bold and expert in petty larceny; and the older the regiment too, the more undisciplined and disorderly, and the less inclined to go into battle, or perform the duties of a soldier any way."[20] As a brand-new lieutenant then writing before his first combat, Fiske was much concerned about his men's cleanliness and discipline. The state of veteranness was a palpable threat to his precombat view of the ideal infantry company.

Combat was the rite of passage from greenhorn to veteran, but the full transition demanded a process soldiers called "hardening."[21] It was both physical and mental. Ben reported his progress proudly to the home folks. Becoming hard partly involved grasping the wisdom he referred to. It involved stronger resistance to sickness, getting a good night's sleep on the hard ground, thriving on army rations, and standing up well to long, hot, or soggy marches. On the other hand, sorting out the soldierly public portrayal of emotions over close friends' deaths had only just begun after Antietam. Most of the Rockville boys were still alive; no green strangers had shown up as replacements. In early December, Ben happily pondered the continued presence of "good and true men here, such as Dave Whiting, Albert Towne, J[ohn]. Williams and a many others that I could mention. of such I am glad to be with."

Chums vs. Others

Ben's and other men's social networks in the army formed a series of concentric circles rippling horizontally outward from themselves at the center. The innermost circle comprised his chums—his closest friends and two younger brothers. Depending on the type and size of shelter available, these friends slept together and cooked together. They were to look out for each other's welfare, including sharing food arriving in boxes from home, passing along messages and news about each other in letters, and doing whatever they could in combat to see that the wounded among them were carried to the surgeon's tent and well cared for. They lent each other money. In his letters Ben drew no explicit lines of rank between him and his close friends. Some were fellow NCOs, some were privates—yet none was an officer. He mentioned close friends by name, not by rank. He and they must have understood the need to compartmentalize the category of "chum" from those of "private" and "sergeant" when there were details to be done or orders to be followed. Blatant line-of-duty favoritism toward one's close friends over others in the company would have earned scorn from the others. Still, one looked after his close friends, and they after him.

Ben's next wider circle was the other enlisted men of his company. These made up the group collectively dubbed "the Rockville boys" for home readers. Company D was his primary unit of formal responsibility in both combat and camp. There were no platoons or squads as formal subunits of the company. Occasionally, he led small temporary task groups that he called "squads."

The third circle was the regiment, whose collective behavior usually was portrayed in comparison or contrast to that of other regiments: "our green regiment" or "our gallant regiment" or "the louzy 14th." Otherwise, there was little discussion of Ben's view of social relations within the regiment, except that focusing on the behavior of its officers. There were no company rivalries and no interaction among cliques of friends in different companies. (Given the localized origins of each company in its early months of war, there was no particular incentive or structural basis for intercompany cliques to form—at least among enlisted men. Both Fisk and the regimental history describe social activities and bonds among the regiment's officers. There were structural reasons for this: There were fewer officers than enlisted men, and, unlike the enlisted men, the officers were typically moved from company to company as they were promoted or as vacancies appeared.) There was obvious pride in belonging to the regiment, especially after its conduct at Antietam. There were symbols of collective regimental identity, the most obvious being the two regimental flags—one the national stars and stripes, the other a dark-blue flag bearing the state's seal. There were insiders' anecdotes and monikers, such as "Old Bunch 'Em." These distinctive traits accumulated as the regiment continued to survive.[22]

Beyond the regiment, there was occasional portrayal of the other, more inclusive, formal boundaries of army existence: the brigade, division, corps, and Army of the Potomac. The more inclusive the circle, generally, the less frequently it was characterized in Ben's descriptions and thus, presumably, the less pervasive it was in his social consciousness.

In addition to the horizontal axis of his social reality, Ben dealt with the vertical axis: enlisted men at his level and officers above (undeservedly, for the most part). Aside from his criticism of specific company and regimental officers, he wrote little about his view of relations between officers and enlisted men as social categories. Samuel Fiske was much more forthcoming. He continually drew distinctions between the life of officers (including himself) and that of privates. He had strong, almost paternal, feelings for the welfare of the men in ranks, but he unabashedly enjoyed assets of his status. For example, he lamented the fact that a private who had been detailed as forager and cook for the officers became ill and they were forced to prepare some meals themselves.[23] He mentioned no informal socializing with enlisted men.

Ben expressed no sense of social isolation. He and the other Rockville boys were at this time surrounded by friends and acquaintances, and there were those friends and relatives he kept meeting in other regiments. In fact, he may have craved some temporary relief from the very public social existence that was army life.

These are the details of some of the basic facets of world view Ben chose to share with the home folks. Some had to be learned, adjusted, and refined as Company D became hardened. Most of them were interrelated, so that different ideal guidelines for being manly, egalitarian, a close friend and a veteran could together prompt a particular pattern of behavior in a particular social context, such as carrying a wounded man to the rear or sharing the eatables sent from home in a box. There were some that clashed, such as the hierarchical system of army rank and the ideal of essential equality. The specifics of the basic facets of the world view changed or were replaced as the war went on, usually in response to circumstances in which they were contradictory or merely irrelevant.

These facets also colored Ben's portrayals of the three main contexts he distinguished in army life: camp, march, and combat.

Portrayal of Camp Life and the March

After Antietam, Samuel Fiske complained bitterly about his company's endless guard, stevedore, and wood-chopping details in October's camp at Belle Plain, declaring, "We came here to fight!"[24] Like Captain Fiske, Ben chafed at performing work details. Combat was what they were there for. Chopping trees and unloading wagons and barges was dreary, toilsome, and demeaning. The demand for this and the more routine drudgery of picket and guard duty was constant. As more of Company D's men were played out from illness or combat, the burden fell increasingly on those who were present for duty. Steadfastness had its distinct drawbacks.

A good many men were evidently absent for one reason or another much of the time, in proportions that would drive modern first sergeants to distraction. Fiske reported his entire company had been pulled from the regiment for extended guard duty in the vicinity of Harpers Ferry, then was marched elsewhere days later to chop down trees that interfered with the artillery's fields of fire. In late November, Ben wrote that there were thirty men present for duty in Company D. The others, he felt, were shirking.

Ben wrote little about the routine of camp life because he felt the home folks wouldn't be interested; it was not a context for "Important Events." He offered no systematic accounts of his daily round of activities, the drill, or the regimental band's evening concerts. In fact, we know virtually nothing of what Ben did for relaxation and entertainment in camp when he wasn't writing letters. Fiske described the gala 1862 Thanksgiving celebration in the 14th's camp: Men wove evergreen boughs into decorative designs and made an arch for Lieutenant Colonel Perkins's tent. Then, the regiment was assembled in front of the arch for expressions of "prayer and praise and patriotism." Although the fare for the day was hardtack and salt pork, the next day the officers dined at a sumptuous meal in their garlanded dining hall. The leftovers were made into soup and served to the enlisted men.[25] There was not a word of any of this in Ben's letters. Either the home folks wouldn't be interested or it was too frivolous to be worth writing about. He wrote little about drinking. We know he was not a temperance man, and resourceful soldiers managed to get booze under almost any constraints. Given that he was constructing his letters for a fairly wide circle of readers, it is consistent with his image that he left out descriptions of diversionary drinking—his or others'.[26]

Like virtually every other soldier on both sides, Ben wrote a good deal about the weather in camp, particularly when it was bad. Wet weather was not only miserable, it increased the soldiers' chances of "taking cold," which could lead to lingering night coughs like his and to far more serious illness. The influence of the bad weather of November 1862, coupled with the dreary stevedore duties at Belle Plain and the inadequate shelter, gave Ben much to complain about. His downbeat shadings might be dismissed as individual emotional idiosyncrasy were it not for similar tendencies in Fiske's dispatches of the same period. Fiske and Ben complained about the same things, particularly the poor shelter, wretched rations, and wearisome drudgery. Judging from both portrayals, this late fall of 1862 was particularly bothersome to the regiment as a whole. The men were green, the officers were green, the camps were poorly sited, and much had gone wrong. The conditions may have seemed particularly bad because they developed while the men were still new to the army. There was little besides their fresh recollections of home life with which to compare their situation. Nonetheless, Ben typically finished off his grumbling with the conviction that his grit would see him through. Fiske, on the other hand, was more likely to invoke God's help.

Each of them made specific appeals to home folks for political action against the army's incompetence.[27] With a large and mostly sympathetic following of Springfield *Republican* readers, Captain Fiske frequently called for public outcry.

Ben suggested it only once explicitly, but the strident tone of his other criticisms may well have been intended to goad his readers into some kind of protest.

Ben's choice of subjects in his letters from camp reflected his view of what constituted "news" for those at home. What he chose to report and how he reported it seemed to manifest Captain Fiske's observation at the time: it is harder writing to give daily details of life than to communicate the "grand descriptions and the thunder and lightning battle scenes."[28]

The march to a new locale was a most welcome change. Fiske reported that on the march from Bolivar Heights to Fredericksburg, "The health and spirits of the army are better, now that we are in motion; and we hope for a big series of crushing victories to finish out our fall campaign."[29] The march gave Ben something different to write about. There was the cheery letter about the lush and lovely landscape around a bivouac near Upperville, Virginia. But the letter after that took back the cheeriness. He did not typically describe easy or pleasant marches in his letters. As in his camp narratives, he tended to play up the harder details and how well he stood up to them. Both he and Fiske characterized the time the regiment got lost in the pouring rain near Belle Plain as their worst experience so far in the army. Ben explicitly included Antietam in this reckoning.[30]

The transition from camp to march brought a decline in the number of men present for duty in the company and regiment. On the march on 2 November 1862, Ben reported that the regiment included some 300 muskets, 31 of them in Company D. He often mentioned the decreased size of the 14th and Company D at major transitions, such as from camp to march or from march to combat. The numbers seemed to decline steadily and somewhat drastically during the period between Antietam and Fredericksburg; but, in fact, they were hovering. Throughout the war, neither the company nor the regiment ever reached the size it had been when it left Hartford in August 1862. The regiment's effective size in major transitions ranged from less than 200 to just under 300, and the size of Company D about one tenth of that. There were always men absent while serving on detached service or special details, sick men in hospitals, stragglers, and, later, deserters. Those, plus the vacancies caused by deaths, left the typical effective regimental and company strength at about a third—and often less—of its original numbers. Obviously, Ben felt that once the critical mass of the company shrank to about thirty, it was worth writing home about. Later it would shrink further.

Characterization of Combat

Ben drew himself up for his descriptions of the Antietam battle. These were more carefully constructed than the other letters, with a greater sense of conveying important events. He was complimented on his efforts, which obviously pleased him, and the stylistic and content precedents had thus been set. As in the march portrayals, he took pains to communicate events and geography arranged in a chronological framework. He portrayed himself as brave and mostly cool, manfully in charge of himself and others under fire. He admitted no fear in the letters, although he did allow that it was "no pleasant feeling" to watch enemy gunners load and fire artillery pieces aimed directly at him. Mostly he recounted a feisty opposition to Secesh.

Compare his account of combat fear with excerpts from that of Captain Fiske, written during opening phases of the battle itself:

> [T]he situation [of being under fire] is not, I confess, a pleasant one to me. (The firing is over for the present.) I had no disposition to run away, and indeed didn't see any very favorable place to escape from shot which fell in front, on both sides, and as much as a mile in our rear. But the feeling of being exposed to the mangling effects of those murderous messengers of destruction is far from an agreeable one. You can calculate the probabilities as being a thousand to one or ten thousand to one against your being struck; but somehow that one chance looms up rather disproportionately in your view.[31]

Like Ben, Fiske dared not mention fear by name; yet his readers got the message. Fiske's greater eloquence disguises the similarity of happenings and feelings he and Ben both chose to report, using much the same heroic style and vocabulary.[32] There is a difference in emphasis. Ben focused on what he did; Fiske went on more about how he felt. This difference persists in their separate accounts of later battles.

Fiske also chose to dwell on combat aftermath. After Antietam, he wrote: "The excitement of battle comes in the day of it, but the horrors of it two or three days after. . . . The air grows terribly offensive from the unburied bodies; and a pestilence will speedily be bred if they are not put under ground. . . . Waste, waste, ruin and destruction."[33] Ben did not reflect much on aftermath, and even less on its horrific aspects—except the stench, which assaulted every soldier at Antietam. Important events happened in the battle itself, not afterward. Readers would not be interested. Even in his letter accounts of the battle he seemed deliberately to tone down the gruesomeness. If this was to spare Sarah and her immediate network the gory details, it was a contrived, formal gesture—perhaps manly etiquette for addressing a largely feminine readership. Certainly he had no qualms about including some graphic details in his letter to friend Luther Morse and in his journal, and he certainly intended that Sarah read both.

Still, these are virtually the only graphic portrayals of death in his entire original war narrative. He did not mention the appearance of the piles of dead in "Bloody Lane" close by his regiment's position. Evidently he was just then in the process of deciding how much of this to write about and finally concluded that henceforth it was best left unmentioned.

Company D and the regiment dramatically shrank in size once the fight was joined. Ben reported that his company went into the Antietam battle with eighty-four men. By about mid-afternoon, during the movement to the plowed field on the hill, he counted twenty-four men including the three company officers and only two sergeants. The regiment at that point numbered 345 (his exactness here suggests there was a roll call before moving out to the new position). He later placed the company's loss at twenty killed or wounded, the regiment's at 108 killed or wounded.[34] Allowing a percentage of absence due to illness or special details, there were still apparently many who skedaddled or helped wounded to the rear with no sense of urgency to return to the line of battle—as Ben noted in a disgusted aside. Fiske shared Ben's disgust. Reflecting on Antietam, the captain contemptuously declared: "The vile, obscene, blasphemous swaggerers of our regiment, the thieves and drunkards and rowdies of the regiment generally, to the number of seventy-five or a hundred, were found wanting in that fatal cornfield, and came sneaking back for days after the battle, with cock-and-bull stories of being forced into hospital service, and care of the wounded."[35]

Ben constructed the battle using a template of a respectable manly ideal shared with folks in Rockville: facts of movement and time, a brave account of his own actions juxtaposed to a self-righteous blast against skedaddlers and shirks, and a tally of losses (the Rockville boys mentioned by name). He chose not to discuss his emotions at length. Three days after the battle, Ben wrote that he had "carried Wilkie to the rear." In his journal, he wrote that he left him lying along a fence. In both contexts he seemed proud of his conduct. Yet his behavior with Wilkie evidently weighed on him. In a recollection written in January 1863, he had cause to reexamine it closely.

Letters and Journal Compared

Ben's journal portrayals, compared to his letters, were crafted to come even closer to his prevailing ideals of manliness. He described his own conduct, of course, but the others in his experience—except for his commanders—were made anonymous by being collectivized into the first-person plural. We are told nothing of his brothers' conduct at Antietam or of their emotions or opinions. It was as if such information was too trivial, perhaps too personally emotional, for important events in heroic prose.[36]

His preoccupation with health came through more implicitly. It was a reason for the recurrent complaint about missing knapsacks and unfilled requisitions, and for the explicit description of cold, wet weather. He commented on aggregate sickness, however; never his own. Illness was depersonalized.

Manliness was portrayed in much the same terms as in the letters, freely using examples of his own conduct. There was the familiar first-person recitation of adversity and standing up to it. He portrayed anxiety before combat as a trait displayed by others, but in his journal he came closer than in letters to describing his own, such as not being able to sleep much on the eve of Antietam. Manfully he overcame his distraction enough to cook and eat some grub before moving out for the morning assault.

There is a difference between his journal's portrayal of officers and what he wrote in the letters. The shirking accusations were muted, as were the sketches of officers' arrogance.[37] Ben also seemed properly impressed by glimpses of his division and army commanders. Unlike Captain Fiske, he never blasted McClellan for his tragic lack of impetuosity. He maintained a loyalty to McClellan that was shared by other soldiers. He described others' weeping and tossing of hats and caps at McClellan's farewell review. We cannot know from his important events narratives whether Sgt. Benjamin Hirst wept or flung his cap in the air. Nothing of this was in his letters.

Expressions of patriotic emotion are as evident in the journal as in the letters, even though—as we will see—he was probably not feeling very patriotic at the time he was recopying the journal pages. This adds to the impression that the journal was single-mindedly crafted so as to embody basic ideals.

Like the letters, the journal painted camp life at Bolivar Heights and Belle Plain as dreary and unhealthy. Either he wrote little about it in his original journal notes, or he retrospectively cut out portions as he recopied them. There and elsewhere in his camp descriptions he conveyed more about himself. He wrote about his interest in exploring Harpers Ferry and about how, during the melancholia following the religious service in camp at Antietam, he occupied himself by writing his account of the battle. He was not deaf to the regiment's excellent band. He simply never wrote about it in his letters. And, in keeping with its greater emphasis on the ideal, the journal did not so much as hint at swearing or drinking alcohol.

In the journal, Ben recalled general directions and sequences of the regiment's combat movements—to the left here, across there—but "what our position in line of Battle was I did not know." His letters noted no such problem with orienting himself. Fiske, too, commented on the "astonishing . . . ignorance of us, who are actually playing the soldier's part here, of what is going on around us."[38] This is a common theme in the combat portrayals of other Civil War soldiers.[39]

Portrayals of home, or relations with home including the cherished boxes and mail, were by definition not to be included. He wanted the journal to be an account of his army experience, and, more specifically, his marches and battles.

Interacting with the Home Culture

These letters give us a first glimpse at gender relations between wife and husband as Ben would have others see them. We cannot know what emotions he would have expressed to Sarah privately. We can assume there was warranted written restraint in keeping with Victorian respectability and the possibility of a wider readership.[40] Still, a well-contrived hint at erotic urgings could flatter the spouse and elicit brief knowing smiles from other readers without violating respectable norms. Thus, Ben's order on 30 October that Sarah send him ten dollars "and I will pay you to suit when I see you."[41] He employed the double entendre at least once again in the spring of 1863. At any rate, the formal writing style prevailed: "your affectionate husband, Benjamin Hirst"—not simply Benjamin or Ben. Beyond this, there were few expressions of endearment.

Instead, Ben's affection came out largely as concern for Sarah's well-being: inquiries about her health, approval of her decision to take in a boarder to help keep her company, his worry about her digging the potatoes. It also was implicit in the single-mindedness with which he dwelt on the subject of boxes from home. To be sure, the items he ordered would make army life more endurable with winter coming, and they would help keep soldiers from usurious sutlers. But the boxes were much more to him. They were a physical manifestation of home and Sarah. Food baked by her. Items selected and purchased or made by her and lovingly packed by her. And best of all, they might include a likeness of her. "Town Agent" Hunt was a scoundrel not merely because he humbugged the patriot soldiers out of their food and comforts; he was trifling with the men's fundamental links with home. Every Union soldier with accommodating relatives sent orders home for box contents, then watched fitfully for their arrival.[42] Boxes in camp did wonders for morale and helped strengthen social and emotional bonds within camp as well as with home. The boxes were carefully unwrapped, inspected, commented upon, and inevitably the eatables—and undoubtedly the drinkables that survived the trip—were shared with one's close friends. As in many non-Western societies, one achieved respect by conspicuous sharing rather than miserly hoarding—at least of food delicacies from home. Tobacco may have been more grudgingly shared.[43]

Letters were another manifestation of the love-with-concern between soldiers and home folks. Not only their contents, but their frequency and length. Ben and other soldiers quickly came to expect balanced exchange. If Ben wrote Sarah at least once a week, she was expected to write to him just as often. There was a tallying in many of his letters—how many he had sent, what he had received, and so on. Once from the Belle Plain camp, where everything else was unhappy, he scolded Sarah for not writing to him more often.

As much as Ben enjoyed the boxes and letters, he would not think of having Sarah herself come to camp for a visit. The constraint of his conception of ideal gender roles was too powerful. Soldiering, he archly reminded her, was "man's work," and an army camp was no place for a decent woman—the enlisted men's areas were not, at any rate. (Officers could send for their wives during lulls in active campaigning.) The logistics involved in providing Sarah with proper accommodations and getting released from duty long enough to be with her were too overwhelming.

In these early letters, Ben's attention as absent household head focused primarily on economics: what Sarah was to do about the pigs (three different letters) and getting in some good cider. This was evidently male business in the prewar household. Sarah had to be told plainly what to do while he was away.

Sarah was also told how to handle the three brothers' money, and was expected to act as their accounting and disbursing agent. As described earlier, this may well have been her role in the household even before the war. Money matters were as popular in Ben's letters as discourses on boxes. Part of the explanation was the delay in the regiment's payroll. This was also virtually the only way Ben and Sarah had of verifying that sums he or she sent had not got lost in the mails. Money was about the only legitimate alternative to boxes as a source of amenities to help relieve camp blues.

Sarah also served as Ben's representative in his efforts to maintain important social relations in Rockville and Dedham. She was to show Ben's letters to Luther Morse and his wife, to mention Ben's gratitude to the Bottomlys, to give his regards to the folks on the hill, in the mill, and all inquiring friends. In his letter closings, some of this was pro forma—the sort of thing one put in proper letters as a nonspecific flattery of all potential readers. In later months he would become more directive of Sarah's social efforts on his behalf.

Ben fretted not only about his own social image, but about Sarah's as well. The "Try and spel a little better whe you write" postscript in his fourth letter served notice that her letters were passed around to his close friends and probably other Rockville boys. He wanted them to have the best possible impression. This concern was congruent with his emphasis on portrayals of manliness: the respectable soldier as a former respectable laborer.

There was a peremptory tone to Ben's communication with Sarah that seems chauvinistic by modern standards. Yet it was thoroughly consistent with the ideals of gender behavior at that time, as was the suggestion of inherent female lack of physical and emotional toughness.[44] Ben seemed to be guided by the prevailing manly stereotype of women as physically weak and liable to be duped by their emotions into doing something foolish.[45] Paradoxically, he depended on her strength and shrewdness to maintain their home and sustain him and his brothers at the front. This was probably not much of a change from her prewar functions in the household, through the ups and downs of factory existence and major relocations. He obviously cared a great deal for her and her welfare, and avoided writing things to her directly that would alarm her or offend the ideal sensibilities of a woman of her station.

Part II

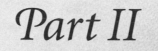

Fredericksburg and Winter Camp
6 December 1862 to 28 April 1863

Chapter 4

The Context

The 14th had little time to enjoy its respite from the labor at Belle Plain. Regimental optimists had started to build log huts for their winter quarters in the Falmouth camp, but these were not completed before the marching orders for Fredericksburg arrived. On 11 December, they left Falmouth and drew up three miles south along the Rappahannock opposite Fredericksburg. They arrived during a heavy Union bombardment designed to drive Confederate sharpshooters from houses on the town's river front. The sharpshooters effectively interfered with the completion of Union pontoon bridges to cross the river until they were finally evicted bodily by Yank infantry ferried across for that purpose. The bridges were ready by about sundown (4:30 P.M.), but the 14th did not cross until the following morning (12 December).

The regiment spent the rest of the day and the night of the twelfth along Caroline Street, between Thirteenth and Fourteenth Streets. Before lights out, the men were assembled for roll call every hour to keep them from wandering off. Col. Dwight ("Old Bunch 'Em") Morris was left sick back at Belle Plain. Lt. Col. Sanford Perkins, commanding the regiment, was nervous much of that night, "unlike his usual confident self."[1]

Colonel Morris was not the only 14th Connecticut officer indisposed for the coming battle. Company D had no officers present at all. Its men were commanded by Orderly Sgt. Frank Stoughton, and only about twenty-five of them—including the three Hirst brothers—were poised to go in. The other companies were similarly understrengthed for the fight, the whole regiment numbering perhaps 325 to 350.

The men fell in for the attack at about 10:00 A.M. on the thirteenth. For the next two hours, they moved along city streets in short spurts, then waited tensely in ranks as Rebel artillery crashed around them. The street intersections offering an east-west thoroughfare were particularly hazardous. At about noon, they finally left the relative protection of the town's buildings, crossed a narrow causeway, and moved out onto the deadly half-mile-wide plain separating them from the Rebel line. Rebel artillery fired canister at them as soon as they cleared the buildings. One man wrote that the projectiles bounced through them like "enormous marbles."[2]

They came onto the plain too far to their left, so they had to maneuver under fire to bring them into position for the charge. The men executed a wheel to the half-right but drew up too close behind another regiment. They had to about-face and move to the rear amidst the jeers of others who thought they were leaving the field.[3] They lay down in whatever depressions they could find and watched as their division's 1st Brigade (Kimball's) charged and was destroyed by the Rebels firing from the sunken road beneath Marye's Heights. The 3d Brigade went in next and was similarly stopped cold. Then, their brigade, the 2d, charged. Survivors remember that Colonel Perkins was seriously wounded shortly after calling out for the 14th to move forward. Mobility was hampered by the heavy overcoats and loaded knapsacks (complete with blankets rolled on top) each man wore. This was no parade-like, well-aligned charge; instead, men wrote of a mad forward dash, with knots of soldiers being blasted to a staggering halt and then flinging themselves on the ground to seek whatever protection they could find. There was confusion as men lost track of their regiment and brigade.[4] Two successive NCOs carrying the regiment's state flag were wounded, and the colors lay unnoticed on the ground until they were later discovered by two other NCOs of the regiment. No one was certain in retrospect just how close the men of the 14th had come to the sunken road.

The survivors came back from the plain individually and in small clusters, furtively, eagerly seeking buildings and depressions for protection only to find scores of others already there. Some wounded waited until nightfall to drag themselves off.

The men were unusually anxious about trying to get the wounded to safety; the Fredericksburg narratives by members of the 14th emphasized this more than did their recollections of other battles. The wounded were surely at unusual risk. One of the color sergeants carrying the state flag was hit in three places and trampled by three successive charges: "But no one had time then to attend to one poor wounded fellow."[5] Corporal Lyman of Company D left two grievously wounded men to continue the charge. After the fighting, he helped some of the other wounded huddled in an excavation for a partially completed icehouse. Lyman wrote, "I have always looked back upon the time spent in that place with great satisfaction, because of the comfort I was able to minister to the poor fellows."[6] The 14th's chaplain stationed himself at the division hospital, making vats of coffee and tea for the wounded. Ben Hirst shared this same general concern, as will be seen.

Captain Fiske reported that scarcely 100 of the regiment—less than one-third of its strength going into the battle—were present for duty shortly afterward.[7] Another hundred or so had turned up by mid-January of 1863. The discouraged men dragged into their Falmouth camp on Monday night, 15 December, led by Capt. Samuel H. Davis of Company H, the highest-ranking officer of the 14th present for duty.

Survivors began construction of log huts forthwith, predicting that the army

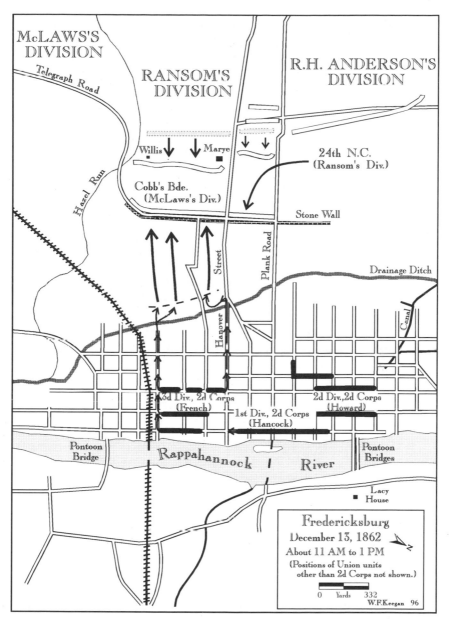

McLAWS'S DIVISION

RANSOM'S DIVISION

R.H. ANDERSON'S DIVISION

Telegraph Road

Willis

Marye

24th N.C. (Ransom's Div.)

Cobb's Bde. (McLaws's Div.)

Hazel Run

Stone Wall

Street

Plank Road

Drainage Ditch

Hanover

Canal

3d Div., 2d Corps (French)

2d Div., 2d Corps (Howard)

1st Div., 2d Corps (Hancock)

Pontoon Bridge

Rappahannock River

Pontoon Bridges

Lacy House

Fredericksburg
December 13, 1862
About 11 AM to 1 PM
(Positions of Union units
other than 2d Corps not shown.)

0   Yards   332

W.F. Keegan 96

would now finally settle down into winter quarters. The high command, however, steadfastly refused to describe the Falmouth camp as "winter quarters," choosing instead the phrase "long encampment."[8] Presumably this was part of the struggle to evade the slightest similarity to McClellan-like inactivity. By any name, Falmouth was a muddy, depressing, drawn-out existence.

For the 14th—if not for others—January's Mud March from Falmouth provided some momentary farcical relief. Assigned to the rear guard on the march, the men packed up the tents covering their log huts. They had not yet left camp when the gooey calamity descended on the main body. They watched with grim, head-shaking amusement as the march came to a full-stuck stop.

Troops' morale was at rock bottom. Burnside was out as the Army of the Potomac's commanding general by the end of January 1863. "Fighting Joe" Hooker, his successor, brought rapid improvement in rations, which helped reduce some of the inevitable winter illness and improved morale. Then came four months' pay in February, evidently their first since leaving Hartford.

The regiment was commanded by a rotating series of captains most of that winter. No field officer was present and nobody was promoted to field rank until late April. One captain recalled that the officers found occasional diversion in quaffing punch made by Lt. Fred Doten: "It was at some of these gatherings that Captain Lee used to give swan like imitations and that [Company] 'G' officers used to trot out little 'Uncas,' the stuttering teamster, as a spiritual medium, who used to go into trances and therein deliver addresses on didactic subjects, but who got mad when Lieutenant Fred Seymour asked him to take a drink in his spiritual not material character. Quartermaster Dibble used to say that when Uncas got mad at his mules he could swear in the most unspiritual manner without stuttering at all."[9] There was no similar anecdote about amusements for the enlisted men. After all, they were officially not to be trusted with alcohol.

Connecticut politics created a more persistent diversion for all ranks in February and March. The state's Republican governor, William Buckingham, had been a staunch supporter of the war. He was being challenged by Democrat Thomas Seymour. Samuel Fiske was an outspoken Buckingham supporter and used his dispatches to castigate the opposition. He was outraged, for example, at the Democrats' campaign efforts to use the 14th's sagging morale as evidence for widespread disaffection with Republican war efforts.[10] President Lincoln reviewed the army on Sunday, 5 April, an event that caught Ben Hirst just coming off picket duty.

These intervals of distraction could not offset the unhappiness of the Falmouth camp. Men whiled away gray, soggy days on guard or picket duty, which came frequently now that the regiment was less than a third of its original size. Thoughts of home became an obsession manifested in long letters to loved ones, persistent finagling for furloughs, and impatient waiting for boxes of home-packed sundries to arrive.

Chapter 5

The Letters and Journal

~~~

Dec. 9. Went to see some of the boys in the 72d Pennsylvania, and to hear the news about Fredricksburg. I was told no attempt had yet been made to take the city and that the rebels are there in force, and are building earth works night and day, in plain sight of our army. Walked over towards the Lacy house and could see lots of Johnnies walking about over (the river) into the city.[1]

~~~

Letter File #22

Camp near Falmouth Vir
Thursday Dec 18.th 1862.

Dear Sarah,

I write you these few lines to let you know that ~~that~~ I am safe once more. but I have not the heart to give you a detailed account of all our Regiment has had to pass through during the past 7 days. our John got here just in time to have a hand in it. he got off safe. but I am sorry to say that Joe got wounded in 3 places at once. one is in the thigh, another through the same leg in the Calf, and one through the other leg. his bones are not hurt so he will in all probability get well again. the loss in our Company and Regiment is very severe as you will see by the Newspapers to which I must refer you for the present, as I cannot write at this time. Love to all. your Affectionate Husband

Benjamin Hirst.

~~~

Letter File #23

Camp near Falmouth Vir.
Saturday, Dec 20.th 1862

Dear Sarah,

Mr Towne [Albert Towne's father] arrived here yesterday morning, and he delivered the things that you and others sent by him. they came at a good time as the boys needed the things very much.

I am very sorry that you took the step that you have [see below—ed.], as it was a needless journey for you to undertake, and I can see no posible chance of getting to see you at present. as for your coming out here to see me, you must not do it as you value my future happiness. I wrote you at Harpers Ferry what I thought about your coming to see me. the difficultys are greater now than they were then. you must not think that I blame you for what you have done, because I think you done it under the idea that I was sick or wounded [p. 2] neither of which I am at present. Mr Towne can explain to you why you ought not want to see me here, and some of the reasons why I cant get to Washington to see you there. Nevertheless I shal try all i can to morrow. if I suceed (of which I have no hope) you will see me. if not, you had better go home until a more favourable oppertunity. if you do not hear from me in 2 days, you had better go home where i will send my next letter. in the mean time it is posible you might find Joe who was sent to Washington yesterday. he is wounded in both legs, but not fattaly. if you find him I should like to have his direction as soon as posible. our Reg.ᵗ suffered severely in the Batle last Saturday. out of about 325 men we took in it, we have lost in Killed Wounded and Missing 120 men. our Company out of 25 men losing 14 but I am happy to say that I did not get a scratch. John the same, Tom [Butterworth] and [p. 3] Sam Barrows staid in Camp sick. I enclose you in this, 2 pieces of Patch work, that I brought from Fredricksburg, and the Feather is from John to Maggy. if you see aunt Mary again give her my respects, and tell her I have not seen cousin Ben since leaving Bollivar. I must now conclude for the present hoping you will take this in the same Affectionate spirit as it is written in

I remain your Affectionate Husband
Benjamin Hirst to his
Beloved Wife.

Dec 24th. I was surprised to hear someone calling my name and to be told that a lady was looking for me. I crawled out of my dog kennel pretty quickly and found my wife standing before me. I could not invite her to come in very well for want of room, so she told me to report with her at Gen Sumner's headquarters right away and that

he had sent for me. I got ready as soon as possible and started for the Lacy house, my wife relating to me how she came to be here.

She knew Joe was wounded and she could not find him in Washington so she came on here in company with a Mr and Mrs Lowe, from Massachusetts, who were looking for a son wounded in both feet. . . . At this time it was very difficult to get passes to the army, and it was only through the kindness of the Hon Dwight Loomis, then member of Congress, who gave my wife a letter to Secretary Stanton[2] that she was able to procure one.

The party arrived at Aquia Creek the night previous and staid in the sanitary commission tent until the next morning, when they reported to Gen Sumner[3] at the Lacy house. The general, after hearing what they had to say, quietly turned to an officer in full uniform and said, (he was his son)[4] Sammy, go . . . ride around to the 14th Connecticut and tell Sergt Hirst to report to me. He then conducted them to another room

Gen. Edwin V. Sumner, commanding the Right Grand Division at Fredericksburg. Box 2, PG 85, #2227, Edward B. Eaton Collection, Connecticut State Archives, Connecticut State Library.

The Lacy House at Falmouth, General Sumner's headquarters in December 1862. Box 1, Vol. 1, PG 85, #S698, Edward B. Eaton Collection, Connecticut State Archives, Connecticut State Library.

and told them to make that their quarters while they staid here. Mrs Hirst got tired of waiting and found her way to our camp, and so she brought the general's order herself. We arrived at the Lacy house just as an ambulance drove up, and I assisted in carrying out the son of Mr Lowe. Gen Sumner was looking on with a great deal of sympathy. . . . Then turning to us he said to Mrs Hirst, "Ah, I see you have found your husband," then looking at me as I saluted, he continued, "you are excused from duty for the present and can make your headquarters with the rest of the people here. Good morning, all, I will see you again." Such was the kindly reception given to the common soldier and his friends by the gallant warrior, Gen Sumner. (Since then I have often had occasion to contrast his bearing with that of some popinjay clothed with a little brief authority without having brains to comprehend that it was possible to be in the army and yet be a gentleman.) In the evening Gen Sumner conversed with us for some time and led me on to speak of our regiment's experience across the river, etc., and as I mentioned the incident about the two officers on the night before our crossing,[5] his eyes snapped like fire as he said something to himself about the scoundrels. In another conversation with the General I ventured to remark I would like to escort my wife back to Washington, and it was with some hesitation as he replied, "I am afraid it cannot be done; I myself need rest and would like to go home for a little while, but must not think of it. We need all our well men here." After two days and

nights at the Lacy house we took our leave of the kind hearted General, my wife go-
ing back to Washington, and myself to camp.[6]

Letter File #24

Camp near Falmouth
December 30.th 1862

Dear Sarah,

We have just got marching Orders, but where we are going to I cant say. we have got every thing ready to leave at once, the moment we get the word. enclosed in this you will find an order for 10 dollars. when you get the money for it send it to me.

I sopose you would like to read what the 14th Con Vol done at the Batle of Fredricksburg it aint too late I hope to tell you.

On the morning of the 11 inst we got orders to get 60 rounds of Amunition and be prepared to march into Fredricksburg, where we understood the Rebs were in force. at daylight we started, our Company under command of the orderly Sergeant [Frank Stoughton]. We numbered 28 muskets, our 4th Sergeant being Color Bearer [Charles Dart], and having one man with the Doctors tools, so that Com D. had 31 men to start for the fight. one skedadled the first day. another was sent back to camp [p. 2] while a third one hid in the City until the fight was all over. however we all started at the time appointed. after making a detour of a few miles, we rested in Front during one of the most Tremendous Canonatings ever heard on this Continent. we had to encamp here until next morning, owing to our Pontoon Bridges not being laid as soon as expected. the next morning we entered the City without losing a man, the Rebels not seeming to care about hindering us. we encamped in the City one day, during which times we had ample time to View the Havoc made by shot and Shell from both sides, and such a sight I never want to see again. I cared nothing for the ruined Walls, but for the wanton destruction of Furniture and other household articles, by our troops, made me Curse the War more than ever. I cannot tell how i did feel. [p. 3] after a restless nights sleep, we arose in the morning of the 13.th ready for the Slaughter prepared for us. how slow the hours seemed to pass, while a shell from the Rebels ever and anon, warned us of what would soon be the Fate of a many. We were marched to the uper street and our Division was Formed in line, we being ordered to lead in the Bloody Work. Why dont our guns shell the rebs asked one, wait a bit boys and youl soon see em says, another. See that man in the Church Steeple waving the signal Flag. our guns will soon give em Fits, but Alas our Guns are worse than useless here. Fall in Boys. Forward Double Quick March and away we go our Reg leading the Second Brigade in the fight. soon we are from under cover of the houses, and are running at

The 14th charged here on 13 December 1862. The house on the left is at the center of the old fair grounds. The front fence indicates the front of the fair grounds. The sunken road and Willis's Hill are at the rear of the house, and the Marye House on Marye Hill is in the background toward the right. H. S. Stevens, Souvenir. Washington, D.C.: Gibson Brothers, 1893, 84.

a rapid gait through the rail road Depot. *We reached a street running to the depot, when we filed right and went by the depot, over the railroad track and across a small bridge laid over a waste way partially filled with water.*[7] when we emerge in ful view [p. 4] of the Rebels, and in good range of their shot and shell, they were fully prepared to give us such a reception, such as was never before seen. hundreds were allready lying on the ground Killed and Wounded while others were taking off the Wounded as Fast as they could. away we whent for about 1/4 of a mile when we laid down on the slushy ground, to get our wind and reconoiter our position. We were on the extreme right, and subject to a raking fire from the Rebel Batterys, which sent a many to their long account. *Some distance to our front and left, was a high board fence which partially shielded us from the rebel musketry, but the guns in our front sent shot and shell right through the fence and into our line. . . . [A] shell bursts near the head of company D, and Corporal John Symonds is in total darkness for evermore in this world. His brother-in-law at his side is fearfully wounded in the face and arm. Poor Oliver Dart. As he rolled over he looked as though his whole face was shot away. Men were being killed and wounded all along the line where we lay, and we could do nothing in return.*[8] Fall back is the next word and the Regiment fell back about one hundred yards, in came Hancocks Division, the Irish Brigade in our front,[9] and away they whent when we got the word forward the 14.th Forward, Forward, Forward. said our Col. and Waving his sword with his Face to the Foe he fell gallantly urging on the men. [p. 5] such of our men as whent rushed along with a will the Rebels giving it to them at every step, while our only chance lay in getting under cover of the rebel works, but few ever got there, and of the few even less came back again, the Irish Brigade were already giving way and some had broke through the 14.th when the Remnant of the Regiment fell back bringing of[f] the Colors in safety,[10] but it was a fearful sight to see. thousands now lay on the Field and still the carnage whent on until night put an end to the Slaughter. of our Regiment, most of our efficient officers were either Killed or wounded, while of the men we lost about 50 per cent. the list of our Company Killed and Wounded you have already got, so that you can satisfy all the people at home who was in the fight and who was not. if you are asked about our present strength tell them that we today can carry [p. 6] about 180 muskets, out of 950 that we left Hartford with just 4 months ago. if the good Folks at home do not take hold and demand a rest for us, the 14 Con Vols will be played out before spring, never to be heard in Batle any more.

your Affectionate
Husband Benj Hirst.

⁓⁓⁓

Journal Excerpt #10

December 11th

The Bombardment of Fredricksburg comenced early this morning, and it was kept up all day. such a Canonading was never before heard on this Continent, and it must have caused the Rebels considerable suprise, to have over 200 Canon playing on them at once. at early day our whole Army was in motion and we soon learned that our division was [to] be one of the leading ones; there was a perceptable differance in the size of our Regiment as compared with it on the morning of Antietam. then we took in the Fight 780 men, here, we left Camp with less than 300 muskets, and the differance in Officers was more disproportionate. For instance our Company had a Capt and two Lieuts at Antietam, here, our only Lieut on duty got the Dim Flims,[11] and we marched under the Command of our Orderly Sergt [Frank Stoughton]. We made a Circuitious march to avoid showing ourselves to the Rebels, and arrived about 1/2 mile in Rear of the Lacy House, about 10 oclock A.M. here we were halted the Pontoons not yet being laid. about 4 oclock a mighty Cheer aroused [p. 2] me from a slumber I was having by the road side (for I can sleep amid the Roar of Canon) and announced to us that the Bridge was laid. we were instantly put in motion Hancocks Division leading ours, but only one Brigade was crossed, owing to the lateness of the hour; We finally Encamped where we had rested during the day, and I had a good nights sleep.

December 12th, 1862

We were up early this morning and our preparations for marching was soon made, and not a bit too soon either, Fall in 14th Fall in sang our Gallant Lieut Col Perkins, and we were soon marching for the Rhappahanock. *We met some of the troops returning who have been in Fredricksburg over night, where they made sad havoc with the ladies' wardrobes, for some of the men had on such finery as old gingham poke bonnets, old hoop skirts, calico dresses, and one fellow who seemed about 7 feet high was dressed as a nigger [?] bride, from his head down to just above his knees, where the ruffles ended, and his dirty old blue pants began to show. Tobacco was at a discount, one pound plugs being offered for 25 cents, with few takers.*[12] a short delay behind the Lacy House and we soon rushed down a ravine at the right of the House and were crossing the river in a moment, the Rebel shells bursting on each side of us. once over and [p. 3] we felt comparatively safe, we were drawn up in line on the first street next [to] the river, while Thousands of our men crossed over without loss so far as I could see. after a while we advanced higher up into the City the shells from our own and the Rebel guns flying harmlessly over our heads. here we stacked Arms and had a chance to look around. the City was a deserted one the Inhabitants having fled God knows where, every house had some special mark of the preceding days Bombardment. it seemed to have been bombarded from and by both sides as the houses were battered both ways. *There was one building near the river I was glad to see looted. It was filled with tobacco in blue papers, labelled "Bull Run tobacco," and underneath the words was a cut, of a lot of Yankees running and a few confederates pursuing them in the back with bayonets.*[13] . . . [O]ur men were soon loaded with Trophys of the City. too many of them Alas never lived to bring them away. We were quartered in a house for the night, but I did not rest much, being detailed to cross the river, for rations. I finally got to Bed (the first I saw since leaving home) at 12 P.M. [midnight]. . . .

December 13th 1862

We were on hand this morning before daylight and we soon knew that our Division had to Lead the Assault on the Rebel Centre. we were marched to the street next in rear of the City, and there awaited with what patience we could the Order to advance. I have before wrote you an account of this Battle and it is unnecessary to repeat it here only to say, that We completely failed in our attackt, our own 14th losing in this Batle 123 Rank and File, in Killed wounded and missing, and this was not our only loss, as the two leading Divisions, were to some extent demoralised by the failure to carry the works of the Enemy. it was the first time the Rebels had ever seen the Backs of the second Army Corps, and I pray it may be the last one.

[p. 2] December 14th was devoted to taking care of the wounded, and reorganising our broken Colums. there was but litle firing during the day, and as it was Sunday, it seemed as neither party desired to renew the Battle on this Day. *John Hirst procured an old gig with broken shafts upon which we placed Joe and wheeled him up to the pontoon bridge where we got him into an ambulance.*[14] December 15 it was understood this morning that the Rebels were going to try and Shell us out of the City, and it created great comotion amongst the friends of the wounded; we soon had orders to have the Wounded removed before noon, and such a sight I never before saw; wounded men were being carried off, on every conceivable thing, some in chairs, on Beds, settees, Boards, Stretchers, doors, Carts, Coaches, Wagons and Weelbarrows every thing was brought into requisition; . . . I think all of our wounded were removed before the hour given. towards evening our men made a feint as though we were going to renew the [p. 3] attack, but it was determined by our Genl not to do so, and at night we began to Evacuate Fredricksburg.

December 16th Every thing was on this side [of] the river, and our Pontoons were taken up, to the great suprise of the Rebels who thought they could anhiliate us at their Leisure. we were marched back to our respective encampments, to recruit our wasted strength, and spirits. This defeat virtualy ended the Winter Campaign of 62 and 63, as we have done but little since.

~~~

Letter File #25

Friday January 9th 1863
Camp near Falmouth.

Dear Sarah,

I wrote you 10 days ago, and guess you got my letter, about 3 days after you got home, but devil a line have I had from you. what is the reason. all the Boys in the Company can tell me my Wife got home, but when or how Dam me if I can tell.

We are yet encamped in the same place, as when you were here, altho we have been under order to leave since I last wrote you. where we are to go to or what we are to do we cant tell. two of those express Boxes came to hand all right, but the Victuals were all spoiled. I am in the same luck [?] as i [p. 2] as ever, the Box that had my things in did not come. nor has it yet been heard from. Tom [Butterworth] got nothing either so that I had good company to help me Swear. tom is gone to Washington to see if change of Grub wont do him good. John got a letter from Joe yesterday, Joe is doing very well. John is not as well as i could wish, the least thing tires him out. I am about the same as usual. Sam Barrows wants his money, as he may get his discharge any day, and I got cleaned out buying that check i sent in my last letter. John has just got that letter with the 5 dollars in it, that you sent to Alexandria. the money [is] all right. Write as soon as you get this, I remain your Affectionate Husband

Benjamin Hirst.

[p. 3]

P.S. We have heard nothing from Albert Towne [Jr.] as yet. I have visited most of the Hospital Grave yards, this side the river but have not seen his name. there are scores of graves, that are marked unknown. he may fill one of these. B Hirst.

The fate of Albert H. Towne was not known for several months after the battle, when a letter came to Rockville directed to his friends. The writer, Col. Chamberlain of Maine, stated that on the afternoon of December 13, 1862, he saw in front of his brigade the dead body of a young soldier with a testament by his side. He picked up the book and afterwards saw written upon the fly leaf, Albert H. Towne, Rockville, Conn. this testament was finally returned to his parents and all doubts as to his fate cleared up.[15]

P.S. [the second in this letter] I forgot to write you that I received that parcel you sent by Plimton, all right. the Lady packed it in a litle Box and I got it about 2 weeks ago. the Tobaco and Cigars that Myron Jesting sent to Joe Jesting, we Confiscated as Joe had been gone home over his time.[16] you can tell Myron that the Cigars and Tobaco was first rate and you can settle with him for them, or if that dont suit him tell him to come on here and I will settle with him myself a much better Plan as he might as well come first as last. you will see by Bottomlys letter, that they would like to have you visit them, if you can make it convenient to do so, I should like it. the Present that I sent Bottomly was a Wooden Chain, a very pretty one, that took a man 3 days to make. he gave [p. 2 of P.S.] it to me, and I sent it to John Bottomly,[17] and also a Laural root Ring to Forbes. I send you a Washington Paper along with this. send me some Stamps in your next and give my respect to enquiring Friends, I remain yours as Ever

B. Hirst.

Letter File #26

Camp near Falmouth Vir
January 11.th 1862 [1863].

Dear Sarah,

I received your long expected letter last night, and was much pleased to see the sucess you had in doing your business in Washington, and that you got home all right and found things to your satisfaction.

And now for what Mr Towne says about me in conection with Brigham, I showed Frank Stoughten your letter, and he will write to his Wife that he knows about the matter. for myself, I can laugh at all the yarns, that can be told about me. I done just as I meant to do under certain circumstances; at Antietam, I just moved poor Wilkie and left him to his Fate. after his Death I blamed myself for not taking [p. 2] him to the Hospital, and swore never to leave another man as i did him; and when I saw the same men at Fredricksburg playing the game of Antietam I whent in too, but with no idea of leaving the Fight. when [Pvt.] O. Dart and Simons [Cpl. John Symonds] were wounded, I saw [Sgt.] Brigham and [Cpl.] Hyde, and [Pvt.] Newel (3 Yankees) take hold of Symons to take him off. I jumped to my feet and took hold of Dart calling Hyde from Symons to assist me. we took them to the Hospital, where I ordered Hyde and Newel back to the Regiment, and to tell Stoughten I would be with them in a few minuets, after the Dr looked at Dart and Symons. it was me asked Brigham, to come with me to join the Regiment. he said John wanted him to stay by him, then Dart said he wanted me to stay with him a little while. I done [p. 3] so because, I just then heard of our Regiment coming down the street having been relieved. I then made myself easy attending to Dart, as F. Stoughten knew where he could find me at any moment day or night. after our Joe was brought into Hospital, Brigham came to our John and

me and said the Regiment was a litle ways down the street. I asked Brigham to go
and see Frank Stoughten and tell him where I was, and also to tell him, that if the
Regiment moved I wanted to go with it. he said he would do it, but did it not. our
John can Witness this. Stoughten came to me soon after that and told me to Stick
by Dart. I then was satisfied that Brigham had told him as i asked him to, but Frank
says Brigham done no such thing, but that he asked him (Brigham) if he could
not join him. he [Brigham] said John Symons Wanted him, and whent into the
Hospital. I have since asked [p. 4] Frank why he did not ask me to join them. he
said because he thought I was ready to go at any moment, and he could depend
on me. I want you to show Jerry Rhodes this letter, and tel him that any man that
says I did not do my Duty at Fredricksburg is a Liar. I have never been excused
from duty for sickness (altho I have often been worse than those whose place i had
to take). and tell him if i was the only Comisioned Officer in a Company i would
not go to a Doctor to get excused on the morning of a Batle, also tell him if the
War is conducted in this way very much longer I shal be able to play Yankee as well
as Soldier. What Brigham writes home I care nothing about, he was as Brave at Fredricksburg as at Antietam.[18] a few days after you left here I wrote you an account of
the Batle of Fredricksburg. hope you got it, as it is as near [p. 5] correct as I can
make it. I also sent you a check for 10 dollars that I bought. We got an agreeable
surprise last night by the arrival of that Box with the Boots and other things in
them. the Bread was all mouldy but the Liquour was all right, and the Loaf Sugar
is also first rate. I shal try to Sell Tommys [Butterworth's] things and send him the
money, as it will be Spring before he is fit for duty. give my respects to all the Folks
at the mill, and tell them that I do nothing through Fear, or Cowardice whatever
others may do. I got 10 dollars in your letter and want you to send Sam Barrows
money in your next. also the money for that check I last sent you. I must now
conclude for the present hoping this will find you in as good health as myself.
    Yours Ever as always Benjn Hirst.

Letter File #27

Camp near Falmouth Vir
Sunday January 18. 1863

Dear Wife,

    I received your long expected letter this morning. it had 10 dollars in it. this
makes 2 letters with 10 dollars each in them. I have not got the second letter you
sent, but soppose it may be all right as I this morning got a letter from Bottomly
Dated on the P.O. mark Dec 6. I have settled with Sam Barrows, and in this you
will find enclosed another Check for 10 dollars, which I borrowed from John. get

the money and send it as soon as posible with 5 dollars for myself. I dont see what you want going in the mill for it will do you no good, but I sopose you are buck cat at present, so you will do what suits you. if it does not agree with you I must insist that you quit it at the first oppertunity. [p. 2] (if I could quit mine as easy you would soon see me at home.) you did not tell me if you got my last letter in which I told you about the Battle at Fredricksburg (I mean the last letter but one) as I last wrote you about myself and Brigham. What does Frank Stoughtens Wife say. as soon as I finish this letter I shal write to sister Kate [Smiley] as she in her letter seems anxious I should do so. I am sorry to say that John gets no better. I wish he would be lucky enough to be sent to Alexandria again. he will never be able to stand a Winter Campagn, and if we march tomorrow as is expected we shal have to leave him behind again, and I hope he will be sent home like the rest of the sick. I have just heard that Irvin Stoughten has got his discharge, and Lieut Emery has tendered his resignation. hope when he gets home, that Cap^n [p. 3] Hammond, Lieuts Vinton and Emery will organise a home Guard of our returned Patriots. they will make a good representation of the Fight until Death kind. (in a Farce). Dear Sarah, you write me to take good care of myself I shal endeavour to do so, and i want you to do the same, so that when I come home we shal be able to have our health and Strength such as God has heretofore given us. I for myself do not envy some of the returned Volunteers from Rockville. some are sick and some are Cripled for Life, but others are there from the sheerest Poltroonery. these last I envy the least. give my respects to all my friends and keep up your own good Courage I remain

> your Affectionate Husband
> Benjamin Hirst.

Letter File #28

> send me some letter Stamps

> Camp near Falmouth. Vir
> Monday January 19. 1863.

Dear Sarah,

I write you these few lines, because in looking over my effects last night, I saw that I had not sent you the check that I meant to. you will find it in this. it is now 12, M. and we have not marched yet, and it seems to me that we are as far from it as ever. I think John will be sent to Alexandria or Wash^n in a few days if he does he will write you; when we march again I shal be the only one of the 10 that tented togather in Hartford. the other 9 will all be played out. I must close this as the mail is about closing. give my respects to Bugbee, Frink, Morse, Smith, Holgate and all the rest of my old Shop mates.

yours in Love and Life B Hirst

Journal Excerpt #11

January 20th 1863, had an Address from Burnside read to us, and gave 3 cheers for the Rhapahanock; but there arose a great storm that rendered it imposible to move. hundreds of horses and men were disabled in the attempt, and after the greater part of our Army had been floundering in the mud 3 days it was given up, and we have been Virtualy in Winter quarters ever since. Benj Hirst

Letter File #29

Camp near Falmouth.
Saturday, January 24 [1863]

Dear Sarah.

I send you these few lines in Murrys letter he is going to have a box sent him you can put a parcel in it. send me 2 Pocket Handkerchiefs and one neck tie, some Brandy, and a Needle Book if you can get a chance to make one, and anything else that you would like I should have. the great Army move that we were going to make has proved a failure on account of a great Storm that comenced the day that we began to move. Horses, Wagons and Canon are Stuck fast in the mud for miles around here. respects to all. more in my next. have not heard from you since my last. B Hirst

Letter File #30

Camp near Falmouth, Vir
Saturday January 31.st 63

Dear Sarah,

I received your Welcome letter last night, and was truly glad to hear from you as I was getting uneasy about that last check I sent you. I got a letter from you the day before containing 5 dollars, and the letter last night had 10 dollars in it, and some postage stamps. I have not yet got that second letter you sent me, so I give it up as lost. I should have made 8 dollars on those two checks, if that letter had come to hand. as it is I do but lose 2 dollars. I borrowed the money to buy that last check off John, so when I pay him I shall have 4 or 5 dollars left. There is some talk of the [p. 2] of the paymaster coming to see us pretty soon, but he has not got hear yet. I received a letter from [Joe?] Smiley the other day, they are all well. I saw Tom [Quinn?] last week, also Aleck McKinley, young McFate, Brien [?] Kelly, and others of the Del Co [Delaware County, Pa.] Boys. they came to see us one night during the Big Storm when Burnside meant to cross the Rhaphannock. as I had a little medicine in my knapsack, we passed an hour or two, as happy as though the morrow would never bring trouble. the Boys got wet through in going to their Regimental Camps. the next day it rained all day, and the day after, they are marched back to their old Encampments about 9 miles from here. John is in the Regimental Hospital he is getting a litle better. I think he will get along, when the weather gets pleasant, but at present the changes [are] so sudden it is a wonder [p. 3] that any of us keep our health. we have made a fire place in our Tent and by bringing Wood on our backs, about 1/2 mile we make out to keep our toes warm. I wish you would tell me in your next how you direct your letters to Joe. the last 2 letters I wrote him came back to the Reg^t and one I sent to Tom also came back. I shal send them again to day. enclosed in this you will find a letter I got from Mr Bottomly. I have wrote him to send his box along. I guess we can soon demolish it, as I can eat every day, what would formerly do me 3 at least. you will see by the Newspapers that Gen Sumner has got through with the Army, as has also Franklin and Burnside.[19] does the Government think they did not get men enough killed at Fredricksburg, if so why dont they let us know it.

[p. 4] I told Frank Stoughten, what Mr Towne had said he told him; Frank says there is some mistake about it for he knows that he never said it to him or any one else. I care but very little about it, at present; but to say that whosoever said it, is a Damned Liar. and I can Prove it.

I am well at present, as ever I was in my Life, and if I should not happen to get very sick, I shall never try to get Home with the Chronic Diahrea. that is the way some Chickens are hatched, and Dave Whiting and me are watching another one or two on the Roost.

Give my love to Mother and Maggie, and tell Frink I want to hear from him. why Dont Morse write me. give my respects to all my shop mates and tell them, I am the same young Cuss as ever. if Azubah [?] Whiting should happen to get asleep just tell her she is asleep again. no more at present, your Affectionate Husband B Hirst

Letter File #31

Camp near Falmouth
Friday Feb 5.th 1863

Dear Sarah,

I write you these few lines to let you know that I am well in health, and Pocket, having been paid off, up to the first of January. I received a litle over 75 dollars; 40 of which you will find in this letter; I have not heard from you this week, but I got a Mercury the other day, and it is a ever Welcome visitor. I have not heard from Bottomly since I last wrote you, but think uncle Sam ought to have that box along by this time. why dont Mrs Murry and you send that box along. John is getting a litle better and I think he is quite comfortable in his present quarters. I have not heard from Tom or Joe since my [p. 2] last, I sent a letter to each of them the day I last wrote you.

there has been quite a list of promotions in this Regiment, and Frank Stoughten may thank Lieuts Vinton and Emery for keeping him in the Ranks; I have just found out that at an examination of more [?] Commisioned officers, held at Belle Plain 2 months ago, (of which I never heard until now) Lieut Vinton, sent Corp Lyman and Frank Stoughten, and in particular recomended his Friend Lyman for promotion to a Lieutenantcy. he has now got it, and Frank is still Orderly Sergeant. *How it [Lyman's promotion] came about we do not know, but he is a good man and will make a good officer.*[20]

For myself I never expected anything from our Officers, since Burpee left us in Hartford, and being that the others are now safe at home [p. 3] it is well enough to let you know what was done by them this litle time Past, on the morning when we were ordered to march to Fredricksburg. Lieut Vinton whent to the Doctor to be excused from duty. the Dr would not excuse him, and Vinton then whent to the Col who left him in charge of Camp. the consequence was, that some of our Company, pretended to be sick, and that is the true reason, that Co D, did not have more men in the Battle of Fredricksburg; Vinton was very glad to let Stoughten Command the Company then, and when we were ordered to March a few Weeks ago Lieut Emery done the same thing day after day. neither of them wanted to be hurt before their Resignations were accepted, and I kind of reckon they will take good care of themselves now.

[p. 4] I must conclude this rather short as the mail is closing.

I remain your Affectionate
Husband, B Hirst.
Respects to All.

Letter File #32

Camp near Falmouth Vir
February 10.th 1863

Dear Sarah,

I received your Welcome letter on the 8,inst also one from Joe, one from Tom, 2 from Bottomly so I am chock full of Business in answering letters this morning. we are on picket and lolling around in the sun, it is as warm as a May Day and I was never in better health in my Life, than at present. I am about 12 lbs heavier than I was when I left Hartford, so you can judge by that, that I dont let trifles worry me, but I was very much displeased when I read your letter in regard to x x x conduct; it may be that I shall get home for a day or two in the course of 6 or 8 weeks. if there is any more of that conduct I shall regulate things a litle differant. in the mean time [p. 2] if you think she will do so again, you must quit working in the mill and take care of the house yourself; give x x x to understand that I wont be disgraced by any one, particularly in my own house. Dear Sarah, I shall be sorry if you cant send me that box, as you have been to so much trouble in getting it for me. I did not intend you to send me a lot of Victuals, but they would be Doubly welcome at this time, as John is getting better quite fast, and begins to eat like a Horse, and I can eat like two. Frank Stoughton started for home this morning on a 10 days Furloug. they are going to let a few go home each 10 days if the others come back again all right. from our Company there is several applications ahead of mine so I cant tell for certain [p. 3] if I shall get one or not, but hope I shall, as I would give a good deal, to be with you for one short Week.

Joe writes me that he got my last letter and he is getting along nicely, he thinks he will soon get to New Haven. Tom says nothing about going home or that Boss [?] job, but writes as though he would join the Regt again as soon as he gets well enough. he is getting better. Bottomly sent me that Box by Harndens Express last Wednesday and mailed me the Receipt and a list of the contents of the Box. it contains 2 Christmas Loaves 3 mince Pies some Cheese, Tobaco, Cigars, Pipes, matches, Dried allibut, pot each of Pickles onions, Cabbage, and a Pot of Potted Beef.

if I should get his box and yours [p. 4] a couple of Weeks before I get a Furlough, you may look [?] out for a better looking Chap than you saw out here. give my Love to Maggy and respect to Mother[21] and all enquiring Friends

I remain as Ever
your Affectionate
Husband Benjn Hirst.

PS. You will find in this a sheet copied from my Diary. I will send you more as fast as I get time to copy them, and want you to keep them, as they may be of use to me some day. [These comprise the journal excerpts here incorporated into the preceding text. —ed.]

BH.

Letter File #33

Feb 10th. I have just got from Picket Duty and received yours of the 5inst and if I was home I would soon settle things. you must stay at home and see that there is no Liquour brought in the House and if that dont do you must pack up the old Womans things and start her to Philidelphia. you can pay her Fare and what will keep her a few months for I will be Damd if I will be disgraced by a Drunken Woman. you must look to it, for I shall know the truth, and shall not be triffled with in this matter, as it concerns our future Happiness, and your and my present Peace. if she is determined to go on, she must suffer alone as she assuredly will.

am glad you wont have to work nights any more[22]
I returned that Check where I got it. it was genuine as the Officers of his Company say. i got my money back from him. write me by return Post
your Affectionate Husband B Hirst

Letter File #34

Camp near Falmouth Vir
February 23.d 1863

I write you this late letter with my regrets for not writing you sooner, but I should have done so if I had not wanted to inform you of the safe arrival of those boxes. I am sorry to say that we have not yet got them, and can see no signs of them yet. the Express Companies are like the Government, they dont care a dam how they humbug the soldiers. Frank Stoughten got here on Friday Evening, and brought me that Parcel you sent by him. those night caps are first rate to sleep in, and that Diary will be very useful. Frank says that the folks in Rockville sent so much Talk by him, that he has got it all mixed up togather and cant unraval it, to save his life. so you must write me what you told him [p. 2] I should like to get a Furlough first rate, but there is so many ahead of me that I cant say if I shal be able to get one or not. Dwight Loomis has wrote for Mike Fay, and it is likely he will come next, then comes Allen, or Thrall [a wagoner], Joe Muray, then me, which will bring the time up to the last of April, and by that time there will be something else up.

Our Joe writes me that he has had a Relapse owing to their dressing his Leg with Iodine instead of Tincture of Iron; he was going to come Home with Mr. Loomis and Lady, but he will not be able to do so at present. When Mr. Loomis comes Home you might interest him in getting me a Furlough. tell him what you want done around the house at Home and that I want to see Joe in Washington. John is got back with us again [p. 3] and is a great deal better. I am first rate, notwithstanding the exposure that we sometimes undergo. Last Week I took Johns place on Picket and was exposed to a snow storm for 19 hours and was wet through and through, my feet was so wet and Cold, that I did not begin to feel them getting warm until the water began to scald my feet. If I had kept my boots in the fire much longer I should have burnt them off my feet. after one day in Camp I was all right again. so much for getting used to things.

We now Picket on the River, and I was posted at the place where we crossed our Pontoon to Fredricksburg. the Rebels were on the other side of the River and were quite sociable with us. when they found out that we had been over there, they invited us to come again, but we [p. 4] [could] not see it. I hope you have got things at home regulated to suit you. I calculate that while I am out here that you are Boss and can see what is for our mutuale good, as wel as I can; and I hope if it is needed, you will do so. if I should not be able to get a Furlough, I want you to get that stone wall next to Carrolls built right past the wood shed and that side walk completed along the road, and get the Fences put up so as to keep the Damd Niggers[23] out. I think if that stone wall is built it will keep the wash out of the wood shed.

I must now conclude, hoping to soon
　　　　　　　see you I remain your
　　　　　　　Affectionate Husband
　　　　　　　Benjamin Hirst

Letter File #35

[Letter to Sarah written in pencil on back (i.e., 4th panel) of journal sheet describing Antietam]

　　　Tuesday March 3d, 1863

　　　Dear Sarah why dont you write me, I have not had a letter this 3 weeks, and cant make it out. I wrote you last week about Frank Stoughten getting back. I have not got those boxes yet, although they got to Falmouth last Saturday. they are being opened at Couches head quarters.[24] they will then be sent to Divisions, then to the Brigades, and then to Regiments, so we may posibly get them in the course of 6 or 8 weeks, (if the Army dont move).[25] John is pretty well and I continue first rate. have not time to write you much today, but will write you as soon as I get yours which I sopose is on the way. Love to all your Affectionate
Husband Benj Hirst

One day, while we were on dress parade, an officer came riding along and halted in the rear of our acting colonel. He was a delicate looking man without any insignia of office about him, and carried in his hand a small riding whip. Of course we wondered who he was and thought he would see before him a clean, well dressed, fine looking regiment. We were all well shod, and about one-fourth of the regiment wore good home made cowhide boots with our pantaloon legs tucked inside them, Yankee fashion. Did he admire us? Well, he said a few words to the captain commanding, who called for

Gen. Darius N. Couch, commanding the 2d Corps at Fredericksburg and Chancellorsville. Box 2, PG 85, #S3768, Edward B. Eaton Collection, Connecticut State Archives, Connecticut State Library.

the adjutant, and after a short confab the adjutant about faced and came to the right of the regiment with a book and pencil in his hand. I began to think that every thing was not all right, and standing still as a poker began tugging at my pant legs to get them outside my boots. I just succeeded as the adjutant came to the rank of file closers, and was saved from having two hours extra drill per order of the officer in our front, Major Gen. Couch, our new corps commander.

. . . Perhaps you would like to know what a sutler is. Well, he is a man who follows the army for the sole purpose of making money, and owes his appointment to a deal made with the heads of a regiment, that he will furnish the officers with supplies, at a small profit, with liberty to charge the privates all he can get.

... Our sutler is named Sprinkler and hails from Hanover, Pa. He is a temperance man so far as selling to the men is concerned, but the boys get it just the same.[26]

⌒〜〜⌒

Letter File #36

Camp near Falmouth
March 6.th 1863
My Dear Wife,

I received your letter last night and was very glad to hear you are well, as I was getting uneasy at your long silence, but I sopose it was all right. I got those boxes last Tuesday, and taking the 'time' they have been in coming they got here pretty safe. the cakes and doughnuts are good and the Liquor was all right. the Handkerchiefs were safe in Fact I lost nothing but the Bread and Sams Pies which were mouldy. the box from Bottomly was first rate. there was Nothing in it spoiled, owing to the manner in which it was packed. they packed everything seperate, with press board [p. 2] partitions. this is what kept every thing in the box good.

I dont know how this Furlough business will work, as they are not giving any in our regiment at present, owing to the bad faith of the men in getting back. If I could see Squire [Dwight] Loomis I would try to get one from the War Department, for I feel more like coming home to kiss, and enjoy you, every day; indeed it is a great disapointment to lay down at night, and dream I am hugging you to my heart, then awaken and find myself lying in this damd place. it makes me swear some, but that does no good. I would not be in a hurry about getting a Ell put on the house, because you must not run all the money [p. 3] away. you may want to use one hundred dollars at any day, that you are not aware of. Still I would see what it would cost to put an L on for. it wants to be about 10 by 14 feet clear inside, corner posts 8 feet high, roof to pitch each way, and to have a Vernandah from the Front door to the Front of the house. if you could find out how much it would cost, I will try and draft you a plan of what I want, and should want to let the job whole, so that it could be done with the least trouble to you. give my respects to all my shop mates, and tell Frink I can see him at work on the gass [?] works, and he dont look very well pleased, but I hope to see him in good humour when I get back to old Rockville. [p. 4] I am in good health and spirits at present, and John keeps pretty well. Sam Barrows has been troubled with his x x x but the doctor took him to the Hospital last night and done something that has relieved him a great deal. How has your mother been in this past week or two, you forgot to write me in your last. give my Love to Maggy, and respects to all enquiring Friends I remain
your Affectionate
Husband B. Hirst

⌒〜〜⌒

Letter File #37

Camp near Falmouth. Vir
March 13.th 1863

Dear Sarah, I received yours of the 8th inst and I hasten to answer it as soon as posible, for I know that you look for an answer to your last letter before you write another one. I hope you got the 2 Ambrotypes I mailed you last Tuesday. I sent you two because I thought you'd want to send one to Kate [Smiley], and I want to know which is the best one, and what you think about them. I am glad to hear of so many Yankees getting home. if they will only vote according to their experience out here, this War will soon be at an end. I hope to hear that <u>Conn</u>t will soon repudiate, the miserable Policy adopted at Washington.[27] if these men [p. 2] after getting their own necks out of the noose, go to Vote, to tighten ours, it will go to show you the Damnable selfishness of some of them. There is not a man in this Company that does not Curse the hour that sent us out here.

We are expecting a move every day. yesterday we were kept under arms all day, but did not see what it was for, as the Rebels out here are quite peaceable only scareing our Cavalry once in a while, and taking a few of them Prisoners just by the way of amusement. But I sopose old Hooker don't like it, and will soon try to put a Stop to it, and by the time he does that, we shal want a New Commander. John is about the same as usual and has just had his likeness taken. [p. 3] I sopose he will send them home. the second man from our Company, on Furlough as only just started for home, so you will see by that, that my turn will not come until about the 4th of July. if Loomis can get a Furlough from the War Department, I should like it very much, and I know that I deserve one. let me know what he says about it. I wrote to Butterworth last night. I hope he will get home, as it is the Fashion. We had 3 Rockville boys join us yesterday. 2 of them were wounded at Antietam (Waldo, and Orcut) and one we left sick at Bollivar—(Dick Reed). they all 3 look first rate, but are devilish sorry to be here, and the rest of us dont care who comes or goes. give my respects to all the boys at the [p. 4] mill. I hope the Birds will keep a singing and you sing some yourself, and I should like to join you in the Chorus. I must now conclude hoping you are in as good health as this leaves me. I remain
your Affectionate
Husband Benj Hirst

P.S. Send me some Stamps

Letter File #38

Camp near Falmouth
March 17.th 1863.

Dear Sarah, I last received yours of the 11th inst, and was glad to hear you are in good health, and that you have been to see Loomis. if it does no good it can do no harm. you will see by my last letter what my views are in regard to getting a Furlough. if Loomis cant help me to one we must wait the course of events and no doubt I shal come out all right. I want you to make me another Flanell Shirt and drawers, that is all I want in the clothes line. I last night got a letter from Joe he is doing very well again, and is in good spirits. John is the same, and I shal mail you his Likeness [p. 2] along with this letter. the one you like best is for you, the other one, he did not say who it is for. You will find in this letter 2 cards one for you and one from John to Maggie. I have got a couple to send to Kate when she next writes me. what do you think about them. did you get my Likeness, if you did I hope you like them, for they are good likenesses, that is for the Army. that old Hen you enquired about Left his nest too long so the Eggs got Haddled [?], and he dont know how to begin to feather another nest; if there is another attempt I will tell you who it is. Joe Murry [Murray] has been a Sergeant about a month. he was made so like a many others, for staying at Camp while the rest went to Fight at Fredricksburg. I dont want you to say any thing about this, as I [p. 3] believe he got ready to go, and would have whent, but for Lieut Vinton.[28] When he saw Vinton back out, he Murry backed out too. you must excuse the shortness of this letter as I have not closed my eyes this 31 hours, and I am tired, having just come of[f] guard. My health is good and if I thought yours was as good I should have very litle to trouble me at present. I hope Mother is better and I am glad you have left the mill as you can take care of things yourself; give my respects to my old Shop Mates, and tell some of them they will soon have a chance to know what Soldiering is. we are looking to see such men as Millo [?] Pember draughted. if we get them in the Bully 14.th we will give them a front seat. must now conclude yours forever and Ever. B. Hirst.

Letter File #39

Camp near Falmouth
March 17. 1863

Dear Brother [Joe],

I have just received yours of the 13th inst, and it gives us great pleasure to hear you are getting along so well. I last night received your letter of the 9.th inst, it had been missent or I should have got it sooner.

With regard to the changes in the Box Weavers [?] in Rockville you need not fear but you will get a job as soon as you are able to take up one, there will be plenty of chances open to you, and to myself if I ever get out of this. I got a letter from Sarah last night. she has been to see Squire Loomis and Lady, and they had quite a long talk about you. Loomis says you will be discharged as soon as you are fit to take care of yourself. if I was you I would write him once in a while as he may befriend you.

All is quiet out here with the exception of a litle Canonading to day. What it meant we cant find out . . . . Several of our detailed men have . . . joined us so we have about 25 men in the Company now, but some of them wont be of any account to us. . . . John Joins me in sending Love to you, your Affectionate
Brother Benj Hirst.

~~~~~~~

Letter File #40

Camp near Falmouth, Vir
Sunday March 22, 63
My Dear Sarah,

I received yours of the 15.th inst in due season, and was very happy to hear that you are well. I was in hopes to have heard that you had received those Ambrotypes. I hope you have got them, and that you like them; I also received the Mercury, and the reason I don't always mention having got the Mercury, is because I get them very regular; I got a letter from Miss Isabella Smiley, that had been 4 weeks in getting here, they want to get my likeness; I wrote her that I had sent 1 to Aunt Sarah and I thought you had, or would, soon send them on. I hope you have done so. That is if you received them yourself. I am very glad to hear Margret [p. 2] is such a good girl; she wil never regret it, for the Habits she forms now are the ones, that will rule Her always; Sam Barrows is a little better, he is going to the Division Hospital in a day or two; he received a letter from his Mother the other day. he says he will write after a while, in the mean time he wants some [money], and John has let him have it. Sam wants his Mother to give you 10 dollars which you will put to Johns account, and keep it for him. mention it when you get it; I never got that second letter with the 10 dollars in it. you had better get that side walk done as soon as posible, and clean up around the House as soon as the weather will allow. have the Pig Pen cleaned out, the manure put in a heap, and get a Pig, if you think you would like to take care of one. if you get the garden Ploughed, before I get to [p. 3] to come home, have the stones moved by the Wood house, so that you can have the stone wall brought down past the Wood House; a good Wall there will keep you from being drowned out another year; I have not yet had time to Draught the kind of an ell I want put on the House, and I hope you will be in no hurry of getting it done; for it will be a long time before this war is brought to a close; and if I live to serve 3 years that is a long time too; I reckon Brigham wont get Home as soon as he thought he would; when Stoughten whent home Brigham cared nothing about it, and did not apply to go home until after Stoughten, Fay, Thrall, Billson, Allen, Murry and myself, had applied. but he wanted to go first and got a Blank Paper then filled it out for himself. he failed in getting that through, and then comenced [boring?] the [p. 4] Liut to let him go next after Thrall. the Lieut to get rid of him, wrote his papers out, but did not send them to be sighened. he had before told me we should go in the order of application. I whent to him yesterday and found out how Brigham was trying to work it, and the Lieut said he would have to wait his turn. I gave Brigham a piece of my mind, that I hope he wont forget in a hurry. I expect Allen will go home next, then Murry, after him myself. I hope you got my last with the 2 cards in it and Johns likenesses. i was a litle sick yesterday, but feel well this morning. about Hooker I have formed no opinion.[29] we have soft Bread and Fresh Beef 4 times a week and are better supplied than we have been heretofore. Love to all I remain

your Affectionate Husband
Benjamin Hirst.

Journal Excerpt #12

March 23, 1863. Co D 14 Con Vol Falmouth
[p. 4] PS. I think I had better send you an account of the strength of our Comp at this time. We left Hartford with a ful Company, viz 98 Privates. Now we have but 57 names on our books, of which number 16 are in Hospitals at a distance from here, 4 are in Hospitals here which leaves us 37 men for duty and of this 37, 4 are Teamsters, 3 in the Band, 1 drumer, and 2 men on detached service, and 2 men in the Pioneers; thus leaving the fighting strength of our Company at 25 muskets. Our Company is about a fair Average for the Regiment. I have not yet the chance to see the Regimental Book, but I know we draw about 400 rations, and taking out Teamsters, Band, pipers [i.e., fifers] and drumers, men on detached service Etc. the Brave Fourteenth cannot number more than 250 muskets for service. Benjn Hirst

March 24th 1863

Letter File #41

Camp near Falmouth Va
March 30.th 1863.

My Dear Sarah,

I received yours of the 26.th this Evening, and I received two other ones since I last wrote you, but I finished my Narrative and sent you the last sheets last week. I am glad you like the Likenesses. I reckon they Flatter me as they do most of other People, still a few pounds of Flesh on a man makes a great difference in his appearance. John has not been well as he was at Home, but the Likeness he sent you hardly does him justice. . . . I got a letter from Tom [Butterworth] on Friday. he is in Hospital at West Philadelphia [p. 2] and has had a relapse. I also had a letter from Joe he is doing nicely and sits up every day so if no more mistakes occur he will soon be able to be moved to New Haven or Home. I am sorry to say that the 10 day Furlough business has been stopt again, and for the present I see no chance of getting one as I have not heard anything of Loomis; but as long as I have my health I shal not let that trouble me much, if my anticipations are not realised. Brigham was trying to play a pretty game. he was determined if he could not get home, that no one else should if he could help it. Allen might have gone home a week ago but for him. the consequence is that neither can go at present. I think we shal move from here very soon, as everything indicates that as soon as the Weather will permit we shall try issues with the Rebels again, and I hope we [p. 3] shal be successful. You did not tell me in your last how the Strikers made out in Rockville. The Stay at Homes do not mean to suffer much for their Country if they can help it, but I reckon the Conscription will bring some of them up to their milk. With regard to Building I think we had better not do so, at present. Labour is so high that I can not afford to pay so much as it would cost. When this Devilish War is ended prices will tumble down faster than they go up, and if I can get nothing else to do I can at least do that myself. John says he would rather you would keep his money than put it in the Bank. Get Treasury Notes for it, and keep it. he wants to know how much money he gave you in Hartford, as he has forgotten. You had better write in your next what sums he has [p. 4] paid you. I am very sorry to hear you have had such a time around the House, and I hope you will soon be able to get things righted. if you get that Wall laid as I before wrote you, it will save you from getting in such another scrape. get it done by all means as soon as the Weather will permit, and if there is stone enough in the Garden to do it, have it carried down to the Gate Post, then we shall get only our own wash.

In one of your letters you say you have felt like singing since you have got my Likeness. it does me good to hear you say so. I hope you will sing outright fully believing that all will yet end Well. if you should see Holton [?] the American Mill Carpenter tell him that some of the Boys would like a Hartford Times. We get plenty of the other Hartford papers. give him my respects and ask him how he likes the new Term CopperHead. I am First Rate and Remain Yours as Ever. Benjamin Hirst

---

Letter File #42

Va
Camp near Falmouth
April 2, 1863

Dear Brother [Joe]

I received yours several day ago, but I have not had time to answer it before now owing to the constant Drill, and other work we have to do. altho we expect to move every day, we are Building Huts as though we were just going into Winter quarters. we have just got our[s] done it is 11 feet by 7 1/2 and 5 feet High. We have 2 tiers of Bunks in it. So you see we shal be pretty snug if we stay here any length of time. yesterday morning we were all under Arms from 3 oclock until daylight expecting to meet the Rebels, who had forded the river, but when they saw we were not to be suprised they whent the way they came. [p. 2] We are very glad to hear you are getting along so well, and I hope you will soon go home, for I expect the 14.th will have enough to do this coming Campagn. I got a letter from Tom he is in West Philadelphia, and dont seem to get much better. Sam Barrows is still in the Hospital, getting no better. John and I keep first rate, and I hope to do so. I got my Likeness taken and sent it home. Sarah says it is first rate. she sent it to the mill, and as soon as the Weavers heard of it they came runing all around to see it. they were all suprised to see that I was looking so well. They are having a high old time in Conn about Politics, but I think Tom Semour[30] will be the next Governor if they do call him a Copperhead. They got up some Humbug Resolution [p. 3] in our Regiment the other day in which they try to make it appear that the 14.th are to a man in favour of Buckingham but I think if they will Vote the Regiment by Ballot they will find it a litle differant to what they expect. We had a speech from Capt Davis in which he asserted that the Republicans of the 14.th whent to Fredericksburg while the Democrats stayed in Camp. What do you think of That. There is another Call

So I must Conclude
I remain your Affectionate
Brother B. Hirst

[The following written in pencil beneath Ben's signature:] Captain Davis is a damned liar it was the abolitionists that stayed in camp Lieutenant Vinton and others of his stamp

Joseph Hirst

As Captain ———— [Davis?] was standing at the head of Co. D avenue some one sang out, "three cheers for Tom Seymour." The captain made a bolt down the street until somebody between two huts gave him a [trip?] and he tumbled through one of the canvass roofs amid the laughter of all who saw the trick.[31]

———✦———

Letter File #43

Va
Camp near Falmouth
April 6th 1863

My Dear Sarah

I received yours of the first of April this evening and I hasten to answer it to-night. late as it is as I have to go on Picket at 6 oclock to morrow morning and then I could not write you until Thursday as it will be Wednesday afternoon before I get back to Camp. I am sorry you were disopointed in regard to not getting as many letters as you desire. I write almost every oppertunity I have, as you know that I have occasionaly to write to our Relations and Friends. for instance last week I wrote you. also answered Tom Butterworth and Forbes, and wrote Kate besides sending a small wooden Charm to John Bottomly and a letter to the [p. 2] Place. this with drill every day and Picket and Guard Duty is no Joke. I also wrote our Joe the same day I wrote you last. in addition to all this we have to carry our Wood over one mile and a quarter to keep our fire going, so you see we are not kept in Idleness. I cannot tell you, when you will get a letter. I keep writing you, but you do not tell me the Date of the last letter you get. you ought to have had a letter the day but one after you got the last [one] of (our Campaign). I am very glad that you are in good health and hope you will continue so. I am in first rate health at present and should be very happy if I could come Home for a season to dry up your Tears. you must not Fret when you do not get a letter at the expected time [p. 3] because there are various reasons why you cant get them. some letters are lost and sometimes they come all in a heap. I shall keep you posted as well as I can. I hope you liked the account of my Travels. I finished them to fill up a gap in your Corespondence hoping to Please you. I got Sam Barrows to get his Likeness taken. he paid for it himself, and it is a good one. you will find it in this and can hand it to his mother as soon as posible, with Sams Respects, but he says he cant find time to write yet. I got a letter from Kate to night in which she asks me to Come to Leiperside[32] at Easter and she will give me some Egg Nog, and a lot of other good things. I should be very happy to do so, but I should be happier still, to have a little [p. 4] good old Fashioned time with my own little Wife in my own house. I'll Bet High, I could make you sing and Curly Bark, in no time. Let us Hope to have the Pleasure of meeting yet. you ask in one of yours about our Grub. I can tell you I can eat anything that is to be got. yesterday I had 2 Plates full of mush to my dinner and very good it was with a bit of Sugar on it. today I eat 7 Potatoes at the same meal and a pinch of Salt to them is not bad. Kate and Joe [Smiley] were suprised to see that I was looking so well in the Likeness you sent them. I must conclude for the present as I have to pack my Kit before I can turn in. I spilled my ink so you must excuse this Pencil letter for the time. I remain your Affectionate Husband Benjamin Hirst

Letter File #44

Camp near Falmouth
April 9th 1863

My Dear Wife,

    I write you these few lines to let you know that I am yet kicking, altho I was badly used up last night. Some of the Wolley Heads at Home think we have nice times of it out here, and I see by the Papers, that they represent us all, but, Dying to get Killed. but now they have carried the Election they will probably change their tune, and when the Draft commences, they will have all the Infirmitys that Life is afflicted with. I hope the Draft will be Rigidly enforced and the 14th filled up with such a lot of Wolley Heads, as i can see are now at Rockville. if they were here they would learn more in a month than all their Philosophy ever teached [p. 2] them before. when I last wrote you I told you I was going on Picket the next morning. we started for the Lacey House at 7 Oclock A.M. and I had to be awake until the next morning at 10 A.M. when we were relieved. but instead of going back to Camp we were marched about 4 miles out of our way to join our Regiment at a Grand Review, at which, Lincon was present.[33] I reckon there was some swearing while we were going, and coming back, just imagine us; all our Regiment that could be got together were there, with their best Bib and Tucker on, showing off to Kill, and us Poor Devils after being on duty a day and a Half, were formed in a Division by ourselves. we had our overcoats on, and our Blankets in a coil around our shoulders, besides our Haversacks and Dirty Cups hitched to them [p. 3] and we were all dirty and sleepy, and some of us had Axes to carry. I had one, a five pounder on one shoulder and my gun on the other (a pretty looking Devil for a Right Guide of our Division) but so it was. and it was nothing of a suprise to me, to see the President (after a great many Thousand of troops had passed him in Review all in Parade Rig) should come a litle more to the Front as we approached him, to see what Damnation kind of men would come along next, however if he or his Wife or Daughter (Both there) asked any questions, I think they were somewhat suprised to hear that we were in the Approved Light Marching Order of the Army of the Potomac. However it was a Big thing, and I saw the Rail Spliter, and he did or might have seen me, so we are square on that point. I hope the next time he comes he will send his pay master, who would [p. 4] be a first rate substitute about these times. just after we passed the President we were put to the Double quick for a quarter of a mile, to show the Stamina of Old Hookers soft tack. after that we made tracks for Camp and arrived here about 5 oclock P.M. and I was not sorry to tumble in my Bunk to rest my wearried Bones on the soft ground. to night I am all right again and ready for the next thing that comes along. I must now conclude this rambling letter hoping you are all in good Health I remain

your Affectionate Husband
Benjamin Hirst

I am not sorry [the] election resulted as it did. I think the democratic party placed themselves in a false position by [not representing] ... the war democrats of last year. The people you name who have skipped to Canada are a cowardly lot and would do no good here.[34]

The Grand Review at Falmouth in the winter of 1863. Lincoln is on horseback in middle left of image. From a sketch probably by Edwin Forbes. Robert U. Johnson and Clarence C. Buel, eds., Battles and Leaders of the Civil War. *Vol. 3. New York: Century, 1887–88, 120.*

Letter File #45

Camp near Falmouth Vir
April 14.th 1863.

My Dear Sallie,

I received yours of the 5.th inst, last Friday night, but as I wrote you the day before, I delayed answering it until this morning. on Saturday Murry [Joseph Murray] and I got a Pass to go to Stafford Court House, to see the 5.th Conn and we also saw Wm Coffee in Bests Battery. Wm looks first rate, and so did the Boys in the 5.th I saw Node, Simmons, McGuire, and several others. we had a pleasant visit and got back to our Camp Sunday at noon. Price Kelly [of the 72d Pennsylvania] came to see me yesterday. he has been home [to Chester] on Furlough and got Married on the sly, to a Miss Johnson. *[He] ... gave me a silver plated medal with my name, company and regiment engraved upon it. He said it would be hand[y] to have in case I got killed.*[35] ... Anthony [Quinn] is working at Croziers [Crozer's?],[36] well satisfied to be out of this, and I guess will try pretty [p. 2] hard to stay out. you speak in yours about your improvement in writing. you now write first rate, but your spelling would puzle any one but myself to make out. I can read your letters straight along and am glad to see that you do so well. still you can easily improve yourself, by taking Notice when you read any book or Paper how words should be spelled for instance in directing your letters to me you spell Washington thus Washinton leaving out the g. you must not be vexed at this, it is meant for your benefit. and you will never regret trying to do your best each time you write to me. you no doubt think I write without any trouble, but it is not so. I am afraid to read over my own letters lest I should get mad at them and put them in the Fire. John says your account of money is correct and is satisfied [p. 3] with his money being in the Bank. he is well and sends his Love to you all. We heard all about the Election as soon as you probably, as the Washington papers had the result in last Tuesday morning. I am sorry Hyde was Defeated, but for the rest i don't much care. I think the Election was carried on under false pretences on both sides, the Republicans with their Humbug Loyal Leagues pretending that all who differed with them were Traitors and the Democrats by having such men as Bill Eaton, Schnable, and Toucey Electionering for them, placing the mass of the Party in a false position. I see by a paper you have a Ladies Loyal league in Rockville. now the Ladies may be Loyal enough and some of them I know are Kind and Good Women, but in the list of Officers, I failed to discover one who had a Husband or son in the Army, and it will [p. 4] be the aim of this society to send other Poor Devils in their Places and get Great Credit for their Patriotism. but enough of this for the present. I think we are on the Eve of Important Events, the Spring Campaign is about to open and we are under marching orders to move at any hour. I will write you frequently as I can, and hope you will keep up good Courage. never

fret at Newspaper accounts of Probable Events, for it makes me laugh to see the Humbug accounts pretended Corespondents send them. I am in good health and spirits, and if i can keep my health, I am satisfied to go as far as any Wooley Head as ever left Rockville; Sam Barrows is going to some General Hopsital. When he gets there he will write Home. have you got his Likeness yet, I sent it some time ago. give my respects to all enquiring Friends and to Mother and Maggie and for yourself you know what to expect when I see you. your Loving
Husband Benjamin Hirst.

Letter File #46

Camp near Falmouth Vir
April 16.th 1863

Dear Brother [Joe],

I take the present oppertunity of writing you a few lines it may be the last for a short time, as we are under marching orders, this few days past. We have 3 days rations in our Haversacks, and 5 days in our Knapsacks. I reckon one half of the Army will be sick before they go many miles with 8 days rations on their backs, in addition to a change of under cloths and a Ruber Blanket, Blanket, Shelter Tent, and 60 round of Cartridges. I shal go it, as long as I can and when I cant I shant. John is as well as he usualy is, but coming back onto hard Tack and Pork is knocking some of the boys down already; we hope you will [p. 2] soon get Home to Rockville, where I think as soon as you are able, you will get Work. I got a letter from Sarah last night. all is well there at present. I also heard from Tom. he is having a time shaking [?] himself at West Philadelphia. I am in hopes he will also get Home. Sam Barrows is going to be sent to some General Hospital also Corbit, [and] Waldo. We have 4 other excused from Duty each morning. how they are going to march I cant tell. Perhaps you would like to know the strength of our Company at this time. We have 2 Lieut. *one is sick and the other one under arrest* and 25 [or 26?] non Commissioned Officers and Privates. 6 of these are sure to be used up the first days march, as 4 of them get excused every day now. *Poor Co D is like a little runty pig, not of much account anyway. This you know is private and I would not allow any one else to say it.*[37] I am well at present and hope to Weather [p. 4] [the] coming Storm. write us occasionally, whether we get a chance to answer you or not.
I remain your
Affectionate
Brother Benj Hirst

Letter File #47

Camp near Falmouth Vira
April 18th 1863

My Dear Sarah

I received your[s] of the 10,inst with great pleasure and am glad to hear you keep your health. We expected to have moved from here before this, but it seems to me that all our Efforts are coming to a dead lock for want of a head capable of managing Great Armies like ours. In the West and South West we are doing nothing, and at Charlston we have been Defeated. this is all through the Imbecility of some of our Head men. Now I dont care how soon we can make an Honourable Peace, but as long as we Fight, I want we should Win. and I also think we ought to Win. Dear Sarah how about that Furlough business. has squire [p. 2] Loomis done anything about it. we have men going from the Regiment all the time, but our Company has had only two. this is owing to the Officers looking after their Friends. Company D has no Officers that are interested in getting us our Furloughs, because their Friends and Townsmen are in other Companies. they know these mens circumstances but ours they are unacquainted with. that is the reason we do not get our share of attention. I heard that Squire Loomis had wrote to our late Acting Col. [Captain Davis?] but whether he answered him or not I could not find out. will you see Mr Loomis and find out and ask him about a Furlough from the War Department. if there is no chance of getting one there I want to know it, so that I can compose myself, in regard to this business. give Mr. Loomis [p. 3] my respects and tell him I am one of the only few in our Company that has not at some time or other been excused from duty since enlisting. I believe I told you in my last that we were held in readiness for a move somewhere. we have 8 days rations to each man, that is Hard Bread, Pork, Sugar and Coffee to do us 8 days without drawing on our suply Train for more. how well we can travel with such loads on our backs is hard to tell but I am afraid the experiment will be a Failure. I am glad that Mrs Barrows likes Sams Picture but she gives me too much Credit in getting it, I only asked him once for it, and in a day or two I got it. give the old lady my Respects, and tell her I think Sam will soon get Home again without much trouble. [p. 4] John is well and sends his Love to you all, and you will find in this two rings that he has made one for you and the other for Maggy. I need hardly tell you the Bone came from a Army Critter and that we eat our share of it. I still keep my health, and feel grateful for it. give my respects to all my Friends, and if you should see Frink tell him it would give me pleasure to hear from him. I got a paper from Mr Holton and I am obliged to him for it. I sent Holgate a queer envelope. I hope he was not displeased with it. give my respects to Morse when you see him, I hope the 2 Babies and mother are well. Love to yourself.

I remain your Affectionate Husband Benj Hirst.
P.S. got the Postage Stamps in your last. B Hirst

Letter File #48

Camp near Falmouth Vir
April 21.st 1863

My Dear Sarah,

I received your double letter last night, and was very glad to hear you are well. I hope you have had Luck enough to get the work done around the house. I would advise you to use some exertion to have things done in good shape. If Christy cant get time to fix around the house and Garden get some one else to do it. I would have the upper part of the Garden stocked to Grass, the lower part of the Garden you can take up yourself. I should like to come home when I have served a year as you intimate. but things dont look as they did 9 months ago and if I keep my health I kind of think we shall have to stay a year or two longer. [p. 2] You seem to think the Copperheads will resist the Draft. I have no Idea, there will be any resistance to the Draft in Conn. there will not be any by the Democrats I am certain and if the Wooley Heads resist I should not want better Fun than to do Provost duty in Conn, and have to take care of them. they would have more kickes than Pence in a short time.

We have not moved yet and I cant see that we are any near moving than we were a week ago. There is a dead lock some where, but where we cant tell. I only hope they know in Washington. We have Thousands of Men going out of Service the next month. the 2 years men are begining to get through and the 300,000 nine months men will begin to go out next week, so you [p. 3] need not look for any big things in the way of fighting unless it is done within a day or two. you say you would like to go on Picket with me, but I reckon you would only want to go once. I will try to tell you why. the Picket is divided into 4 reliefs. the first go on the Posts for 6 hours, during which time you are not allowed to have any fire. you are then Placed in rear of the Posts for 6 hours more. if you can make a little fire where the rebels cant see it you may do so. you are next marched of[f] to the Grand reserve which is Posted in a Ravine. here you stay until you are relieved the next day. I want you to send me some money in your next say 10 dollars and I will send you a check in a day or two, same as those you got when here. you want to know [p. 4] if I got Tight when I had got my Likeness taken. I answer No, I told E Johnson to direct it, because I wanted to suprise you. and I hope I done so. John is well and sends his love to you all. I am well and send my Love to you all.

yours Truly and Affectionatly
B. Hirst.

Letter File #49

Vir
Camp near Falmouth
April 26.th 1863

My Dear Sarah,

I received yours of the 21st inst, last night, and I am very glad that you are all well, and that this leaves John and myself in good health. I am very much obliged to Squire Loomis, for his exertions in trying to get me a Furlough but there is too much Red Tape (I soppose) for him to succeed at present. If he had been a member of Congress Elect, he would probably have had better success.[38] I shall not get sick thinking about it, and hope you will keep well too, for it is sopposed that when a man Enlists, he Sells Body and Soul, but I have a notion of keeping as well as posible for my own convenience, and hope Uncle Samival will [p. 2] keep so too. with regard to writing to Govenor Buckingham, I dont think it would be of any use at present, and I should be very much mortified to have a letter of mine served as Mike Fay had one of his. He wrote a very nice letter to Gen French complaining of the Furlough business as conducted in this Regiment. the Gen wrote a line or two on the Back of it and sent it Back to the Lieut of our Company, telling him to see to that mans case (so Mike was just in the same place as before). the first time the Lieut saw Mike he asked him what he got by writing to French and that was all he was allowed to know about it. Loomis also wrote, in Mikes behalf, and that letter was shown to different persons too. and Mike gets laughed at for it. they have kept very still about the letters or letter that Loomis [p. 3] wrote on my behalf, well knowing that they cant ridicule me without trouble to themselves. I am not sorry that we are yet encamped here, but the War will never end by our sitting still, and when the Lord wets our Jackets with rain he dont let the Rebels go dry. I have no desire to go in another Battle, but I do not Dread it, and I think when we do have one, the Rebels will get the worst of it, so dont you Fret yourself about it. what must come will come, and you and me are as nothing to it. I am sorry to hear of such mean Cowardly Scamps as Clem [?] Dowling and Barney Brothers, naturalised Citizens running from [?] their Country the second time. I could Shoot one of them with as little Compunction as a Rebel. I hope they will be compelled to come back, and the Draft Rigidly enforced [p. 4] until the Wolley Heads themselves Cry enough. I should like to come Home as well as any man living, but I will never willingly come in Disgrace as many now in Rockville have.

I am glad Mr. Holgate likes his Envelope and I should like to hear from him occasionally. you did not tell me how Morse and the Babies are. I reckon he feels very big on that account. It is pleasant to think that you and me are not yet too old to follow his example after this War is ended. what do you say. you think I am teasing you, and I can see you half Laughing and crying over this letter; and I would willingly give a year of my Life, to steal in behind you; and place one arm around as of old. I shal write to Leiperville today. give my Respects to all enquiring Friends, to mother and Maggie, and when I can Embrace you, you will know how well I Love you. I remain your

Affectionate Husband Benj Hirst.

Chapter 6

The Narratives and World View

This was the most depressing period of the Union so far in the war. Ben and others wanted respite, at least, if they could not have an end to it. To get home just for a visit became the preoccupation after the shock of Fredericksburg. For Ben, this had to be accomplished by using honorable means. A "French leave" was out of the question, even though thousands on both sides were quietly making tracks from camp. Nor would he attempt to deceive the authorities by using poor health as a justification.

Falmouth was not quite the excremental, debilitating place Bolivar Heights had been. Ben himself was mostly thriving—putting on twelve new pounds by February. Sickness was eating away at his circle of comrades, however.

In one letter, Ben described his health and strength as "God given"—an atypical religious reference, but one that underscored a growing fatalism: God wills it, what must come will come, "you and me are as nothing to it." It was an attitude to help cope with the capriciousness of serious illness and death. More and more, he prefaced his hopes and predictions with the obligatory hedge that if only his health would hold, then . . . . To write the words was akin to knocking on wood. No sense in attracting fickle sickness by ignoring its potential for bringing tragedy.[1]

The distinction between true illness and poltroonery was becoming harder to draw consistently, as was the more fundamental distinction between courage and cowardice upon which it rested. His sick friends could never be called cowards, yet their infirmity kept some of them out of combat, like those—mostly the company officers—whom he continued to revile as shirks.[2] If the criteria of cowardice were becoming less clear, however, Ben's testy vigilance remained an important component of his social image projected for the home folks. The officers had long since been written off as hopeless malingerers. Ben and one of his chums had turned to watching others in Company D for telltale signs of strategic sickness even while lamenting the loss of more friends to "real" disease. Still, it was a troublesome dichotomy. There was his friend Joe Murray, for instance. He was promoted to sergeant soon after sickness supposedly had kept him out of the Fredericksburg fight. Ben resolved it by declaring that Murray would probably not have stayed behind had it not been for the cowardly example set by Lt. Chelsea Vinton. It was unsettling, however, and Ben uncharacteristically asked Sarah to keep his portrayal of Murray's behavior quiet, which must have signaled her to keep the entire letter to herself.

After Fredericksburg, Ben was forced publicly to recalculate the dichotomy between courage and cowardice. His own courage during the battle came under direct attack. His efforts to choke off the allegations show how powerfully the manly ideal had informed his constructed reality in the letters. It was curious combat behavior even as Ben described it. Two Rockville men were hit—both seriously, one horribly—fairly early in the assault against Marye's Heights. One, John Symonds, was a corporal; the other, Oliver Dart, was a private. Company D had no commissioned officers with it. It was led by Orderly Sgt. Frank Stoughton. When Symonds and Dart were wounded, four able-bodied men—Sgts. George Brigham and Hirst, Cpl. Elbert Hyde, and Pvt. Kilbourn Newell—left the attack to carry them back to the medical station. By Ben's post-battle reckoning, only twenty-five men from Company D were in the assault at the outset. The absence of four men, three of them NCOs, carrying two wounded accounted for one-quarter of the company's strength. This was evidently before the regiment had reached its position closest to the blazing Rebel muskets along the stone wall. Moreover, Ben and his fellow sergeant Brigham were persuaded to stay with the wounded men until the whole regiment had retreated into the city's streets. While Ben was sitting with Dart in the aid station, Ben's brother Joe was hit three times. John Hirst brought Joe back for help. Except for Joe's wounding, none of this was written into Ben's initial accounts of the battle. In view of the frequent mention earlier of how he had helped his chum Wilkie at Antietam, this omission must have been deliberate. Ben was not proud of his conduct. On the face of it, it was exactly what he had so outspokenly criticized the shirks for at Antietam.[3]

The manly ideal had to be maintained. Ben had acted with cool deliberation under the circumstances, he declared. Explicitly, he did nothing out of fear or cowardice. This set him apart from others he had accused. He had not played sick to shirk the battle entirely. It was that his conscience would not let him leave these two as he had done Wilkie at Antietam. As for the rumors of his conduct, he had two manly responses: to laugh at them as being unworthy of his serious consideration and then take them seriously and counter them with testimony of his own corroborated by Orderly Sergeant Stoughton (as communicated to Stoughton's wife).

Moreover, Ben had a self-righteous falling out with Sergeant Brigham. It is not clear that he and Brigham had been close friends at first. Both were from Rockville and enlisted on the same day. Both had served together in the same militia company before that. Both were mustered in as sergeants. At any rate, Brigham had let Ben down by not quelling the rumors from Fredericksburg. Brigham had not met his gentlemanly obligation as Ben saw it. Ben had jumped to help the wounded only after Brigham and others had already done so. Brigham, Ben hinted, had behaved questionably at Antietam as well: "[H]e was as Brave at Fredricksburg as at Antietam" (11 January 1863). Then Brigham later spoiled the chances for others' furloughs by trying to intervene in the selection process. That was deceitful and selfish. Ben felt called upon not only to give Brigham a piece of his mind, but to tell the folks in Rockville about it.[4]

Reid Mitchell describes the impact of critical commentary in letters to home: "The army provided little escape from the prying eyes of small-town America. News of a man's conduct, moral and military, was too easily sent home. . . . This communication created strong constraints on soldiers' conduct. Discipline, bravery, perseverance, and good moral behavior all could represent an attempt to maintain the respect of civilian society as well as adaptation to frontline conditions."[5] This aptly characterizes Ben's general posture throughout his narratives. More specifically, it aims the Fredericksburg allegations right at the heart of his constructed image.

The allegations were brought back from Fredericksburg and kept alive by Albert Towne Sr., who had vainly gone there to find his son's remains. The father had brought parcels from home for Ben and others, and Albert Towne Jr. had been one of Ben's close friends. This made the accusations all the more galling. They did not die quickly in Rockville. Ben had to go over the defense more than once. Yet he voiced no regrets and made no apologies. He never sent home further reports or asked for more information on Symonds's and Dart's recuperation from their wounds. He wanted to get the incident well behind him. But he stewed about whether his courageous image was intact (18 and 31 January 1863).[6]

After Fredericksburg, grumbling but dogged steadfastness had at last shoved aside naive patriotism in Ben's portrayed world view. Three months after Fredericksburg, he was particularly explicit: "There is not a man in this Company that does not Curse the hour that sent us out here" (13 March 1863). It was depressingly clear to him and others that the war would not be over soon after all. But the unhappy steadfastness still had to be linked with courage: "Now I dont care how soon we can make an Honorable Peace, but as long as we Fight, I want we should Win" (18 April 1863). A week closer to the spring campaign, having awaited marching orders for days with packed haversack, he was moved to write that he was not sorry to be waiting in camp, but the war would not end by sitting still. He had no desire to go into another battle, but he did not dread it (26 April 1863). Fiske, in his more public portrayals, sketched the newly acquired measure of steadfastness:

> We grumble, indeed, as soldiers will, and as these soldiers have had good reason to grumble. I have done my share of it (I am ashamed to think, a little more than my share); but I grumble henceforth no more. And all we grumbling soldiers, now we find that the people of the North are usurping our (as we supposed) exclusive privilege, or rather following our bad example, are going to shut our mouths, and relieve ourselves in

hard blows at the enemy, instead of hard words at our friends. I believe this is coming to be the spirit of our army, what is left of us.[7]

Three weeks before Ben wrote his gloomy 13 March note, Fiske reported: "Talk about demoralization of the army! Well, we have fallen pretty low. We haven't the same strain of lofty patriotism in our talk as when we first came out."[8] Both men were writing partly in response to escalating campaign rhetoric in the coming Connecticut gubernatorial election, which was itself a microcosm of the national clash of war ideology between Republicans and Democrats.[9]

Steadfastness had its limits. As a quid pro quo, the government should be obliged to give individual soldiers a temporary break from monotony and violent death. Ben, in fact, wanted the entire regiment to be given relief after Fredericksburg and wanted home folks to pressure the government to do so. That failing, individual furloughs would do. The furlough business thoroughly frustrated Ben. Although he complained, he still strove to control his emotions.[10] He wanted Sarah to give him news about his chances for a furlough so he could "compose" himself.

His portrayal of authority continued to be largely negative. There was the familiar grumbling about company officers after Fredericksburg, with an added insight: "For myself I never expected anything from our Officers, since Burpee left us in Hartford" (5 February 1863). Not only were they shirks, damned fools, and tragically unconcerned about their men's condition, some of them were also deceitful, luring volunteers into the company with manly patriotic rhetoric then quickly abandoning them for selfish gain. Burpee left the company for a higher rank elsewhere—a reasonable act by army standards but an abandonment of manly responsibility by Ben's.[11]

Nonetheless, Ben's views on officers were changing. So were the officers themselves. Lieutenant Colonel Perkins in Ben's perspective was transformed into a gallant leader by his behavior at Fredericksburg. Courageous conduct overcame mean-spirited authoritarianism. The following spring, new company officers were being promoted from the ranks of enlisted men. By this process, Company D received two new lieutenants, both former sergeants from Company C. This was the first major break in the geographical integrity of Company D's Rockville corpus. These officers, who replaced Captain Hammond and Lieutenants Emery and Vinton, must have been more competent. Ben did not criticize them as frequently. In fact, he did not even give their names to the readers at home (they wouldn't have known lieutenants from Waterbury, anyhow). Although he might not have seen them under fire earlier, their reputations for courage certainly would have been carefully examined by Ben and the other men of Company D. Whatever their other faults, they evidently met this singularly important criterion or Ben would have written home about it.[12]

The furlough game intensified Ben's prevailing ambivalence toward his officers. On the one hand, he felt the company's new first lieutenant, James F. Simpson, was unfairly interested in helping his close friends in Company C get furloughs

while ignoring the Rockville men of Company D—even though the former officers from Rockville had earlier done precious little to help Company D. On the other
hand, Ben had to stay on Simpson's good side while trying to get his own furlough.
The new lieutenant had to be made aware of Sergeant Brigham's untoward efforts
to get special consideration, yet could not be given the chance to reject and ridicule Ben's own efforts to jump channels.

In Ben's letters there is a strong new hint of envy as other NCOs became officers. Corporal Lyman, who also helped wounded at Fredericksburg, might not have
become lieutenant but for his friendship with certain officers (not merely envy
here, but the ambivalent suggestion that one must hobnob with officers to become
one). Ben implied that he himself had been kept in the dark about the round of
examinations of potential officers. But would he have put himself forward had he
known about them beforehand? He did not say.

His portrayals of general officers remained mostly noncommittal—when he
bothered to sketch them. This was a marked contrast to Captain Fiske's angry
public denouncements of McClellan, Burnside, and their staffs. So far, the more
remote the authority from Ben's mundane daily round, the less the criticism.[13] Even
the opening of boxes from home by 2d Corps headquarters was merely mentioned.
Captain Fiske later would become outraged at this intrusion into the soldier's most
cherished link with home. Ostensibly, the boxes were being opened to seize ille-
gal liquor. Possibly, it had not yet become sufficiently wanton to create much of
a stir.

As his hardening continued, Ben once again referred to the wisdom instilled by
army service, especially army sleeping arrangements and army food. There was
the virtually universal veteran's reaction to the conscription laws. Ben heartily
wished the able-bodied men still at home would be drafted and sent to the front,
preferably to the 14th, where they would be properly welcomed. The contempt was
scarcely concealed.

Hardening was becoming apparent in Ben's portrayals of social relations as well.
Rockville boys who had been sick or wounded were reluctantly coming back to
the company. Their reluctant return was met by an indifferent reception: "The rest
of us don't care who comes and goes" (13 March 1863). His close circle of comrades
had dwindled drastically. On 19 January 1863, he wrote that if the company was
then to leave on a campaign, he would be the only one left to make the trip out of
the original Hartford group of ten tent mates. The toll on the Rockville boys in
the first five months of service had been staggering. He did not write about finding
new friends. Presumably, he and John were the minimal necessary social unit (one
had to have at least one chum, if for no other reason than to construct a complete
shelter tent). Conceivably, the capricious disappearance of one's close friends
helped create the social indifference and an emotional numbness—not caring who
came and went. Yet it is doubtful that this indifference had built to the point that
wounded friends would be ignored under fire.

Competition for furloughs created social tension within the company, despite officers' efforts to organize the process fairly. It was socially unacceptable to try to jump the list by deceit, but it was foolish not to use every available legitimate means to get special consideration. The social peril was getting caught at it, as the unfortunate Mike Fay did. There was an even more reprehensible social transgression: to overstay one's furlough, thereby delaying and possibly canceling that of the next man on the list.

The winter camp at Falmouth was a vast plain of waiting men. Ben and others waited for boxes, for mail, for furloughs, for spring.

Company D drilled and pulled guard and picket duty. Politics leavened some of the monotony. The gubernatorial campaign in Connecticut was heating up, and the men followed the newspaper accounts avidly. In March, one of the state papers published a statement declaring that the 14th Connecticut Volunteers were sick of the war and favored Seymour and the Democrats. Fiske detailed the reaction in camp: a resolution was drawn up and read at the evening parade on 24 March, firmly supporting Buckingham and the Republicans and scourging the Democrat Seymour as a traitor. Only one officer and "five or six enlisted men" dissented, two or three of whom dissented because they couldn't properly hear the proclamation as read.[14] The acting commander and adjutant of the regiment then signed the proclamation and sent it home.

Ben was keenly interested in all this. While he and his circle of readers may not have favored Seymour, and plainly did not care for Copperheads, he felt that the true Democrats would have voted to end the war as quickly as possible—honorably. He obviously felt the "humbug" resolution had been presented so as to trump many soldiers' true feelings. It had portrayed those opposing it as cowards. Later, ever-vigilant for affectation and hypocrisy after the Republicans' victory, Ben earnestly hoped they would now show up at the front to have a more direct role in the fight they, the "Wooly Heads," favored. He did not say whether or not he was one of the few enlisted men who publicly opposed the proclamation at the dress parade. It would be out of character for him to endorse it; but it would be equally unlike him to speak up and thereby be labeled a traitor by others in the regiment.

Possibly, Ben used "Wooly Heads" here as he would "lame brains" or "morons." More likely, he employed it as a racist moniker for Republican abolitionists, much as "Black Republicans" was used by others.[15] He looked down upon the "damd niggers" in Rockville. However, his political comments never clearly touched upon abolition as an issue. For him, what mattered was the Union and winning an honorable peace. To that end, no hypocritical Republican war cry by civilian politician-shirks could be countenanced.

Otherwise, Ben fought boredom by writing his letters and copying his journal. The letters themselves said relatively little about camp life. There were glimpses: the deforestation of the Falmouth area; his log hut dimensions; his conversations with Rebel pickets across the Rappahannock; the review for Abraham Lincoln; picket duty. But these he conveyed as isolated anecdotes, rather than part of a consistent effort to portray the camp existence. It was for him and others a long, monotonous interlude between important events.

There had been a story to tell about Antietam: the men's first combat; exposure to death in stages, beginning with the march over South Mountain; tactical ma-neuvering under fire; and diverse terrain. From Ben's and others' perspective, it was a victory for the Union. There was none of that at Fredericksburg. There was, by comparison, little to write about. For the 14th Connecticut it came as a single wallop, although everyone on both sides of the Rappahannock saw it coming well beforehand. They marched gallantly forward, were blasted, lay down, then with-drew. Ben wrote his letter narrative of Antietam on 20 and 21 August 1862, three and four days after the battle itself. His account of the Fredericksburg battle was not written for the home folks until 30 December—two weeks after the fight. To be sure, he was distracted by Joe's wounding, the withdrawal and reencampment, and Sarah's surprise arrival in camp. And, it had not been a Union victory.

Twice he mentioned being too emotionally overwhelmed to write details: first in the brief letter informing Sarah he was safe and later in the narrative of the battle where he could not tell the home folks how he felt about the destruction in Fred-ericksburg. Manly emotional control, again. Best not to try to describe one's feel-ings when they are not under control. It was enough to let folks know the emo-tions were deeply stirred. Significantly, in this last instance his reaction was sparked by the flagrant loss of manly control by others.

He continued to mark the shrinking size of Company D. About twenty-five seemed fairly standard for both march and combat, with a daily roster constantly changed by individual soldiers' comings and goings. Before the war's halfway point, the 14th Connecticut Volunteers already hovered at the "late-war" regimental av-erage of between 200 and 300 men.[16]

Although he continued his disinterest in battle aftermath, he felt obliged to re-port trying to find his chum Albert Towne's grave on 6 January 1863. He could not find it, but the effort itself was important as part of the ritual concern with proper homage to the dead—the details of the cause of death remaining less important than observing proper mortuary protocol.[17]

Ben continued to leave himself unexposed emotionally, as in the Antietam nar-ratives, with one exception: he spent a restless night before the assault, even though he was kept at work transporting rations until past midnight. The next morning, time passed slowly for him as the men waited in the streets. There was nothing about the circumstances of Joe's wounding and no accounts of cool bravery un-der fire, save that displayed by Lieutenant Colonel Perkins. It was ultimately a distressing, demoralizing defeat—and he had not been in the thick of it very long. Samuel Fiske did not dwell on details of the battle, either. He was more concerned about the senseless waste (recall his "Waste, waste . . ." soliloquy after Antietam). Even the regimental history, with forty years of retrospect to draw upon, was rela-tively terse.[18]

Interacting with Home Culture

For Sarah, the winter of 1862–63 must have been hellish. Ben's letters in the fall suggest she was depressed. Then came Fredericksburg and no immediate word about Ben. Albert Towne Sr. packed up to go find his son. Alarmed, Sarah left for Washington, D.C., hoping somehow to locate her husband. It was a womanly, emotional thing to do. Foolish, in Ben's view.

Virtually everything we can learn about Sarah's sojourn with Ben in the Lacy house comes from his later newspaper account. Even there, besides his initial surprise, we are not told much about his overall reaction to her presence. It must have been ambivalent. Ben did not explicitly mention their meeting in letters afterward, but made some passing references to "when you were here." He never declared it had been good to see her, even under the circumstances. He never reminisced about what went on between them at the meeting, other than that she received some checks. Instead, he upbraided her for not immediately writing that she had returned safely to Rockville.

She must have been tormented by the furlough game. Ben left to her much of the responsibility for organizing outside influence favoring his application, then bombarded her with comments about how fruitless it all seemed. (Indeed, as he portrayed the furlough allocation process, it merely increased demoralization for the majority of the regiment who couldn't get one.) Captain Fiske's ebullient newspaper column about how much he had enjoyed his own furlough during this time must have chafed homesick enlisted men.

Sarah had taken in a boarder to help keep her company and to fight depression. Then she took a job in the mill after Fredericksburg, evidently to keep her occupied. Ben's reaction indicated there was no pressing financial need. She had scarcely begun work when her mother's drinking problem erupted. The mill work ended after two months.

Ben was concerned about her state of mind. In April, he wrote to her more frequently than ever when she complained he was not writing enough. (He had declared he was writing as much as he possibly could, but nonetheless increased his output.) He had finished copying his journal by then, so it is possible that he had more time for writing letters to Sarah. There is a strong suggestion that his greater effort was based on his growing concern about her depression. In his letter of 6 March 1863, he was worried because Sarah had not written for an unusually long time. That could well mean she was ill, as Ben's failure to write from Bolivar Heights had meant five months before.

His letters to her from Falmouth were occasionally more passionate—compared to those of the fall—about his yearning to be with her. (This could either have heartened Sarah or made her more depressed—or both.) The passages were still restrained, controlled; but they conveyed intense feeling. There were three in particular: 6 March, 6 April, and 26 April. The 6 March letter was written just after Ben had received a box from Sarah—the palpable reminder of her and home. The lament that his dreams of holding her were shattered by his waking "in this damd place" was concluded in manly fashion: "it makes me swear some, but that does no good."

Variations on the boxes-from-home theme were a regular feature of his winter letters. He finally received the box got together by Hunt—the one with the boots in it—weeks after it was to have arrived. The box discussion then withered away as the army made ready for its spring campaign. Their contents would have been extra burdens for the soldiers to carry on the march. Boxes were mostly a seasonal happiness.

Traffic in likenesses was another way for Ben and others to freshen their ties with home. The photographic process was still novel enough, and the product offered such a vivid reminder of loved ones. Ben fussed about them in his writing, first to send word that his had been made and sent, then to inquire anxiously about what Sarah and others thought of them. He even saw fit to add fun and surprise to the interest by getting one of his friends to address the envelope containing the likenesses. It pleased him immensely that Sarah liked them, and that she sent them to the mill to show his coworkers. Ben proudly wrote Joe about how the weavers flocked around to see them. Thus, they were a valued means not only for remembering loved ones, but also for maintaining important social ties.

Ben continued to use Sarah to maintain his ties with others in Rockville. He wanted her to socialize with the Bottomlys of Dedham, Massachusetts, who had been kind enough to send Ben a box. (Ben used the discussion to give Sarah a quick lesson in how to pack boxes properly.) He enclosed Bottomly's letters in his own for Sarah to read. There were also his more urgent objectives in sending her to influence Congressman Dwight Loomis. Ben revealed some of his thoughts about social strategizing in a letter to Joe, urging him to write Judge Loomis "as he might befriend you." Influence was an important social commodity to Ben; yet having to traffic in it must have increased his ambivalence toward authority.

Besides the gossip about the Fredericksburg incident, Ben's social image at home was imperiled by his mother-in-law's drunken behavior. He was quick and emphatic in his instructions to Sarah. He would not have his image as manly head of household subverted by a drunk, and a woman to boot. Damage control must have been effectively handled by Sarah because Ben heard nothing more about it for a time, then was relieved to learn that the woman was "feeling better."

Once again, Ben tried to improve Sarah's spelling. She was concerned about her writing because she knew Ben was showing her letters to others and did not wish to create an unfavorable social impression. She evidently was defensive about her progress. Ben made a real effort to take some of the edge off his criticism (14 April 1863). (Captain Fiske made a condescending comment about the poorly spelled letters received from home by the common soldiers. It was the kind of aside that Ben and others of his respectable-worker background would not have found entertaining.)[19]

In other contexts, he continued to portray himself as the man in charge of the household, even if in absentia. As before, this meant giving orders about what needed to be done. Sarah was to continue to pack boxes and handle money trans- actions for the brothers, fix the wall, buy a pig, finagle a furlough for Ben, and so on. But the peremptory tone was subverted by his disarming admission that she was "buck cat" in his absence and that ultimately she could do as well as he could in managing things there. The relative lack of peremptiveness reflected a broader shift in world view. Now that it was clear the war would not end soon and a fur- lough was chancy, his posturing as household head became more ambiguous. That did not stop the flow of instructions, however.

Ben did not want Sarah to work in the mill partly because he feared the work might ruin her health, but probably also because it was beneath her social station. It was common. Unless they had an acute need for money, women should not be bound to manual labor. For Sarah to work was to suggest Ben could not provide for her and the household properly—another affront to his carefully maintained image at home. Nothing in Ben's letters indicated the household was in dire financial straits. Yet he let her do it, again with the observation that she was in charge. Only if her health were threatened would he really put his foot down. And her health would be affected if she tried to do things that were too hard for her— manly things.

If Sarah had no pressing need for money, Ben did. It was evidently not so much the amount Ben was paid as a sergeant, but the very long intervals between pay- days. He borrowed money from his brother John and from Sam Barrows to tide him over. Sarah was to send money to repay them both.

Obviously, all Ben's orders for goods and instructions for behavior were impor- tant to his peace of mind; he chewed on them. In his view, there was little else to write about in letters. Much of what he wanted to portray of army culture was going into his journal of important events.

The Journal Account

Camp life was described no more in the journal than it had been in letters. It was a most un-newsworthy existence. Virtually all of his effort went to constructing the prelude to the assault on Marye's Heights. The wounding of Symonds and Dart and Ben's response are left out of the journal's heroic prose. There is, in fact, less than one line about the assault itself: "We completely failed in our attackt." As with his Antietam entries, he referred readers to his letters. There is the typical lack of detail about his own emotions. His few allusions to his own bravery, steadfastness, and hardening were inserted prior to the brief description of the assault, mostly as asides. For example, he could easily fall asleep amid the roar of the cannon. But again, he wrote nothing of his conduct during the assault. He could not lie, but he could construct important events selectively.

The thinning numbers of the regiment were cause for reflection in the journal as in his letters. After Fredericksburg, the 14th could muster "scarcely 100" fit for duty.[20] The day Ben ended his journal (24 March 1863), the regiment's strength was about 250; Company D was at its "hovering" size of 25 men—out of the 98 privates and 12 officers and NCOs who left Hartford for the seat of war six months earlier.

Ben manifestly had lost his enthusiasm for keeping a journal by the time he reached the account of the Fredericksburg assault. It was not the same anymore. Its events lack his earlier attention to details and vocabulary. It sputters along to end with a bare-bones sketch of the Mud March. "We have been Virtualy in Winter Quarters ever since. Benj Hirst"—there was nothing more worth writing about. Heroic, boastful prose was played out, at least for now.

By about mid-April, Captain Fiske began to feel twinges of regret at the prospect of leaving the Falmouth camp for the spring campaign: "[I]t is somehow a little hard to pull up our stakes, and tear down our walls for departure, after all. We have something of a home-feeling for our poor little mud-built cities. . . . It is with a sort of shrinking and momentary reluctance that we push out from the little eddy where we have lain so snugly for a time, and commit ourselves again to the raging current of war."[21] As he and others continued to languish packed and ready for the coming campaign, Fiske changed his view of camp. It was, he concluded, "a dull, monotonous, stupid, indifferent make-shift of a life, soon to be broken in upon by the excitement of a great and eventful campaign. If I write you nothing, dear 'Republican,' it is because I have nothing to write you."[22] Ben agreed wholeheartedly. He expressed no sorrow at leaving Falmouth. But he and John did not tear down their hut when they left—shrewd foresight, as it turned out.

Part III

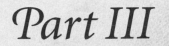

Chancellorsville and Gettysburg
28 April to 6 July 1863

Chapter 7

The Context

The 2d Corps marched west out of Falmouth to cross the Rappahannock at U.S. Ford, about four miles as the crow flies north of the Chancellor house and road junction of the Orange Turnpike and the Orange Plank Road. The 14th was now commanded by its former adjutant, Theodore G. Ellis, who had been promoted to major a month earlier.

The regiment was moved from position to position during 1 and 2 May, but spent most of its time in a large field just to the west of the road leading to Ely's Ford, about a half-mile north of the Chancellor house. It was held in reserve until the evening of 2 May, when "Stonewall" Jackson's attack caught the 11th Corps troops by surprise, stampeded them, and began to roll up the right, or west, flank of Hooker's line. Amid the fleeing men, the 14th's fine band formed up, under fire, and began to play patriotic music. It was an astonishing spectacle: the band standing still in formation playing "The Star Spangled Banner" as exploding shells drowned them out, fragments showered them, and the torrent of terrorized skedaddlers flowed around them.[1] Neither that nor other courageous efforts could stop the rout. The regiment was moved south to the road junction at the Chancellor house, then a quarter-mile westward along the Orange Turnpike, to form a new line against Jackson's onrushing Confederates.[2]

That night the regiment again changed positions several times, but remained on the extreme right of the 2d Brigade's line of battle. There arose a bothersome suspicion in the darkness and tangled woods that nobody was supporting the 14th's right flank. Lt. Walter M. Lucas of Company A, who later would command Company D, was sent to General "Old Blinky" French to find out what was happening. French angrily kicked the young lieutenant out of headquarters; the flank protection was "his [French's] business and he would attend to it."[3]

Early on the morning of 3 May, the regiment began to take intense fire from Rebels who had shattered the first line of battle to its immediate front. The 14th's men could see neither the enemy nor the retreating Yanks in the dense woods, but figured that if they returned the fire they might manage to hit someone, hopefully a Reb, and slow the Rebel attack. Just as they began to fire to their front, bullets began thudding in from their right. Their anxiety the night before was justified.

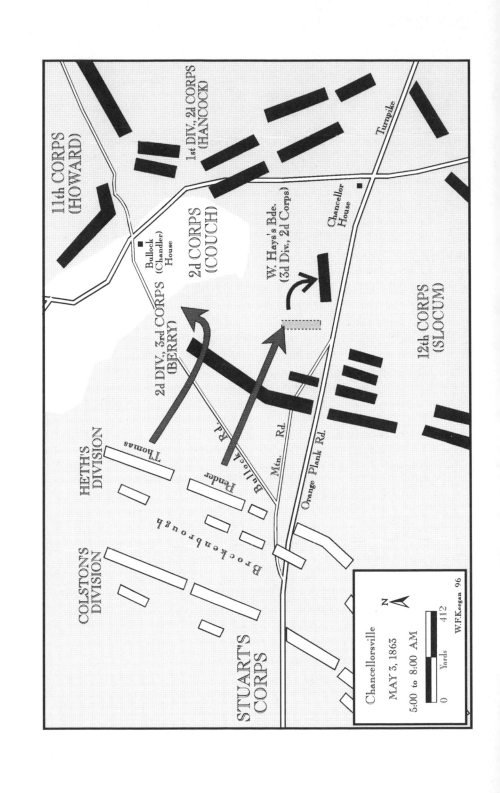

11th CORPS (HOWARD)

1st DIV, 2d CORPS (HANCOCK)

Turnpike

2d CORPS (COUCH)

Bullock (Chandler) House

2d DIV, 3rd CORPS (BERRY)

W. Hays's Bde. (3d Div, 2d Corps)

Chancellor House

12th CORPS (SLOCUM)

HETH'S DIVISION

Thomas

Pender

Bullock Rd.

Mtn. Rd.

Brockenbrough

Orange Plank Rd.

COLSTON'S DIVISION

STUART'S CORPS

Chancellorsville

MAY 3, 1863

5:00 to 8:00 AM

N

0   Yards   412

W.F.Keegan 96

Their right flank was indeed in the air. "Blinky" French had not attended to it and Confederates were now shooting at them from two directions. To add to the lethal confusion, the 12th New Jersey, supposedly on line to the left of the 14th Connecticut, had in fact formed up behind and partially overlapped the 14th's left. The New Jerseymen now began to blast into the thicket to their front, at least as apt to hit 14th men as to hit Rebels. Thus, assaulted from three sides, the 14th picked up its wounded and calmly fell back.[4] Carroll's brigade of the 2d Corps helped choke off the Confederate advance in that sector a short time later.

They went into reserve again north of the Chancellor house, near where they had waited the day before. There they remained, under occasional but harmless fire from Confederate sharpshooters, from Sunday night until about 2 A.M. Wednesday morning (6 May). They pulled out quietly, hoping to deceive the Rebel pickets, and stumbled and slopped through cold, rainy blackness until they recrossed their pontoon bridges on the Rappahannock at daylight. The regiment's leading elements dragged into Falmouth Camp by mid-morning, but stragglers kept trickling in for the rest of the day.[5]

The 14th's strength was 219 on the morning of 3 May. Only one man—an officer in Captain Fiske's Company I—was mortally wounded in the battle. Otherwise, there were thirty-six wounded and nineteen missing. One of the missing was Captain Fiske, who was taken prisoner while serving as a staff officer for the 1st Brigade. The missing from Company D included Lt. James F. Simpson and a Rockville private, George W. Morton, who was serving as the lieutenant's cook. Their fate is described by an amused Ben Hirst in the following chapter. Pvt. John Williams of Rockville was also missing. He was the man left to guard the regiment's knapsacks on the evening of 2 May. The regiment's knapsacks once again turned up missing. The men had dropped them in ranks before double-timing off to stand against Jackson. In Ben's account (5 May 1863), the knapsacks were overrun and presumed lost in the Rebel advance.[6]

In mid-May, the 14th shifted from its old winter turf in the Falmouth camp to move into some pine woods about a mile farther from the river. On 28 May, they were restricted to camp and told to be ready to move out at a half-hour's notice with three days' rations. They waited each day for momentous orders, but it was not until seventeen days later—14 June—that they finally marched out of Falmouth. It was just at sunset, and the men must have wondered cynically how long they would be gone this time.

Then came two weeks of marches to the north, paralleling Lee's advance toward Pennsylvania. The weather had turned hot, and the men suffered. They moved by way of Dumfries, Wolf Run Shoals, Fairfax Court House, the old Bull Run battlefields, Gum Spring, and across the Potomac at Edward's Ferry on the night of 25 June. By 28 June they were camped just outside Frederick, Maryland. On 29 June, they had the most arduous march of their army career thus far: some thirty-two miles to Uniontown in one day, passing through Liberty, Johnsville, and Union Bridge.[7] The footsore men bought refreshments at nominal prices from citizens in Uniontown and rested while receiving a congratulatory message from the 2d Corps commander, Gen. Winfield Scott Hancock, on their conduct during the hard march. They also learned "with satisfaction" that Gen. George Gordon Meade had replaced "Fighting Joe" Hooker as commander of the Army of the Potomac.[8]

They rested until 1 July, then were marched rapidly through Taneytown, Maryland, and arrived within two or three miles of Gettysburg by 8 P.M. There they were ordered to picket duty along the Baltimore Pike. The next morning, 2 July, they were marched to the vicinity of Cemetery Hill, halted in a field near where the Federal line turned sharply to the south, just to the left rear of Woodruff's Battery of regulars, and stacked arms to wait until about 4 P.M. Then, they were relocated about 200 yards farther south along the line, behind a low stone wall running south, and faced west toward Emmitsburg Road and a mile-wide plain of meadow and growing wheat. Almost halfway across this plain (about 800 yards away), and slightly to the right of the regiment's front, stood a house and large barn belonging to a farmer named William Bliss.

Along the stone wall the regiment was ordered to support Arnold's Battery A, 1st Rhode Island, drawn up in position to the regiment's left. To their right was a small house used as headquarters by Gen. Alexander Hays, who had succeeded "Old Blinky" French as commander of the 2d Corps' 3d Division. The men lay down behind the wall, their heads resting on their knapsacks. They listened to the heavy firing to their left, over by the Round Tops, then to their right after nightfall, where the Louisiana Tigers' and North Carolinians' attack against Cemetery Hill was eventually smashed. By about 10:30 P.M. the battlefield became quiet for the night, including Arnold's Battery, much to the gratification of the tired soldiers of the 14th (although at least one other NCO besides Ben Hirst claimed, retrospectively, to be able to sleep through the racket of a friendly battery firing only a few paces away).[9]

The next morning, 3 July, Companies B and D were ordered out to relieve those on the skirmish line about 400 yards to the front. They left their reserve along the depression and fence line along Emmitsburg Road, some 200 yards forward of the wall, then, under fire, quickly moved through the tall wheat out to the advanced skirmish line. This was another north-south post-and-rail fence line running toward the Bliss farm perhaps 250 yards to the skirmish line's right. The men were posted about thirty feet apart and could not see each other while hugging the ground in the tall grain. They were under fire from Confederate skirmishers along their front as well as intermittent fire from Rebel sharpshooters using the protection and excellent field of fire offered by the Bliss barn.

The persistent Rebels were several times driven away from the barn by Yank units, only to move back in as soon as the Yanks withdrew. Rebel sharpshooters in the barn were picking off mounted officers moving along Cemetery Ridge, and harassing the cannoneers of Arnold's Battery almost a half-mile away.

Later that morning, the remaining companies of the 14th were ordered out to occupy the Bliss farm and keep the Rebels permanently away. The regiment attacked in two waves, under intense fire the whole distance, capturing first the barn, then the Bliss house. To their consternation, they found there were no windows in the barn facing the Confederate lines to the west. They continued to take heavy fire as the men bunched up in the barn for protection. Finally, Captain Postles of the brigade staff was ordered to get word to the 14th to set fire to the buildings and fall back. The captain mounted his horse to dash the half-mile out to the farm with his message. His ride was pure gallantry. Under terrific fire both out and back to his lines, he made it without a scratch on him or his horse.[10]

The eight companies of the 14th quickly and effectively fired the house and barn, then gathered up their dead and wounded and scuttled under fire back to the line behind the stone wall. The other two companies, including the Hirst brothers and Company D, remained on the skirmish line along and beyond Emmitsburg Road.

At midday came a lull in the fighting. The heat and humidity were building. At about 1 P.M., both sides opened tremendous artillery barrages across the plain. The Rebel shells tended either to overshoot the 14th's main position or to spang off the rock ledge to their immediate front without doing further damage. The skirmishers were less fortunate.

About an hour later the artillery fire ended. Arnold's Battery, out of ammunition and badly shot up, limbered up and pulled out, leaving one gun behind. In the barrage, that gun had been moved to a position about ten yards in front of the wall, down the gentle slope toward Emmitsburg Road.[11] The 14th's men extended to their left to fill the position vacated by the battery, then lay down behind the stone wall. To the regiment's immediate left, the wall turned abruptly westward for eighty yards before turning again to the south. This latter corner was "the angle." Pennsylvania troops there would presently receive a mass of Pickett's and Pettigrew's Confederates, emerging just then in long lines of battle from the tree line on the other side of the plain. Minus forty or so skirmishers still out front, the regiment at this time included about a hundred men fit for duty along the wall.

Chapter 8

The Letters

⌒~~~⌒~~~⌒

Letter File #50

[written in pencil]

Somewhere in Virginia.
April 30. 1863

My Dear Sarah

I recieved your letter of the 26.th inst, while on the march last night. the money was all right, and I was well pleased that you were so prompt in sending it. I am much vexed that you have so much trouble in getting a man to do the work i want done. when I enlisted i had no idea that you would have to turn Navigator. it is too bad. and may the Devil or the Draft get the mean cusses before long. you must mind and not hurt yourself for I would rather the whole Place was like a Virginia House than that you should hurt yourself. you will see by this that we are on the move again. Monday we got orders to be ready at daylight to leave and we whent to work getting ready. [p. 2] about 10 oclock P.M. the Paymaster got here and Paid us two months Pay. Tuesday morning we marched a few miles and encamped. we were started again about dusk to go and build a road leading down to the river. we were kept at it all night. yesterday we resumed our march and came about 6 miles. we are somewhere in the Vicinity of United States Ford. you will find 30 dollars in this. 20 of it is Johns. we did not get them checks yet. I must conclude this as soon as Posible for I expect to have to fall in each moment. our Company has got 21 muskets on this march. the names of the men are F Stoughten, GM Brigham, B Hirst, Joe Murry, A. Hyde, J Billson, Dainty, Wm Goodell, J. Hirst, A. Horn [?], Menn [Hemmann], Hills, Hotsposky, Julian, Scott, Stafford, Reed, Jackson, [p. 3] J. Williams, D Whiting, Morton (cook), Ch[arles] Morrison, Kilburn Newel. so that nobody need be alarmed whose Friends are not in this list. John and myself are well. give our Love to All.

your Affectionate Husband
Benj Hirst.

Letter File #51

> Battle Field
> in Rear Fredricksburg
> May 4. 7 A.M.

[written in pencil on paper scrap about two and a half inches wide and five inches long]

Dear Sarah

up to this time John and myself are all right. the Army is in a body [?] all right, altho we have had some desperate Fighting and have not yet Captured the Rebel Army. we have them where we can whip them if they will come out. Rockville Boys are safe as yet. yours as ever Benj Hirst.

Letter File #52

> Camp near Falmouth, Virginia
> Wednesday May 9 [May 6] 1863

My dear Sarah,

It is with a sad yet thankful heart that I am able once more to assure you that both John and myself have again been through one of the greatest (and I fear one of the most disastrous) Battles yet fought without getting a scratch from the thousand destructive misiles, that were showered upon us. When I last wrote you (April 30) we were just about to cross the Rhappahannock at United States Ford, about 9 miles above Fredricksburg and effected a crossing at about 5 oclock PM where we heard read an order from Gen Hooker, in which he stated that owing to the Brilliant movements of the 3d, 11th, 12th Army Corps, the Rebels had refused to Fight us on their own ground, and that they would have to fight us on ground of our choosing, or skidadle in Which Event certain Destruction awaited them. this made some of the men cheer like the Devil, but the Fourteenth seemed to take it as a matter of Form. we had a very Fatigueing march and effected a junction with the rest of the Army about 10 P.M. (May first) the Ball was opened by the advance of our men to meet the Enemy, and soon the Fighting began on our Left, with what success I am unable to say. our Corps Commanded by Gen Couch was kept in Reserve, to be thrown on any point that might be threatened by superior Forces of the Rebels. we had nothing to do until about 11 AM when we were pushed rapidly across the Gordonsville and Fredricksburg Plank Road (this road was the Rise for which both sides were contending). it already looked like a Battle Field, being strewed [p. 2] with overcoats, Blankets, Letters and lots of other things that I have not time to mention. After gaining our position it was soon seen we were not needed at that Point, and our Brigade (Gen Hayes [William Hays])[1] was marched back at our Leisure. in the afternoon fighting commenced on our Right, and it soon became general along the Line; but we could see but litle of it, in fact nothing but a shell once in a while that came among us at that distance we being about 2 miles in rear of the Battle. it lulled down at sunset and our Brigade whent on Picket but had nothing to disturb us during the night. Saturday morning [2 May] were marched to Front of Gen Frenches Head quarters (about 1/2 mile in Rear [of] Hookers) where we were kept engaged all day in listening to the incessant roars of Muskets and Artillery which grew nearer and nearer each hour; towards sunset our anxiety grew intense and it soon became evedent that our turn had come to try and stem the Rebel Flood that had already turned our right Wing, and Threatened the Destruction of our whole Army. (The Reserve consisted of the 1st & 3d Divisions of the Second Corps). at about 6 1/2 oclock the whole 11th Army Corps, gave way almost without firing a shot, the Panic stricken runing about in hundreds and thousands.[2] We soon Fell in, unslung knapsacks, capped our Rifles, and our Brigade was the first ready, and the first on the Road to the scene of Disaster. Double Quick we whent, a thin streak of men four abreast through the hundreds of wretches that blocked the road. About every few seconds a shell would burst in the road which would help to clear it for us. arriving at Hookers Head Quarters, things [p. 3] looked bad. Hooker and his whole staff was here. on the right and Front men and Artillery were coming in in disorder; some brave men yet stood bravely to their Posts who received us with loud Hurrahs, and with shouts of derision for the Rebels to again come out and show themselves. (the Rebs lined some woods on each side of the Gordonsville road and had a Battery Planted in the road at a distance of not more than a mile from Hookers quarters; a Brass Battery of ours was run out to oppose it and our Brigade was to take position in the woods on the right of the road and about half way between the two Batterys they being not more than 1000 yards apart. Hooker directed in Person.) the fourteenth never behaved better than they did on this occasion. Marching slowly and steadyly on the Right of the Brigade, down the road until we reached our Position, when Mr Rebel gave us one dose of Grape shot which luckily wounded but 3 of our men. our Battery then opened, and the grape and Canister seemed to go in every direction. It was a regular Artillery Duel and was kept up until we had got into our Position in the Wood, then it gradualy grew still for a time. It was a stillness that preceedes Death to a great many of our Corps on the Left of the Turnpike; at about 10 PM oclock they again opened (it being almost as light as day) and renewed the attack on our Centre. the shouts of the Rebels were awful as they pressed upon our lines. our men met them firmly, and in about 15 minnets drove them back amidst loud Hurahs.[3] the men on our side of the Road laid still all night expecting each minnet to be attacked. but we escaped [p. 4] until daylight [on 3 May]. when we were about to cook some Coffee and had just made fires for that purpose, the Rebels began to move upon us. we fell in with alacrity and laid low until they came within range. I had here better state our situation. our Brigade was in

Gen. William Hays, commanding the 2d Brigade (including the 14th Connecticut), 3d Division, 2d Corps at Chancellorsville, where he was wounded and captured. Box 1, Vol. 2, PG 85, #1727, Edward B. Eaton Collection, Connecticut State Archives, Connecticut State Library.

line of Battle the Left resting on the Turnpike, the Right as Far in the Woods as our Brigade extended. there was another line of men [of the 2d Division, 3d Corps] in front of ours, and none behind us. the Position was inperfect, because the Rebel line was the longest and their Left Flanked our Right. this will account for the indiferent exertions made by our Regiment and Brigade. the engagement soon became general along our Front, and after some resistance the line in our Front gave way to the Rebels, and came in walking over us to get to the rear. I was never in better Humour for a Fight than at this moment, and never felt better able to take care of myself, than I then did during the minuet that elapsed before the Rebels showed themselves. Soon the bullets began to Whistle among us, and most of our men opened Fire before they could see the Rebels. this made our Resistance less strong than it might have been, and did not hurt the Rebels half as much as it otherwise would have done. we pegged away at each other for some time, in fact until the Rebel Left lapped our right, when the Boys broke, at the very moment, as I thought, when we ought to have stood firmest. We fell back with some litle show of order until we reached the Place where we started from the evening before. Sarah, I dont claim to be ever Brave [p. 5] but, I would have been shot, rather than have given way at the moment we did. I do not know where the blame rests but I think it was with the men opening fire too soon and giving way before learning the real strength of the Rebels. the Officers used no particular exertions to Rally the men, or try and add anything to the Reputation of the Regiment. taking everything into consideration I think we done Well but might have done Better. We fell in again at our starting point of the night before, and Rallied to about 100 strong, when we were sent to a new position. this closed our share of the Fighting altho we were under Fire in Second Front Line, until 2 A.M. this morning [6 May] when our Corps (being the last) began silently to skeedadle. I cannot tell our loss in this disastrous Battle but it must be heavy. our Regt lost in wounded 34 out of about 180 men engaged. Co D. was fortunate in having but one wounded while engaged, out of 16 men. his name is Thomas Stafford, he started for the Rear, since which time we have not seen him. Pat Jackson fell out being lame, and has lost 2 or 3 fingers, but how we cant tell, not having seen him since. John Williams was left to guard the Knapsacks, and he is missing ever since then. These are all the casualties of our Company. the Rebels will have a fine time on our 8 days rations, overcoats, Blankets, and all the Plunder of a Battle Field. We have lost everything. all I brought back with me was the clothes on my back, Rifle, and 80 rounds of Cartridges, one Ruber Blanket, and a Fine Coat of Mud. it is getting dark so I must conclude for the present I remain as ever

    your Affectionate Husband Benj Hirst.

～～～

Letter File #53

Battle of Chancellorsville 2nd   Camp near Falmouth, Vir.
                                                     May 9.th 1863

Dear Sarah,

I received your welcome letter last night, and was very sorry to see that you have had such a hard time with your head. I hope that you are all right again. for myself I am as well as could be expected after the Terrible trial us have undergone. I think i wrote you in my last that after our Engagement Sunday morning [3 May], we returned to the place from where we started the night before. here we found our knapsacks as we had left them, but our Camp Guard had fled to a safer place.

here we tried to reform the Reg.t but could only get about 80 men to gather, so we fell further back behind a new line of Battle and got the men togather as fast as we could, leaving our Knapsacks on the now disputed Ground. A large amount of Artillery was now concentrated on the Wood we had left behind us, Grape and Canister was poured into it, and the Rebels were soon compelled to give way in their turn. but not until the Large House used as Gen Hookers head quarters was set on Fire. (it was burnt to the ground). *It would have done you good to have seen "Old Blinkey" (Gen French) astride his horse, in the middle of the turnpike watching the rebel line, both as immovable as statues, except when the general winked his eyes, his heavy eyebrows would come down and the lower part of his face would go up like a nut cracker. Neither shot or shell seemed to disturb him as he watched the road . . . .*[4] About noon things looked bad for us, the Rebels got some Canon to bear upon us, and after Shelling us a little time we fell a little ways back into the Woods, once into the woods the timid ones began to make tracks for the Pontoons, and soon the narrow roads were backed with thousands. the Rebels shelled the Woods at a Furious rate, but after a time our pieces silenced them. some of the Fugitives began to return and order was once more restored and now we began to Act like men again, trees were cut down in our Front, a Breast work was thrown up all along the union lines (Lieut [Charles] Lyman of our Regiment with myself as Serg.t and 25 men completing our Section of the Work by midnight). We laid down about 1 oclock in the morning [4 May] completely used up, had just got to sleep when a False alarm called us up again. after that had subsided was allowed to sleep until daylight. Monday morning [still 4 May] [p. 2] Every preparation was made for meeting the Rebels. our Lines were rectified, and a change made in the Formation of our men so as to make success certain in case the Rebels should attact us. Orders were sent to the different Regiments to find out the missing men and Skidadlers. Cap Davis[5] with 10 men and myself as Sergeant, were sent from our Regiment to Scour the Woods, and Hospitals, and arrest all belonging to our Regiment we could find. I might have declined going on this service on account of being detailed on the intrenchments the night before, but it was a Complimentary job, and I was glad to go tired as I was. We traveled all along our Front Line, and I am satisfied I might have been in the Service 5 years and not seen as much as I saw that morning. I was soon satisfied that it would be impossible for any amount of Rebels to drive us any further back. we traveled clean back to the Pontoon Bridge, and at 8 oclock P.M. got back to our Regiment with about 30 Skidadlers in our charge. There was a great Battle going on, in as we soposed Fredricksburg.[6] but we were well satisfied that our men could hold their own there. we were mistaken. the Rebels won and our Position was now untenable. Tuesday morning [5 May] had roll call each hour expecting an attact from the Rebels but nothing occured until about 10 oclock when they tried to drive in our Skirmishers. some of the Bullets whistled amongst us rather near but no one of our Regiment was hurt. directly after dinner it comenced raining like Mad, and soon we looked like a lot of drowned rats. it rained all afternoon and night, and I think if the Rebels had any notion of attacting us it helped to postpone it. The Boys of our Company had just got a Sheltered place fixed for Sleeping in, and had just got asleep or laid down, when the Word came for Frank Stoughten. after a short time Frank whispered to each man to get ready to Fall in without noise, that we had got to recross the river before morning. it was like a thunderbolt to many, while to others it was like renewed Life. We stood shivering in the rain without a word louder than a Whisper until 2 oclock A.M. [6 May] when we began to leave; a new road had been made in the woods on purpose so that each step we took led us further from the Rebels. [We] reached the Pontoons just at Daybreak and [p. 3] after a Slight delay we began to recross the river. (I was much pleased with Gen Couch who stood at the side of the Bridge giving orders. a Soldier asked what Corps is that, one of our men said the Second. Joe Murry said the second skidadlers. No said Couch, the Second Fighting Corps.) after we had crossed we were marched rapidly back to our old Camp resting but once during the whole way. the Mud was knee deep and most every man had measured his length in it once at least. we got back to our old Camp about 11 oclock A.M. thoroughly exausted with our 6 days on the other side of the Rappahannock. While at Fort Ethan Allen I saw our troops coming in From Second Bull Run, and I saw Burnside stuck in the Mud, saying nothing about our first Defeat at Fredricksburg. but I never saw a Dirtier lot of Poor Devils, than ourselves on arriving at our old Camp. I believe I told you how many men we had wounded. later reports from our Doctor places our wounded at 38 with Capt Fisk killed outright.[7] our missing is quite large, and some of these may be killed. our First Lieut. [Simpson] is missing under Laughable circumstances. on Monday he got sick and took his man Morton (from Rockville) and his Traps into the Woods where the two could live in Peace and security. when the Word came to for us to leave no one could find them. We think if they slept good that Johny Rebel is toting them of[f] to Richmond by this time. our second Lieut [Wadhams] has been under arrest over a week so that the Command of the Company again devolves on Orderly [Sgt.] Stoughten.[8] Dont send me any more envelopes yet, for I made out to save my letter Paper and letters. therefore do not need them. Everything in this Army seems today to be going back to its old place. what our future movements will be depends on the Rebels, and the men at Washington. Joe Hooker is not the greatest man in the World yet, and Will have enough to do to save himself from reproach, and the general impresion here is that the Peer of McCllenan is not yet found.   I remain yours, as Ever. Benjamin Hirst.

Letter File #54

Camp near Falmouth Vir
Saturday May 16.th 1863.

My Dear Sarah,

I received your long expected letter this evening, and am glad your anxiety is relieved in regard to the late Battle. I hope you could make out my writing, in my last two letters, for they looked as though I had been writing with a stick. nevertheless I hope you will take care of them for me and let such of my friends read them as you think proper. In this you will find 5 checks for 10 dollars each. give Tom [Butterworth] his as soon as posible so that he can get it cashed before the State is notified of his discharge. . . . the one for Mrs Barrows, She must write on the Back of it Mrs Samuel Barrows. the one in your name you will Endorse yourself. the other two are all right for collecting. We have just moved to [p. 2] our New Camp. it is about a mile further back than the old one, and is laid out nicely amidst a Pine Grove. I hope they will let us stay here long enough to pay us for our trouble. the Furlough business has been renewed but our Company cant get inside the ring yet, so that if you cant do anything with [Governor] Buckingham it will take a Generation to fetch my turn to the going point. if you think that it would help the matter by seeing the Governor you can do so. With regard to your coming out here to see me, I hope you have better sense than to come again. it would not please me to have you come, especialy in the Company you propose. and I know that you would go home more disatisfied than you now are. with regard to my health it is first rate and to day I am as well able to start for Richmond as I ever was, or will be. [p. 3] You can rest assured that if I should get sick or Wounded I should send for you at the first oppertunity. then you could come on a Dutiful and Sensible Errand, and I know that I should appreciate it. We have got a correct report of our Regimental Loss in the recent Battle. it is 56, of which number 37 we know to have killed or wounded. this leaves us 19 unaccounted for, some of them are undoubtedly Killed. I wrote to Dedham [Massachusetts] about a week ago, giving a short sketch of our operations over the river. If i was you, I would go to Dedum and see the Folks, and I think you would like it, for it would certainly do you good. What do you Say, when will you Start. I have just wrote to Joe. Bill [Hirst] has been to see him. he, Bill, is not expecting the Mill to start this Summer. I hope he will be disapointed. but he had better do nothing for a year than go a [p. 4] Sojering like his Brothers, for if he can get 10 cents per day, and has two bed sheets, he can live and get fat on it. Lord if we could get a few more murphies we should get to[o] Fat to Waddle. I never before knew that Crackers and Pork was such good Eating. but so it is, I believe I could eat a piece of the Devil if he was well Roasted. John is well and sends his love to you and his respects to Mother and Maggy. give my respects to all enquiring Friends and shop mates. Love to you, and do, as I do, believe everything will yet come out right. give my respects to Mother and Maggie. I remain yours. Love, Benjamin Hirst to His Beloved Wife. P.S. send me some stamps.

~~~~~

Letter File #55

Camp near Falmouth Vir
May 16.th 1863

Dear Brother [Joe]

I received your letter last night and am very glad that you are doing so well and also to assure you that John and myself are in good health. I wrote you 8 days ago, giving you a short account of our Campaign over the Rappahannock. I hope you got it. I last night got our third Checks for 10 dollars and would have sent yours to you in this letter but I thought it safer to fill it out and send it to Sarah to be Cashed. you can draw on her for the amount or she can dispose of it as you wish. I hope you will remember me to Russell Miller the first chance you get. I sopose you know as much about our Fighting as I can tell you but I have not yet seen an account [p. 2] Published that I can consider correct. We had the best chance to see a Battle without being Engaged, that has yet occured to us. Our Corps (the 2d) was not acting altogather, the 2 Div being left to Act on the old Battle Ground. Hancocks acted by themselves and Frenches [3d Division] under him.[9] We could see and hear all the fighting until Saturday 6 oclock P.M. when a few Shells dropt amongst us, warning us that we should soon have to go in; the Eleventh Corps breaking about this time without Firing a shot made things look desperate; and as we whent to the Front at Double Quick we passed them coming in like whipt Curs by the Thousand. everything was in Confusion. some of our Guns were in the hands of the Rebels, and we could hear their Exultant shouts as we approached them. Old Hooker was getting [p. 3] a Battery in position on the Plank road as we whent to our Position. Pat Jackson here fell out, and in getting to the Rear lost 2 or 3 fingers. A Big Battle was Fought to the Left of us a few rods at about 11 P.M. which lasted about 30 minuets, during which our men gained ground. Our turn did not come until Daylight Sunday morning, when the Rebels attacked us and after a Sharp engagement we gave way and Fell back. we were under fire until Tuesday night when the whole Army Skidadled from a Position the Whole Rebel Army could not have drove us From, had we still held the Heights of Fredricksburg. I whent all along our Line on Monday, picking up Stragglers and had a good chance to see the Preparations made for them. dont you believe what Newspaper Corespondents say about the River rising and all that Gamen [gammon]. We were simply out Generaled. [p. 4] it did not begin to Storm until after dinner, and our whole Pioneer Corps were put to Work making a new road to Skidadle by. at 7 oclock A.M.

again I saw lots of Amunition Destroyed on this side the river, in the hury to get the Teams out of the Way. our Regimental loss is reported to day at 56, 37 of which number were killed or wounded. Tom Stafford got hit and he is still missing. John Williams is missing and our first Lieut with his man Morton we left in the Wood on Tuesday night, and reckon the Rebels awakened them Wednesday morning. . . . This is all Co D loss at present. so you see we came off pretty lucky after all. send our respects to William [Hirst] and Family. John and myself are both in good health at present hoping this will find you the same

I remain your Affectionate
Brother Benj Hirst

Letter File #56

Camp near Falmouth Vir
(My Birth Day) May 20.th 1863

My Dear Wife,

   I received your letter last night, and am glad that you are as well as usual, but I am sorry to see you writing in such a desponding way. if I have to serve my full term it will be because I cant posibly avoid it. there are 2 years Regiments just going Home and yet they keep all the recruits who expected to go Home with the Regiment in the service for another year.

   Dear Sarah you must not be so desponding. if you could see the Desolated Places, Inhabited by a solitary Woman and 2 or 3 little children that I have seen, Women who would Scorn to see their Husbands at home while We have possession of the Land and at the same time hardly knowing where they will get their next [p. 2] dinner or Supper from, you would thank God, that there are yet men enough in the North to keep the War from our Homes. I am thankful that I have lived through what I have, and if it should be my destiny to Live through such scenes for 3 years, how much greater cause would you and me have for Thankfulness. You must Cheer up, dont work so hard around the House but go around and see your Friends, go to Dedam or to Chester and stay a few Weeks and see how other Folks have to live. you would soon see hundreds of Women, worse of[f] than yourself, and would be better satisfied with your own Lot. To Day is my 35 birth Day and I was never in better health than now. we are living like fighting Cocks this past Week. Brigham got me a Ham and a Lot of Potatoes. this with the small things from the Sutlers is as good living as you can imagine. I got some [p. 3] Oranges this morning, and would have sent you one if I could. but I have a Medal that Price Kelly presented me with, that you can have.[10] I wore it outside my coat, all the time we were over the river. so you see it was all over the Field of Chancellorsville. when I come [home] i will have the names of the Battles put on it. there is some chance of our

getting Furloughs now. Allen whent to see the Major and found out they were cheating us out of our turns. I think Allen will get away next Week. then comes Murray about 3 or 4 weeks after and myself next, after the first [of] July Furloughs will be for 15 days. so if i can get off about then I shal like it. John began to Laugh when he read your letter about his having the Heart Disease. he is getting a face like a full moon and stood our short Campaign like a Hero, which he is (altho a litle Grouty). [p. 4] do you know what I done to day to drink your health with I took and squesed an orange in some water and put some vinegar and sugar with it. it was almost equal to Whyskey and quite as expensive as the orange alone cost 10 cents. Cheese sells for 45 cents per lb. Butter 60. raisins 50. figs 50 and other things in proportion. but we make a smal quantity answer the place of a large one. I am glad you like the letters I send you but it must tire your patience to make some of them out. John wants you to get him a good fish Line and some fish Hooks, send them in your next letter. give my respects to all my Friends and accept my whole Love
for yourself I remain your
Affectionate Husband
Benj Hirst

Letter File #57

Camp near Falmouth Vir
May 28.th 1863

My Dear Sarah,

I received yours this evening and it gives me great pleasure to think you are getting over your sickness, and that you care nothing about coming out here again to see this Blasted Place, that I am tired of looking at every day. it would be a great pleasure to me to see you, at any time or place, where I could be my own master for a few days. but here is worse than the Bad place we read about. I have just got a letter from Babe Quinn[11] which you will find enclosed in this. I shal try to answer it tomorrow morning. she seems to think you ought to have wrote to her before now. [p. 2] Allen might have had his Furlough a month ago if he had looked after it properly. he will go in the next Batch that goes, but when that will be is hard to tell, as they are stoping them again for a short time, or until Old Hooker gets out of the Woods again. We have just got orders to be ready to march at 30 minuets Notice until further orders, but I dont think we shal leave this place for some time yet, unless the Grey Backs come over to see us, in which case we shal try and give them a fitting Reception. I am sorry you have had so much trouble with the garden, but I hope you have made up your mind to let it go to Grass, for I would rather [p. 3] everything was lost than that you should lose your health trying to do a mans work. give it up a [t?] once. John is well and sends his respects to you and Maggie. the Fish line is a good one but he wants a little smaller hooks, those you sent being a little might large. I got a letter from Joe in which he says something about going to New Haven. if he goes there send me word as soon as posible. How is Curly and Dick getting along. I should [like?] to see Curly taking somebodys letter from them, and you scolding him. Dear Wife, I am in good health, and I expect to come out of this 3 years scrape, a Wiser if not a better man, and when [p. 4] it is over, neither you or I will ever regret it I hope. give my respects to all enquiring Friends, and to Mother and Maggie. to yourself my Love. I remain your Affectionate Husband, Benjamin Hirst

P.S. send me a few Newspaper Wrappers, and then I can send you a paper once in a while. Allen is trying to get home again this morning for 5 days. if he should come, get me 2 very light Woolen summer shirts. Plaid or Figured. and send them by him.

B. Hirst.

⌒〜〜⌒

Letter File #58

Camp near Falmouth Vir
June 5.th 1863

My Dear Sarah,

I write you these few lines to let you know that John and myself are both in good health and hope this letter will find you in the enjoyment of the same blessing. I have not heard from you, since I last wrote you. but I hope all is well at Home. We have been ready to leave here twice since my last, each time being called up at 3 oclock in the morning, hardly having time to pack our new knapsacks, then laying around all Day until the Grand Scare would Die out of itself. We can form no idea of what [p. 2] our next move will be, but I sincerely hope it will be a succesful one. We have had a new lot of Officers made and our Orderly Sergeant F. Stoughten is made Second Lieut in Co H. Frank will make a good officer and He has earned his Promotion which is a great deal more than can be said of two thirds of the appointments made in this Regiment; some men have been made Officers, who have never been in Battle yet, and if they can help it never will. Merit is the Last qualification looked for here. therefore Franks appointment is a litle out of the Way, and We have made up our minds to Note it, by Presenting him with a Sword and Belt, every Member of [p. 3] company D. has contributed a little towards it. the money is in my Pocket, and as soon as we can make the necessary purchase, the Presentation will take place. Allen has not yet got his Furlough but expects it every Day. until he and Joe Murray get out of the Way, I can do nothing towards getting mine; our present Camp is in a very nice place compared to what it was, it being in a Pine Woods, and having good Water convenient to it. but the mosquitoes have begun to make fun of me at night which makes me Wish I was at Home sometimes, when I wake up and find them sucking away.

[new pen point, different shade of ink; following probably written later]

An Order has just come for us to have 3 days cooked rations on hand and that all Furloughs are revoked [p. 4] so Poor Capt Allen wont be able to get home just yet. I must conclude this rather short as the mail is just closing. I remain your

Affectionate Husband

Benjamin Hirst.

Edward P. Allen resigned his captaincy in the 5th Connecticut Volunteers. He mustered in with the 14th Connecticut as a musician private in August 1862. He was later returned to ranks in Company D. Photo Group 850 (CWO-Union), Connecticut State Archives, Connecticut State Library.

Letter File #59

Camp near Falmouth
Sunday June 7. 1863

Dear Brother [Joe],

I received your letter last night and take this opportunity to write you a line or two. What the next move will be out here we cant tell but it is not very agreeable to get up each morning at 1/2 past 3 oclock [to] pack everything up ready to leave at a moments [notice] with 3 days rations. this is what we do every morning. this time we have struck tents, but I dont think we shall leave to day. the night before last there was a very heavy canonading on our Left where Franklin before crossed the river and I believe our Folks laid a Pontoon.[12] but amongst so many stories you hardly [p. 2] know what to believe. yesterday there was Canonading on our Right towards Warrenton but what it amounted to I dont know. We have had quite a lot of Promotions made of the old Kind. but they have done Frank Stoughten Justice by making him Lieut in Co H. Frank heard from Rockville that [Thomas] Stafford was in a Washington Hospital. John Williams turned up a[t] Paroled Camp Anopolis. but how he came to be a Prisoner is more than I can tell. our Lieut and Mr [George W.] Morton also got to the same shop at the same time. that Chap who writes for the Papers under the name of Dunne Brown is Little Capt Fisk of ours. he has been to Richmond, and our Brigadier Hayes [William Hays] is still there. Capt Bronson Died a couple days ago of wounds [p. 4] received at Chancellorsville.[13] I saw him shot. all the Boys here are well but Johnson and Gilmore. out of all our Bully Company we have just got 18 men for Duty (that is Fighting Men) John is well and I am pretty fair. give my respects to G Pierce and Lady.

I remain your Affectionate
Brother Benjamin Hirst

P.S. What do you think about the meeting in N. York. Uncle Abe must look out for Shoals. a Spark may inaugurate another Rebellion. . . . *[T]hese copperheads [may] inaugurate another rebellion in our rear.*[14]

B. Hirst.

⸻

Letter File #60

Camp near Falmouth Vir
June 9.th 1863

My Dear Sarah,

I received a letter from Mr Bottomly, last evening informing me of your arrival in Dedham, and I am very glad you have gone, because I think it will do you good. and you can tell me how all the old and young Folks are getting along and what changes have been made there since Forbes and myself used to go the rounds, after Huckleberries (faith I should like to do it again, just now). give my respects to all my old Shop mates, I reckon there is a lot of them there yet. I think I could name a Lot of them, first comes Forbes and Family, Mrs Allison, Friend Tapley Esq., John Lee, [p. 2] Mr. Brook, Charley Thompson, Friend Yacob, Mr Newson and a whole lot of others that I can see in my mind. give my Respects to them all. I wrote you last Friday morning but of course you did not get it. I have not received a letter from you for almost 2 weeks, altho I received the last Mercury you sent me with the newspaper wrappers in it. Joe wrote me last week, he is about the same. there is no change in Affairs out here that we can perceive. but we are kept in readiness to move at a minuets notice, with 3 days rations in our haversacks. every morning we get up at 1/2 past 3 oclock, Stand under Arms until 4 when most of us turn in again for an hour or two, not caring much whether the Rebs [p. 3] come or not. in the forenoon we Drill a couple of hours, and in the Afternoon the same. not being allowed to go outside our Division Lines we know but very little of what is going on. We were out Drilling almost in sight of Fredricksburg when a part of our Forces laid a Pontoon Bridge, and once more crossed the river, and yet at this moment we cant tell, if they hold Fredricksburg, or the Heights, or if they have yet come back again or not. and us within sight of the whole Scene. give my respects to Mrs Bottomly and the Girls and to John. you will find enclosed in this a few lines to Mr Bottomly. give my respects to Mr and Mrs Forbes, and all enquiring Friends. I remain as Ever, your Affectionate Husband

Benjamin Hirst

———⟨⟩———

Letter File #61

Ocaguan [Occoquan] Creek.
June 17. 1863

Dear Sarah,

I take this stray moment to write you a line. We Left our old Camp Sunday night, and have done some tall marching since, and by all accounts we have got some more to do. Joe Hookers Strategy dont work very well or I am much mistaken.[15] with the exception of being foot sore, John and myself are both well. Shal write you as soon as posible. respects to all. I remain your Affectionate

Husband Benj Hirst.

P.S. all of the Rockville Boys are as well as can be expected.

Letter File #62

Fairfax Station, Vir
June 18 1863

My Dear Sarah,

I am comencing to write you with the hope that I shal be able to finish, during the course of a day or two. I thought I knew all about sojering but the experience of the past few days has convinced me to the contrary. Last Sunday morning all the Officers tents and baggage was sent off, and the men were held in readiness to march every minuet. the Main Army had already cleared out for (to us) parts unknown, and we were thrown out as Pickets all along the whole Line, from 3 miles below Falmouth up to United States Ford, and from thence across the country, reaching clean back about 5 miles from the river, the Old Second Corps covering the [p. 2] Retreat of the Army of the Potomac once more. our Brigade being almost in sight of the Reb Pickets we had all the Calls sounded in Camp, same as usual even to the Retreat.

Company D was stationed in a road leading to the ford, with orders to arrest all persons near our lines. Everything passed off quietly until morning, when a man dressed in blue came into our lines claiming to have lost his regiment during a night march, and that he was out of tobacco and would like to find a sutler's shop, etc. I reported him to Capt [Walter M.] Lucas, who gave him the direction of the sutler's, when the man started in that direction leaving his knapsack in our shelter tent until his return. He came back in less than an hour with his clothes wet through by wading in a brook a mile at least within our lines. He was also out of breath and had evidently been running very hard. I did not like his actions and watched him closely as he opened his knapsack and took out a lot of religious tracts and papers which he distributed among the boys. After resting a while he said he must be going, and started down the road leading to the Ford. I covered him with my rifle and brought him to a halt, when Capt Lucas told me to let the poor devil go. In less than two hours after this incident rebel agents were reported to be on our side of the river. . . . He was no straggler of ours, for that kind of men are not made up as he was, and I think Capt Lucas did wrong in letting him go.[16]

When we began silently to Decamp, we marched a few miles when we laid down in our tracks awaiting further developments. about 3 oclock in the morning our Pickets were called in, and the Rappahannock was once more in undisputed possession of the Rebels. We started at once for Stafford Court House (10 miles from Falmouth) and arrived there without accident. here we had 30 minuets for breakfast when we formed Line of Battle across all the roads leading towards us. were kept in position until about 11 oclock when we once more started. and now the Suffering of the men comenced, the Roads being ground to Powder the Sun at its height. we seemed [p. 3] to be suffocated at each step. the Ambulances were soon filled, with sick and utterly used up men. several were Sun Struck, and Died in a few moments. I saw one man fall down; in 3 minuets he was Dead and in 30 Burried. hundreds would lay down in their tracks and refuse to stir until they had rested, and some had to be pushed along by the Bayonets of the Rear Guard, who were not allowed to leave one man behind them. I kept up first rate, as did John. most of the time I kept a oak leaf in my mouth, and when we came to a halt I would take a dose of Red Pepper and a little water and thought it relieved my Drouth a great deal. at 3 oclock P.M. we arrived at Aquia Creek, some miles from its mouth where we encamped, and our scattered men began to get togather again. there was a good bathing place here, and in a few minuets there was hundreds in [p. 4] the water Frolicking like a lot of School Boys. never, can you imagine the Scenes we passed through. in some places a man would let out a great Oath as he tumbled over something in his path and his Comrades (themselves panting for Breath) would set up a shout of Laughter at his misfortune. Thousands of blankets and overcoats were thrown away. these we placed in piles and [were] burnt by the Rear Guard. it was strange how Generous some men would get. do you want a pair of Drawers or Shirt. No. down it goes in the road. Lots of little momentos from home, would be passed from one to another, but the Road would finally get them. the second Day I Left my Blanket, and that is about all that I can do with out. I carry my Ruber Blanket and piece of tent in my knapsack, over coat on top, one extra pair Stockins in my Pocket that completes my traveling out fit. Ben Hirst.

⚬～～⚬

Letter File #63

[Opening portion of original is missing]

Today I took an inventory of my effects and find the following items: cash on hand $6.75, one patent army knife, fork and spoon, one comb, one-half quire writing paper with pen, pen holder and ink, one pipe and box of matches with one-half pound tobacco, one rubber blanket, one piece of shelter tent, one extra pair stockings in my knapsack which is partly filled with grub; the next on the list are my equipments; rifle, canteen and haversack, besides 20 rounds of extra cartridges in my pockets.[17] So you see I shant lose shirt without my hide goes with it. We started again 3 oclock Tuesday morning for Dumfries (about 21 miles from Fredricksburg) and along the road, the scenes of yesterday were reacted on a more extended scale. early in the morning the men get along pretty well, but after the Sun gets fairly up, it is Awful to see the suffering of some of the men. I can not begin to tell you what they look like. the road we passed over has been used before for the same purpose, and it was all cut up by the passing of Wagons and artilery. old Wagons, Cassions, and Sutlers teams were stuck in several places. other ones had been burnt, leaving nothing but the old iron, to explain to you what it once was. in some places where the Ground was swampy, you would find a passage, made pretty [p. 2] by having round shot and shell filled in it. for when a Wagon Breaks down, the Load has to be destroyed, for no spare teams are allowed, and got out of the way to make room for the next one. at 7 A.M. arrived at Dumfries, a Poor Miserable Place of 3 or 4 houses ready to tumble down with age. here we rested an hour for Breakfast when we got orders to start towards Fairfax. We made a Forced March of it. Gen Hancock[18] swore to reach Occoquan Creek during the day if he had but 300 men with him, (our Corps is about 8000 strong) and he kept his word, we crossed the Creek just a[t] sunset, encamping close by, to give us a chance for another bath. We were soon greeted by men from the 2 Conn Light Artillery who have been Encamped here for 5 months. Some of these men saw us leave [p. 3] Hartford, and were suprised to see the Poor Remnant of the 14th could yet crack a joke with them. Yesterday we started for this place (about 7 miles) and this days work Beat the whole. our Division was in the Rear, and we had to wait until everything had gone along but us. it was about 10 oclock before we got under way, and the men and Officers seemed to Wilt right

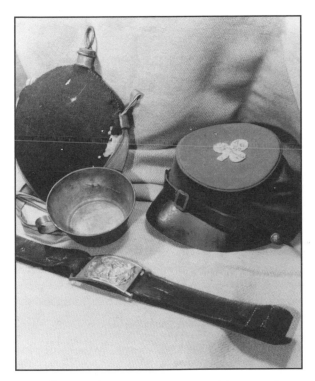

Some of Ben Hirst's wartime accouterments. The canteen is covered with dark-blue wool. The light-blue 2d Corps badge on the forage cap bears his inked inscription, "B.H./Co. D/14th Conn Vols." Courtesy of Alden Skinner Camp #45, Sons of Union Veterans of the Civil War, with special thanks to Bradford Keune.

down as though Blasted by something in the Air, but I kept up Wonderful with the exception of my feet, which Punished me terribly after each halt until i got them limberd again by walking. we got here about 6 oclock P.M. and encamped for the night. When I say, We, I mean Brigham, myself, and the Capt [Lucas] of our Company. (other Companies of our Regiment being here with about the same number) who were all that kept up to the head of the pack. [p. 4] We Left our old Camp with 19 Rifles in our Company, and one man without. the names of our Company is Capt Lucas, Sergts. Brigham, Hirst, Hyde, Murray, Corp[s.] Goodell, Whiting, Dainty, Newel, Privates Billson, Fay, Gillmore, Hirst, Hemman [Hemmann], Hills, Hosdposky [Hodspodsky], Root, Reed, Scott, Julian, Morrison. all hands got here during the night, some of them completely used up. Joe Murray, and Dainty are played out and were sent to Washington this morning. the rest of us are somewhat recruited this morning, and if they let us rest to day, will feel pretty well. give my respects to all our Friends, and send me 10 dollars as soon as posible. We have not had a letter or newspaper for a week, so we dont know what is going on in the World, but if reports are true the rebels are giving us the Devil. I remain yours as

Ever Benj Hirst

⌒⌒⌒

Letter File #64

Gain[e]sville Vir
Sunday June 21, 1863

Dear Sarah,

I received your and Mr Bottomlys letters, on the same day I last wrote you, and am glad that you were enjoying your visit. We rested all the day I last wrote to you. and the next we were ordered to Centreville, where we arrived late the same night. the next day (yesterday) we were started for this place, our Regt being placed to Guard the Division Wagon train. it was after noon before we got started. we passed through Centreville which consists of 8 or 9 houses, and some old Chiminies. but there are plenty of Earth Works and Rifle pits around filled with troops that have never seen a gun fired at an Enemy, and they are strutting around Washington about half the time. We finally [p. 2] started taking the Old Bull Run road, the same road that some of the Boys had Travelled before, with their Faces the other way. We passed over the old Battle Fields and saw some of the evidences of it. here and there was an old musket, broken Gun Carriage, and old equipments. piles of Dirt pointed where rested the Dead, some of these not being altogather covered with Mother Earth. some of the men saw Hands and Feet sticking out of the tops and sides of the heaps. for myself I had no desire to see anything, that I could help: having seen enough of the Horrors of War to satisfy my curiosity. we arrived here about 10 P.M. and this morning are awaiting further orders. we may move at any moment so you must excuse [p. 3] the shortness of this letter. my health is pretty fair and John is the same. he says those fish Hooks are a little too large. he caught one mess of Ells [eels] before we started our Boots from before Fredricksburg. hoping that you are improving in health and keeping good Courage

I remain your Affectionate

Husband Benj Hirst.

June 22d. I could not send this yesterday, so I have just opened it again to add a line or two. our Division did not move yesterday. on some account or other, there was heavy cannonading in the mountains in our front but what it amounted to i cant tell.[19] our present position is about 5 miles from Bull Run on the Manasas Gap Railroad, and the Fields around here are covered with Teams belonging to our Army. I think something Decisive [p. 4] will take place very soon. yours as Ever, B. Hirst.

Letter File #65

Gain[e]sville, Virginia

June 24.th 1863

My Dear Sarah,

You will see by this, that we are still in the place as when I last wrote you. John and myself are both well, and in good spirits altho we get but little rest while here. We are on precisely the same Ground as the rebels occupied after they had Whipt Pope about one year ago[20] and a very pretty place it is. 3 or 4 Planters Houses and Barnes composes Gainsville, but then they have a Railroad runs through it, and yesterday uncle Sam ran two Freight Trains from Fairfax Station to here, the first for some time. It is a very pretty Country, the soil being the Best I have seen in Virginia. away off we can see the Blue Ridge mountains and we know they [p. 2] are infested with Rebels. behind us about 5 or 6 miles is Bull Run with its Hundreds of Unburied Dead, while to our Left the country is overrun with Gurellas, ready to Gobble up any one that comes in their way. a very Pleasant Place aint it. I forgot to tell you in my last that Mr Hills got sick on our last March, and was sent off, thus leaving us with but 17 enlisted men in our Company. one of these does not do duty. (Gillmore.) 3 of our men that whent on Picket night before last, and who ought to have been relieved last night, have not yet come in, and we are beginning to fear some thing has happened to them. but I hope not. I wish you would send me those shirts by Mail. get Johnny Watslong to make them up in a Parcel and direct them, and I will run risk their getting to me [p. 3] sometime or other. put in a Black silk neck handkershief, for I expect some Rebel Major General is wearing the last one you sent me, and I ought to have another one ready

for the next Grand Skidadle. We have not had any letters since I last wrote you, and maybee we shant get one for a few days yet. our Division being detached from the Corps is the cause. our first and Second Divisions are up in the mountains and our duty is to keep open communication with them. every thing that comes along Horse Foot and Dragoons, have to report to Our Old Cock (Major General French) and I hope they will keep him busy doing it for a long time yet.[21] give my respects to all our Friends, and tell them that now is time that they are wanted. [p. 4] John joins me in sending his Love to Mother and Maggie. you will find a little stone in this letter that I picked up in crossing Bull Run. Scores of our men were crushed to Death in the Narrow Gorge, where I got it, at the first Bull run Battle. I must now conclude by subscribing myself as usual your Affectionate
Husband Benj Hirst.

P.s. have that Parcel Directed to me thus. Serg^t Benj Hirst, Co D., 14th Conn Vol. (Frenches Division, 2^d Corps) Washington, D.C.
B. Hirst

Letter File #66

near Sugar Loaf M.t Md.
June 28. 1863

Dear Sarah,

We have again changed our Base (as the papers say) and for the past 2 days we have been in Maryland. the day after I last wrote you, we began to Leave Gainsville to join our Corps. We kept in Position until our Pickets were driven in and then we made tracks for Bull Run, recrossed that Battle Field. then made a New Road through the Woods and were marched under cover of the Woods until we joined our Corps at Gum Springs. this was at 11 P.M. and we were all wet through. but I was very glad to lay down just as I was, and Slept until [p. 2] morning, when we resumed our march in the Direction of Leesburg. We had a very hard march of it all day, and late at night we reached the Potomac at Edwards Ferry. the whole Army was got over before morning, when after a rest we started for this place, expecting to make Fredric City today, thus we have had to go over the same ground we passed over about 10 month ago and all to please old Hooker who I hear has just played out.[22] I hope to God it is true. We have just arrived in Sight of Fredrick City and expect to stay here for the night. give my respects to all Friends. Love to yourself.

Yours as Ever B. Hirst.

Letter File #67

Union town, Maryland
June 30 1863

Dear Sarah,

We arrived here last night, having marched 30 miles yesterday, one of the biggest marches on Record. to day we expect to be in old Pensylvania and I feel ready to go. I should give up on the Road Side, but I want to be counted in if there is a Big Battle in the old Keystone State. This is a Splendid County we are marching through. the Citizens are all Union, and to see a Woman Smiling upon us again give us new Life. John and myself are well. Your Affectionate

Husband Benj Hirst[23]

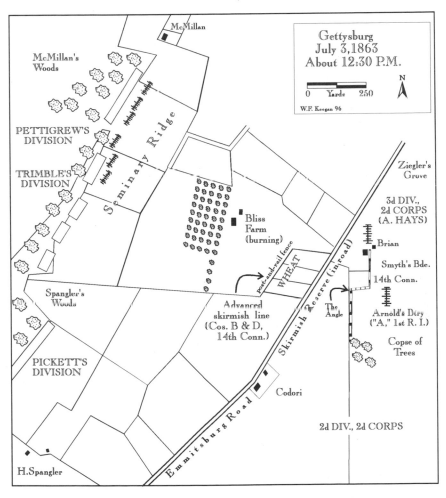

Letter File #68

[written on torn-off sheet of lined note paper in pencil by John Hirst]

July fourth Near Gettysburg 1863

Dear Sister i write you these few lines to let you know how we are as i know you must be very much excited out here as i expect you have had Great rumours by they time this reaches you we have had a very sharp engagement but you need not believe every thing that you here ben Got bruised on they right Shoulder but it is not Dangerous so take my advice and stay at home untill you here for certain where he is as he may be on his way home by they time you Get this i walked him down to they Hospital and he was in very good spirits and said if he could he should come home it was some pieces of [p. 2] Stone that struck him as he was laying behind a stone wall firing at they rebels we give them a good whipping but some of our boys suffered Brigham Got pretty badly wounded also frank stoughton and John Julian them three i am afraid of william Goodell got shot dead as he was loading is gun. Slightly wounded David Whiteing their was others Just got touched but not to mount to anything we got i am allright at present but tired[24] we got four colours from they enemy our regm Got them but they division Got some more but i dont know how many now take my advice and do as i tell you Stay at home untill [p. 4] you here from ben as he told me he should write as soon as he could i must close this for now your affectionate Brother John Hirst Hirst [*sic*]
   Now do as i tell you as ben aint hurt very Bad

⸺⸺⸺

Letter File #69

[in pencil on lined note paper]

July 5.th 1863
Near Gettysburg, Pa

Dear Sarah, I write you these few Lines, so that you can see that I am yet kicking, and am thank ful that I got off so well. The 14.th Conn is covered with Glory having got 5 Rebel Colors in our Posession besides a [word obliterated by stain] . . . of Swords and other Trophys of War [words obliterated] . . . the greatest Battle I have seen for the time we were at it and we Routed three times our number with great Slaughter. I wish i could write you all about it, but my shoulder is too lame to attempt it at present. I Shal be all right in a few weeks, altho I had some narrow escapes. our Company and Co B was out Skirmishing when the Rebels opened about 100 Canon upon the Height our Corps occupied. us Skirmishers [p. 2] had to lay where we were while Shot and Shell was bursting among us from both sides. it was here that John Julian got wounded (and I fear Fattaly). Dave Whiting had a narrow escape, a piece of Shell cut his cap and the tip of his ear. at the same time a piece of Shell struck me on the uper part of the Left thigh. I thought it was all up with me, for a minuet or two, until I opened my eyes to look at the Hole and it wernt there. the place is a little black and stiff but that is all. our Guns were after a while silenced, and our Skirmishers drove in. then I saw the Rebels in 3 lines of Battle moving to attact us. we had but one line to oppose them with but we had a low Stone Wall behind which we laid, until the Rebels [p. 3] got within 30 Rods of us, then such a Volley of rifles we gave them you cannot imagine. soon the first line was Shattered to pieces, and with shouts of Derision we awaited for the next, served them the same way and soon the whole were Flying from whence the[y] came, leaving behind them Hundreds of Killed and Wounded. if our Artillery could have helped us but very few would have got away. as it was the 14th alone took more Prisoners than our own Regt number beside the greatest number of Rebel Flags of any Regiment Engaged. after a while the Rebel Batterys opened again to cover their Routed men and a piece of shell or shot knocked a stone from the Wall which struck me on the right shoulder Blade, and with a yell I thought [p. 4] I was gone for sure. John helped me up and to the Hopsital when he examined me and found I was not hurt as bad as might have been expected. Corp Wm Goodel was instantly Killed by a Musket Ball. Brigham was Shot in the Body the Ball runing around a Rib came out of his back. Poor Frank Stoughten is shot just below the neck and is in a very Critical condition. we had two more in our Company very slightly wounded. the Regimental Loss is as far as known 56 out of about 180. I have just heard that our Troops are again on the move. John is all right, and kept by me all the time until he saw me comfortable here. *Brigham and Stoughton are both with me and we are attended by Michael Fay who thinks he cannot do too much for us.*[25] I think we shal be moved from here in a day or two, when I will write you again. give my respects to all. I remain your Affectionate

Husband Benjamin Hirst

~~~⌇⌇⌇~~~

Letter File #70

This account of the Battle
of Gettysburg was written by
me, entirely from my own
experience of what I saw of
it. October. 1863.

Benj Hirst.

Mower U.S.A. Hospital, Philad. Pa.

Date no matter.

Dear Sarah,

I believe the last letter I wrote you in the Field was Dated at Union Mills [Union-town], Md. and that we were then expecting to march to meet the Rebels somewhere within a few miles of that place; the day before I wrote you those few lines we had made one of the greatest marches of the War. We started from this side of Fredric City and thought we were going to pass through it over the old track to South Mountain, but when we came to the suberbs, we Filed right, until we brought the City into our rear. Forded the Monocacy River up to our waist belts besides several small streams that I did not learn the names of. for the first half of the day, the boys thought it great fun, but after we left the direct Road to Baltimore (as we supposed) the straglers began to be pretty numerous. We passed through Mt. Pleasant a very nice little village, but the Inhabitants were not to be seen, then passed through Liberty and when about sunset we arrived at Union Bridge we began to think we had done for one day, but no; Close up is still the word, and we passed through the Village as if the Devil was after us. Notwithstanding this I had time to notice that the inhabitants we[re] all well dressed and that the Ladies in Particular were very Patriotic, which was testified to in a many ways, but on we go and in a few minutes we have forgot all about them; now we have marched 27 miles since sunrise, and still no sign of Camping ~~and~~ now we ~~they~~ begin to Growl and to fall out. first one gives up, then another, then they begin to fall out in twos and threes, but still I move along as best I can. By and by whole Companies seem to drop out, officers and men together, but still no one can answer the often asked [question]:

how much further & ~~Hebe~~ ilebe Damd if I can go any further, and away goes my Gun over the fence and for a few minuets I give way to bitter thoughts as I rest my head upon my hands. Who is to blame for thus marching us Past [p. 2] all endurance, oh it is our new Corps Commander (Gen. Hancock) who wants to show that we can outmarch as well as outfight anything in the army. But no that cannot be it. It is the cursed Rebels, who not daring to attackt us where we could chastise them have stole a march upon us and now threaten to carry the War to our own Homes. Yes that is it and with the thought I get my Gun again and trudge along for a few more weary miles and I got rewarded for my perseverance for I soon saw that the advance were encamped for the rest of the night, and me and John were soon asleep by the road side, having marched with 3 days rations and 60 rounds of amunition over 34 miles. We rested near here the whole of the next day [i.e., 30 June], and this gave the Straglers a chance to come up, which they did by the hundreds. I supose our regiment was a good specimen of the rest. We had about 35 men in camp that night, our Co having 4 men there, out of 16 on the road. It was here i wrote you those few lines and here that Hancock thanked us in Gen Orders for our Perseverance and endurance during that trying march. The night of the 30 I was on Picket and heard from several sources that the Rebels were in force, not many miles from us, and on the morrow July first we heard heavy firing at some distance from us. it did not take us long to pack up (for most of us had nothing to pack) and soon we were on the march to Gettysburg. about 8 A.M. we marched through Uniontown and took the road to Tanneytown arriving there *about noon and came to a halt along side some enterprising sutler's shop belonging to the 11th corps, and the way that shop was cleaned out, it would never do to tell, as the provost marshal was threatening to put our regiment under arrest, when we were ordered to fall in, and Gen Hancock came dashing by.*[26] We heard that the first Corps was engaged at Gettysburg and that our own Hancock was hurrying to the Front to supply the place of Reynolds who was killed. we pushed along as rapidly as posible the inhabitants along the route helping us all they could. they handed us water and cheered us on at every step. (One old Lady I shal never forget. she came to her door and I saw she had something in her apron. I stept upon the [p. 3] sidewalk with several others and the old lady showed us her Treasure. She had her apron ful of hot biscuit. She gave us one each while with Tears rolling down her aged cheeks she lamented because she could not make them fast enough.) Never before did I see the men march along so gayly as we whent this day, our own little Co of Rockville Boys keeping well to gather, and joking with the rest. towards evening we began to see traces of the Battle. Artillery was passing rapidly to the front and others from the Front, now we would see a small squad of Rebel prisoners coming to the rear, and then the stories we heard from the Skulkers, Shirks, and Camp followers who lined the road side was a caution. Some would have it that our men were all cut to pieces, and they alone were left to tell the tale, while others were equally confident that our side was driving the rebels clean beyond Gettysburg and that they had gone so fast that we stood but a poor chance of seeing head or tail of them. In the mean time we pushed ahead as fast as posible but night overtook us before we got into position. our Regiment was sent to Picket on the Baltimore turnpike where we passed a very quiet night.

July 2nd We fell in just at daylight and were marched of[f] without having a chance to cook our Coffee the only Luxury a Soldier has on active service. We soon joined our Brigade and were soon lost in the thousands and thousands of Gallant men marching to the Front; this was a Great sight to Witness, the long Trains of Artillery were going some ahead, others to the right and Left, while Division after Division took its position for Battle. As far as the eye could reach from Round Top, to Cemetary Hill it was nothing but men Forming for the Decisive Conflict inaugerated the day before. We soon joined our own [p. 4] Proud Corps, just taking position a little to the Left of Cemetary Hill. We got one good look at the Spires of Gettysburg and could just discern the long Rebel lines to the right and Left of the City. Away of[f] to our right fighting had already commenced and our skirmishers were thrown out as soon as we got in Position. The first Deleware of our Brigade doing that duty in our imediate front, they were driven back with some loss, and the Rebels occupied a house and Barn [the Bliss farm] from which they could Pick of[f] our Artillery men at their Guns, then we sent out a part of the 12 New Jersey to clean them out which they did in gallant style, losing quite a number in Killed and wounded, but they inflicted equal Loss upon the Enemy besides capturing a large number in the Barn. The same house and barn was again occupied by the Rebels, when the 108th N.Y. supported by the first Delewares again cleaned them out. In the mean time the Rebels made a many desperate attempts to break our lines, but in each case failed. Sometimes they would try it on our centre and then it would roll of[f] to our extreme right until it seemed to be in our rear, then it would travel all along our left, and once they tried it upon Cemetary hill only to find their crack troops hurled back in utter confusion, leaving scores of their boasted Tigers already tame upon our hands. And thus it whent from morning to night without anything decisive being done on either side, we being satisfied to hold our own in this position, for the Rebels well knew they had either got to drive us away or leave themselves, a thing they knew was somewhat difficult to accomplish. We had had but one casualty in our Regiment[27] and were just congratulating ourselves on our good luck when a tremendous attack was made [p. 5] on our Left at Round Top. One Division of our men being driven in, a part of our Corps was brought in action, and the Rebels were badly punished for their audacity in coming near the old Second Corps. And so it whent until night put an end to the Contest. During the Evening our Regt. changed its position a little to the left and in support of Arnolds (2nd R.I. A) battery. Companies A and F were sent out as Skirmishers and this closed our operations for the Day.

. . . [O]ur brigade was placed in position in the following order: The 108 New York with its right in Ziegler's grove, then the 12th New Jersey at the beginning of a stone wall next to Bryan's barn, which ran along the crest of Cemetery Ridge, then the First Delawares under cover of the same wall, and next the 14th Connecticut, in support of Arnold's Rhode Island Battery, placed in position near a short angle in the wall, and on the left of the battery was the 71st Pennsylvania, which was posted in the angle of the wall supported by the 72d Pennsylvania. Those of you who have seen the cyclorama of the battle of Gettysburg, who recollect the tremendous fighting depicted on the plan of the third day's fight, the brunt of which is borne by the 71st Pa., should remember that the right of the 71st Pa. touched elbow to elbow the left of the 14th Conn. during the scene depicted and that it was owing to the deadly fire of our Sharp's rifles that so quickly cleared our front. You will thus perceive that our brave little regiment formed the connecting link joining Webb and Hays in one continuous line.[28]

July the Third

At early dawn we quietly took our Position in Line, and [at about 6 A.M.] our Co with Co B were sent out to relieve Co A and F and to push back the Rebel skirmishers who were a little too near our lines for our comfort, however we advanced to the *Emmitsburg road* in good order and took the required [skirmish reserve] position in good shape.[29] This was the first time our Company had been thus engaged, and when I was sent with 10 men, to relieve some other ones further to the Front, I felt a little timid about walking erect, with the Balls whizing about my ears from the Rebel Sharp Shooters. But I made out to Post the men (I found one of the men I was to relieve [*Corp. Huxum of Co B*] Dead at his Post. he was shot through the Head and from his position he seemed to be taking aim at a Rebel. I did not know he was Dead until I put my hand upon his shoulder, and spoke to him) and we were soon popping away as lively as Crickets. *I took his post for my own, and it was not long before a bullet came zip into the fence post before me, at the same time I saw a puff of blue smoke rising in the branches of a tree about 200 yards distant, and in the course of 15 or 20 minutes a bundle of something dropped out of that tree.*[30] (I will here tell you of one incident which goes to show how soon we get insensible to danger; my Gun becoming foul, I got a Ball stuck in the Barrel so that I could not get it home or take it out. in this Dilemma, I placed it before me with the Butt resting against a fence rail, and with my shoe string I pulled the trigger fully expecting it to burst, but it came out all right and I was soon firing away again.) In the mean time the Rebels again occupied the House and Barn I before mentioned, and the remainder of our Regiment were sent to drive them out, and to hold it, which was done in [p. 6] as Gallant a Style as could well be. The Regt held on until they got orders to Burn them down, and the Boys soon had a Fire that effectualy kept the Rebels out for the rest of the Battle. In this affair the Regt lost quite a number of good men, and one or two officers were wounded, and thus the forenoon wore away. About noon commenced the Fiercest Canonading I ever heard, the shot and shell came from Front and Right and Left. It makes my Blood Tingle in my veins now; to think of. Never before did I hear such a roar of Artilery, it seemed as if all the Demons in Hell were let loose, and were Howling through the Air. Turn your eyes which way you will the whole Heavens were filled with Shot and Shell, Fire and Smoke. The Rebels had concentrated about 120 Pieces of Artilery upon us and for 2 long hours they delivered a Rapid and Destructive fire upon our Lines, Principally upon the old Second Corps whom they desired to attack. To add to all this was our own Batteries in full Blaze, every shot from which seemed to pass over our heads; it was a terrible situation to be in between those two fires; how we did Hug the ground expecting every moment was to be our last. And as first one of us got Hit and then another to hear their cries was Awful. And still you dare not move either hand or foot, to do so was Death. Once I ventured to look around and just then I saw one of our Cassions blown up, while the same moment a Rebel one was blown up [by a hit] from the same Battery [that had just lost its caisson]. But all this could not last much longer, our fire began to lose its vigour for want of Amunition, and as the Smoke lifted from the Crest we saw our Guns leaving one after the other and soon a terrible stillness prevailed so that you could almost hear your heart thud in your bosom. But what means that shout of derision in our Front. Up men the Rebels are upon us, there they come a Cloud of Skirmishers in front, with one [p. 7] two, three lines of Battle, stretched all along our Front with their Banners flying, and the men carrying their Pieces at trail Arms. It was a Glorious Sight to see, Rebels though they were. The[y] seemed to march as though upon Parade, and were confident of carrying all before them. But away up that mountain slope in our Rear we knew that (biding their time) as Gallant a body of men as ever Rebels could dare to be were awaiting for them. Yes behind that long, low stone Wall is our own Glorious Second Corps so soon to Imortalise themselves by hurling back that Rebelious Crew who brought their Polluting foot-steps to our own dear North. Steady men, and Rally on the Reserve cries our Leader, as we take to our feet; we are driven in, but not in confusion. Sometimes we about Face and return their Skirmishers fire. But still we fall back up the Hill and over the Wall bringing our wounded with us. *As we fell into line Brigham fell in with Company A on account of getting cartridges for his Sharp's rifle. About one-half the regiment had this rifle. Hyde and Newell were sent off with Julian by Major Ellis, and the rest of us were nearly together. Hemmann, Root, Whiting, Capt Lucas and others on my right, Jack [John] Hirst, Scott, Norton A. Reed and others on the left. Goodell, disdaining the shelter of the stone wall, was at my back; Stoughton is with his company further to the left.*[31] And now we have a short breathing spell and can Note the Intense anxiety depicted on every countenance. You can see that: One is looking at the Far off Home He will never see again. Another one is looking at his Little ones, and he mechanically empties his Cartridge Box before him deter-mined to part with Life as Dearly as posible. Other ones you can see are commun-ing with Him before whom so many of us will have to shortly appear. We must hold this Line to the Last Man. The Fate of the whole Army now rests with you. Don't Fire until you get the order, and then fire Low and Sure. It is the Clear Voice of Gen Gibbon[32] as he rides along the Line, and gives a word of cheer to each Regi-ment as he goes along. A few more words from Gen Hayes [Alexander Hays], and our own Gallant Col [Major] Ellis and there runs along the Line Ready, up with our Flags, Aim, Fire. And time it was too, for the Rebels seemed to me to be within 150 yards of us, *just crossing the fences on the Emmitsburg road,*[33] and we could hear their Officers pressing them on to the charge, Fire, Fire, Fire [p. 8] all along our Line. There opened upon them such a Storm of Bullets, Oaths and Imprecations as fully satisfied them we had met before, under circumstances a little more favourable to them. Give them Hell x x x. Now We've got you. Sock it to the Blasted Rebels. Fredricksburg on the other Leg. Hurah, Hurah, the first Line is broken. Never mind who is Hit. Give them Hell again. And soon the second Line is sent Howling back after the first one. Right Oblique Fire, Left Oblique Fire, and the supporting Colums are thrown in disorder and soon seek safety in Flight. *At this time a great number of the rebels threw up their hands in token of surrender and we allowed them to come in, disarming them as they reached the wall. Others defiantly essayed to advance, but opposite the old Fourteenth, none could get over a low rail fence a short distance in front of the stone wall without our permission.*

The color bearer of the 14th Tennessee, with not a man of his regiment within a rod of him advanced steadily until he reached this fence, when he rested his colors before him, then drew himself up to his full hight, looking us calmly in the face. There he stood for several awful moments, when the sharp crack of two or three rifles fired simultaneously sent his brave soul to its Maker.
... Just as the color bearer of the 14th Tenn. was shot, several of our men jumped to their feet with the intention of getting the colors but were restrained by the officers

Gen. Alexander Hays, commanding the 3d Division, 2d Corps at Gettysburg. Box 1, Vol. 2, PG 85, #1645, Edward B. Eaton Collection, Connecticut State Archives, Connecticut State Library.

until Major Ellis buckled his side arms upon Sergt. Major Hincks and gave him the preference of bringing them in They were the first colors taken, and while desperate fighting was going on just to our left, Gen Gibbons [Gibbon] took them, and rode along the crest with the flag at his horse's heels.[34] *Brigham was one of these who started for the flag and was shot . . . while attempting to do so.*[35]

Then you ought to have heard the Exhultant Shouts of our Brave Boys as the whole Rebel Force gave way in utter confusion leaving thousands and thousands of Killed, Wounded and Missing in our hands. What a sight it was, where but a short time before had stood the Flower of the Rebel Army in all the Pomp of Pride and Power was now covered with Dead in every conceivable Posture, and such a Wailing Cry, mingled with Groans of the Dieing [later changed to "Dying" in pencil] is past conception. Oh for a thousand or two fresh men to charge upon the discomfited Foe, and push them Home. Could this have been done the Southron

Army might have been Anhiliated. As it was they suffered a Tremendous Defeat. Our Corp alone Captured 30 Stand of Colers, our Division taking 13 of them, 6 of which were captured by our own little Regt, besides this we took more Prisoners than we numbered men. I did not have the oppertunity to see the whole Fruit of our Victory, but I saw a part of them brought in amid the Exhultant shouts of the Boys, and while i was rejoicing with them I was sent rolling in the Dust being Hit for the third time upon this Eventful day and was this time Dabled [disabled?] for ever carrying a Gun in Active Service again ["again" later crossed out in pencil]. After this I saw but the usual Hospital scenes, which is not very interesting to relate. One thing I ought to do is thank the Citizens of Hanover, Pa. Baltimore, Md and Willmington, Del for their kindness to us in coming from Glorious Gettysburg.

Letter File #71

July 6, 1863 Near Gettysburg Pa

Dear Sister i Just received a mail of three letters and 2 paper for Ben which i sent on to him i am happy to inform you that he is in good spirits and walking around and he told mike fay that he should try and come home i think is chance of coming is very good as their is a great many Badly wounded and they will want all they room for them their is in they hospitals Ben can travel and i think he will come so you stay at home untill you here from him as you might travel a great deal out here and not find him i wrote before on they fourth but i did not know whether it would come or not Ben is not hurt very bad they Back of is shoulder is Bruised but their is nothing Broke i dont know [p. 2] but it is a good Job for him if we are going to have many more days like them as we have had lately frank stoughtons has a very bad wound George Brigham is not so Bad as was thought at first i dont know but John Julian is dead By this time william goodell was shot dead and we buried him on they fourth i got a board and cut is name on it so if any one come after him they can find it our regiment as not had any more fighting since they 3 i was picking up guns all day sunday and Burying Dead rebels which took us all day we are now laying about five miles Back from they Battle field ready to move any time our regiment is very small now only about one hundred and thirty men their is only nine in our company i am well But for a cold i got with Being wet these [p. 4] 3 day you write to me as soon as you have time and send me five dollars so that i can buy some thing i aint got much time to write at present so you must excuse my Bad writing I have Just seen they Chaplin and he say our wounded are doing well i sent a rebel canteen down to ben as i know he did not have any i will write more as soon as i can get a little time from your Brother John Hirst if we stay here to morrow i will try and go and se Ben But you stay at home till you know for certain where he is

～～～

Letter File #72

Chestnut Hill Hospital
July 9.th 1863

Dear Sarah,

I left Gettysburg on the 7.th and arrived here this morning. my health is good. Come and see me if you want to see a good looking chap that is learning to take things in a good natured way. I am in the same ward as Joe, and I should like to get Joe and myself transfered to New Haven, so that we could go home once in a while. if you Come you had better see Mr Loomis about this matter. Brigham was getting along first rate, while Stoughten was somewhat improving. If your mother did not leave Rockville yet, just bring her along with you and leave her to me. hoping you are getting along as well as myself. I remain yours as ever, Benj Hirst.

Chapter 9

The Narratives and World View

Samuel Fiske was right. The men welcomed the change from the culture of the winter camp to the challenge of the march and the prospect of combat. Ben's letters during this period were upbeat, less gloomily self-centered, less laden with chores for Sarah. His discussions of health were more cursory, showing less of the morbid fatalism that had infused his ruminations from winter camp. His concern with health was less tied up with his vigilance and discourses on officers and other shirks—less interwoven, that is, with the ramifications of the courage/cowardice dichotomy. There were more things going on around him to distract him, and they were important events—life-and-death affairs.

His version of manly courage remained the dominant feature of his constructed social image.[1] Once again the interplay of the ideal manly image and the real combat experience guided his prose, which was dynamic with a Victorian working-class notion of appropriate style for portraying important events. Above all, Ben looked upon the important events of spring and summer of 1863 as a chance to reestablish his image of manliness that may have been undermined by Fredericksburg. For all he knew, some home folks were still characterizing him as a ridiculous hypocrite.

His Chancellorsville narratives were a positive start at image reconstruction. He and Company D were portrayed as hardened veterans now, standing jaded and skeptical while other soldiers cheered Hooker's bragging optimism before the battle. When his regiment broke on the morning of 3 May, it was a controlled break—a falling back in good order in contrast to the uncontrolled stampede of some 11th Corps men the evening before. He felt the regiment had done its manly duty for the most part. Neither he nor the other men were fought out.

The image of cool, controlled courage was undermined at one point when he made an interesting tactical observation: the men of the 14th fired too soon, before they could see the enemy. This contributed to their breaking under the Rebs' flanking attack. Fiske agreed, having time in Libby Prison to reflect on the subject. His extensive characterization fleshes out Hirst's more laconic appraisal. It also indicates fundamental shifts in thinking not only about infantry tactics but about the manifestation of true courage:

[W]e don't fight in such a common-sense way as ... [the Rebels] do. Shall I tell you how one of our lines of battle engages? They go in in fine style, steadily, in a good line, and without any flinching; halt at what is held to be a desirable point, and, at the command, commence firing, standing, kneeling, or lying down, as may be ordered. Then, as in all their previous training they have been taught to load and fire as rapidly as possible, three or four times a minute, they go into the business with all fury; every man vying with his neighbor as to the number of cartridges he can ram into his piece, and spit out of it. The smoke arises in a minute or two, so you can see nothing where to aim. The noise is deafening and confusing to the last degree. The impression gets around of a tremendous conflict going on. The trees in the vicinity suffer sorely, and the clouds a good deal. By and by the guns get heated, and won't go off, and the cartridges begin to give out. The men have become tired with their furious exertions, and the excitement and din of their own firing, and without knowing any thing about the effect produced upon the enemy, very likely having scarcely had one glimpse of the enemy at all, begin to think they have fought about enough, and it is nearly time to retire. Meanwhile, the rebels, lying quietly a hundred or two yards in front, crouching on the ground or behind trees, answer our fire very leisurely, as they get a chance for good aim (about one shot to our three hundred), hitting about as many as we do, and waiting for the wild tornado of ammunition to pass over their heads; and, when our burst of fighting is pretty much over, they have only commenced. They probably rise, and advance upon us with one of their unearthly yells, as they see our fire slackens. Our boys, finding that the enemy has survived such an avalanche of fire as we have rolled in upon him, conclude he must be invincible, and, being pretty much out of ammunition, retire. Now, if I had charge of a regiment or brigade, I'd put every man in the guard-house who could be proved to have fired more than twenty rounds in any one battle; ... and in every possible way, would endeavor to banish the Chinese style of fighting, with a big noise and smoke, and imitate, rather, the backwoods style of our opponents.[2]

Earlier in the war, the Chinese style of fighting was considered courageous. While not gainsaying the courage involved, the hardened Captain Fiske declared it had now become stupid and tragic. We cannot know if Ben would have banished the Chinese style of fighting in future battles. At Gettysburg, the tactical demands were not the same as Chancellorsville, and afterward he was out of it. However, there was a reported tendency among Union troops to imitate the backwoods style (some called it "Indian style") in battles over the Chancellorsville terrain a year later.[3]

Many of the shirks were by then winnowed out of the service. Some had skedaddled at Chancellorsville, but most eventually returned to act like men. The

Rockville private left to guard the knapsacks had not run for a safer place; he stood his ground and was taken prisoner when the Rebs overran the area. Nonetheless, some of the skedaddlers from that battle did not come back. Given his earlier preoccupation with cowards and his possible misgivings about his own steel, Ben's pleasure and pride at being assigned to help find and arrest them were perhaps understated in his letter. No coward would be given such duty.

The relaxing of the vigilance was evident in Ben's portrayals of the 14th's officers under fire. The new lot of company officers passed the test of courage, even if they could still not avoid doing damned-fool things. Lieutenant Simpson evidently stood with the men in the thick of the Chancellorsville fight, but then took off into the woods with his attendant, Morton, and got both of them captured by the Rebs. We are not told why Lt. Henry W. Wadhams had been placed under arrest and kept out of the battle. Sergeant Stoughton was again left in charge.

Not all leaders were to be let off the hook. Ben raised his sights to target the division and army commands. The men had fought well, but their division commander, "Blinky" French, had positioned them badly and angrily dismissed their expressed concerns about their right flank. After Hooker manifestly fumbled away the Chancellorsville fight, Ben conveyed a loss of confidence in him and in the army high command in general. As he put it, the stalwart common soldiers had been "humbugged again."

Ben was pleased with his own conduct at Chancellorsville. He portrayed both courage and control in a single statement: "I was never in better Humor for a Fight . . . and never felt better able to take care of myself" (5 May 1863). He implicitly argued that his courageous reputation had been redeemed, even if the army's had not. Would the Chancellorsville narratives suffice to restore his ideal social image in Rockville? He could not be sure, for the regiment and the army had in fact been whipped twice in succession. After a defeat, boasting of one's courage and blaming one's leaders are dubious antidotes for small-town skepticism.

Two themes dominated Ben's camp portrayals: the furlough business, which surfaced again to eat away at company morale, and the long periods of idle waiting after getting packed up for the next march, which had a similar effect. John fought boredom by going fishing and carving finger rings from bone. Evidently, the hard feelings about Fredericksburg had softened between Ben and Sergeant Brigham. For Ben's birthday, Brigham provided a ham and some potatoes. They would also have had a drink or two if only ardent spirits had been available. He reflected on the dwindling numbers of soldiers left in Company D. During this interval, Ben mostly contemplated the odds favoring a furlough.

If the present batch of regimental officers was not cowardly, regimental authority was still manifestly unfair. Men were being cheated out of their rightful turns to visit home. The only way to get special consideration was to join the influence-peddling game—if not by becoming chummy with one's immediate superiors, which Ben clearly did not wish to do, then by bringing important influence to bear from outside the army. If Squire Dwight Loomis had no impact, then conceivably Governor Buckingham would, "Wooly Head" though he was. Authority was manifestly unfair and bureaucracy was inherently indifferent. One needed a strategy for bringing influence to bear if one was going to get any special consideration. Yet it had to be done fairly and honestly, in manly fashion. Ben was quick to suspect others' strategies as devious and unmanly. This informed his views about furloughs and the process of officers' promotions: "merit is the last qualification looked for here" (5 June 1863). The promotion of Sergeant Stoughton was a remarkable exception; it reaffirmed the singular importance of courage as a criterion of merit.

As absentee head of household, Ben's lists of chores around the home and other duties for Sarah were by now almost completely replaced by his growing concern for her health. It is not clear what the problem with her "head" was (9 May 1863), but one of her symptoms was certainly depression. She could not find anyone to do the heavy work around the yard, and when she learned of the Chancellorsville fight, she again wanted to come to the seat of war to find Ben. Again, Ben told her it would be foolish to come and reassured her that if he needed her he would send for her.

He tried several methods of talking her out of her depression. One was to compare her fate to that of the women in desolate Virginia. She was to stop feeling sorry for herself because the women living near the Virginia battlegrounds were infinitely worse off. Another method was to persuade her to take a trip to visit friends. This she eventually did in June. A third method he used was to absolve her from guilt about not being able to perform the chores herself. The garden should be lost rather than Sarah losing her health "trying to do a man's work" (28 May 1863).

There it was again: Men's work compared to women's work, and the physical danger of women trying to work like men. Furthermore, in Ben's blunt consideration, Sarah had let her womanly emotions once again assert themselves as foolishness.

Yet despite her distress, Ben could not spare Sarah the frustrating details of the furlough business because he felt he needed her to marshal still more powerful outside influence. Fortunately for both of them, the flurry of assigning furloughs was relatively brief. Ben continued to expect Sarah to do physically less-demanding tasks, such as sending him shirts and managing the traffic in checks and currency between home and the front.

Ben's letters did not contain the tender passages that had infrequently appeared in those he wrote from winter camp. This may have been yet another tactic for easing her misery by setting an example of manly control and obligation to duty. He undoubtedly continued to have tender thoughts about her.

His efforts may have been successful: Sarah seemed to feel better even before her trip to Dedham, despite the fact that her mother was still living with her in Rockville. After Ben's plain-talking letter on the subject, she reported she no longer wished to join him in the field.

Once Republican Governor William Buckingham was reelected, Ben lost interest in political commentary except for the single politicized issue of conscription. He and other soldiers remained keenly interested in seeing that the draft was fairly and broadly enforced. But now Ben faced a moral dilemma: his oldest brother, Bill, was thinking of joining up. While the countless able-bodied men who were still skulking at home deserved to relieve the burden of the men at the front, and were cowardly for not stepping forward sooner, the hardened veterans could not countenance putting their own close relatives up to the test they themselves had passed. The ideal of forcing every man to try his courage and patriotism persisted—and would become even more strident; but there were important exceptions.[4]

At last, on 14 June, there came a march order that was not countermanded. As in late April, the men welcomed the end to stultifying camp life. Ben and his comrades in Company D were particularly happy to be moving out of Virginia and back into friendly territory. He noted the lushness of the land in Maryland. Fiske agreed: "[I]t was almost like getting to Paradise from—another place; the getting-out of abominable, barren, ravaged Old Virginia, into fertile, smiling Maryland."[5] But as before, the basic theme of Ben's march portrayals was his tough veteran's resistance to adversity. His telling of the shedding of equipment and heat prostration was intended to show his endurance compared to that of others—although if they were all hardened by then, this inadvertently threatened the hardened veteran's image he was constructing. Evidently, it was a canny veteran's tactic of keeping oak leaves in his mouth and lacing his water with cayenne pepper that somehow slaked his thirst. Elsewhere, he implicitly adopted the veteran's condescension in hobnobbing with a Connecticut artillery unit that had seen no combat. Captain Fiske, too, was convinced the 14th's men were now harder: "There is much less straggling, and much less pillaging, than in any march of the troops that I have yet accompanied. Our men are now veterans, and acquainted with the ways and resources of campaigning. There are very few sick among us. The efficient strength, in proportion to our numbers, is vastly greater than when we were green volunteers."[6] The hardened captain's view of hardened veteranhood had shifted dramatically from his earlier callow disgust at "undisciplined and disorderly" veterans before Antietam. (Either Fiske was unaware of the sacking of the 11th Corps sutler by the veterans of the 14th, or he deliberately left his praise unqualified.)

Even these jaded veterans were horrified, however, when they filed through the battlefield of the two Bull Run fights. Ben, Fiske, and the regimental history all remarked on the vista of half-buried skeletons.[7]

A dogged cynicism that went with veterans' status in the Army of the Potomac at that time was also apparent in Ben's march narrative. His sarcastic order to Sarah for a black silk handkerchief necktie was to prepare him properly for the "next Grand Skidadle"; he and his company had been needlessly bothered by a series of

"Grand Scares." All the arduous marching from Falmouth toward Gettysburg, he declared at the time, was merely "to please old Hooker who I hear has just played out. I hope to God it is true" (28 June 1863). (He seemed to forget this in his later narrative of the Gettysburg fight, where he blamed marching on the Confederates' outrageous invasion.) Captain Fiske shared this cynicism of late June. He continued his sarcastic tirades against Hooker and the high command and moved downward to blast his division commander, General French, for bungling a simple river crossing. Fiske then turned his criticism of French and his staff into a general point about the ideals of leadership: nothing was more desirable than "a cordial understanding between the soldiers and officers; officers should care about the comfort of the men, and share in their privations."[8] These were the same ideals Ben used in his earlier critiques of the company and regimental officers.

The prebattle idioms of hardness and cynicism and veteranness for Ben and Fiske became a kind of gauntlet to be flung down before the Army of the Potomac's high command. The men were overdue for a major victory. If yet another defeat awaited them at the end of this hard march, they would not lose for want of being tough, courageous soldiers. Later, after victory, the cynicism could be jettisoned and the tough courage recast as a key to success; but it was too soon for that just now.

With the hardened veterans' disregard for the rigors of the march, Ben and Company D moved out "gayley" toward Gettysburg and the distant rumbling of artillery—pleased at the prospect of combat. Fiske, writing at noon on 2 July, shared their pleasure. His worry was that Lee's army would withdraw before he and his troops could get into the fight.[9]

Ben's Gettysburg narratives were the high point of his important events genre, just as the battle itself was the high point of his army career and perhaps of his life. He put far more emotion into the October portrayal than any of the preceding ones. The euphoria of the army's victory sustained him. Compared to his other portrayals, he took a great deal of time—mostly idle time in the hospital whenever Sarah was not by his side—to think about it and probably to refine the verbiage.

The bright victory of the day gave him, and hundreds of others, free rein to seize heroic words and phrases to describe it for readers afterward. Some of these were in his enthusiastic note to Sarah on 5 July, but they came in a gush in his more reflective October narrative. "Gallant" and "brave" were among the most popular. These he used to draw his theme of personal and collective courage.

He fashioned the detailed description of the skirmish line as his first-person centerpiece of the account. Events during the rest of the day were generalized to the more heroic editorial third person. This particular skirmish line, he wrote, was not a healthy place to be. The strength of each of the two skirmisher companies—B and D—that morning was about twenty men. Each was divided into two reliefs or squads that rotated at intervals between the advance line and the reserve.

Ben wrote that he "felt a little timid" about walking erect through the wheat to the advance line, leaving readers to wonder whether in fact he courageously but foolishly did so. A corporal from Company B, Elnathan B. Tyler, was more explicit: "Those of us detailed to go out on the [advance] line *crawled* out across the wheat field to the fence beyond."[10] The regiment's chaplain, H. S. Stevens, was watching the picket action from behind the wall on the main defensive line:

> When the [picket] reliefs went to their places there was excitement. The relieving squad would leave the reserve rendezvous moving in any way possible to avoid the observation of the enemy, but when a place was reached where exposure was unavoidable each would take to running at highest speed, and upon reaching the fence [along the advance line] would throw himself to the ground. Then must the relieved ones get back to the reserve in a similar manner; and "relieving" seemed a misnomer. The start of the pickets on either side, to or from their places, was a signal for a lively popping all along the line of their opponents as long as a man was in sight. Not many of the runners were struck, for to hit such a rapidly moving object is a difficult feat; but the pop! pop! crack! crack! would go on all the same; and the eagerness to hit would make some shooters careless, so furnishing themselves targets for some hidden watchers.[11]

Men on the advance line lay two or three fence posts apart, more or less hidden from enemy sharpshooters by the wheat behind the fence. In this concealment, it was dangerous to keep up a desultory fire against enemy sharpshooters. The puff of gray smoke from a skirmisher's rifle-musket instantly revealed his position to the vigilant and very effective Confederate marksmen. Thus, when Ben wrote that "we were soon popping away as lively as crickets" once he reached the advance line, he was sending an additional message about his courage.

In case home readers missed his point, he underscored it with the anecdote about his fouled musket. Evidently, he had been popping away so often that the black powder residue had clogged his gun barrel (soldiers were issued special "clean-out" bullets to reduce the problem, but these were unpopular and often thrown away). His aside also tells us more about the armament of the 14th Connecticut in the battle. Companies A and B had originally been issued Sharps breechloading rifles, with a much higher rate of fire than the standard muzzleloading rifle-musket. Regimental strength on the third day was below 200, meaning that if all the Sharps of the regiment had been available then, every man would have been using one. Company D's Sergeant Brigham somehow armed himself with a Sharps, but Ben and about half the regiment still carried muzzleloaders. Years afterward, veterans emphasized the effectiveness of the Sharps in the defense of the 14th's main position.[12]

Ben and his men undoubtedly took fire from the Rebel sharpshooters in the Bliss barn to his right front. The Confederates, however, were more interested in the

Union artillerymen serving the guns on Cemetery Ridge. It was a long shot, but the Rebel marksmen were good enough. Before noon, the enemy were driven out "for good" and the buildings burned by the remaining eight companies of the 14th. The smoke was still rising as the Confederates stepped out on their assault in the afternoon.

Again, the valued courage was a cool courage, and certainly Ben's narrative stressed his coolness on the skirmish line. After the barrage lifted, the coolness again was manifest in the withdrawal of Ben and the other Federal skirmishers in the face of the Confederate attack. The skirmishers fell back in good order, bringing their wounded with them and turning to fire occasionally at the advancing enemy. This was exactly how a defensive skirmish line should behave, even though it was the first time Ben's company had served in that capacity in combat.

The courage was steadfast. Ben lay still with the artillery projectiles flying over him. He didn't mention it, but the sun beating down and the lack of breeze must have added immensely to his discomfort. (At that same time, the regiment's sergeant major back on the main line silently watched the sweat from his face make puddles in the dirt where he lay, occasionally showered by light gravel as one of the guns of Arnold's Battery just behind him joined the barrage.)[13] Once Ben was back behind the low wall on the main line, he noted that men were resolutely emptying their cartridge boxes in front of them. This gave them greater speed in loading, but also symbolically declared their brave intention to hold their position at all hazards. Did Ben, too, empty his cartridge box?

Under emphatic orders, the 14th coolly held its fire until the attacking enemy line came up against the fences along Emmitsburg Road. The portions of the fences still standing were too stout to be broken easily. The Confederates were forced to climb over them, bunching up while waiting to cross and slowed over the rails by their weapons and equipment, so as to make the Federal musketry and canister particularly devastating.[14]

Then came Ben's wound after the Confederate charge had been broken. Ben wrote on 5 July that he was "thank ful" he had come out so well after his close calls. At that time, he and his brother wanted to assure Sarah that Ben was not seriously hurt. In his hasty post-battle note to her, John gave Sarah some manly plain talk about keeping her womanly emotions under control and not—repeat, *not*—to try to join Ben until Ben sent her instructions to do so. John also wrote that Ben "was in very good spirits" as they both walked down to the hospital. Compare this with a generalizing comment by Confederate artillerist William M. Dame: "Wounded men coming from under fire are, as a rule, cheerful, often jolly. Being able to get, honorably, from under fire, with the mark of manly service to show, is enough to make a fellow cheerful, even with a hole through him."[15] But there was no hole through Ben. In fact, it was the classic million-dollar wound. He was moved to a hospital near his old home of Chester. Sarah could visit him there, and he could deal with his mother-in-law personally (if that gave him any pleasure). Three months later, he was certain the injury would keep him from coming back into combat; but the constraints of the courageous ideal prevented him from conveying a sense of relief—assuming that was one of the emotions he was experiencing. Still, an ambivalence must have persisted as the war went on and other men with apparently much more serious wounds—Frank Stoughton, for one—returned to combat after recuperating. Too, Ben lacked the visible scar that could be worn as the lasting emblem of his courage. Nonetheless, the wound was honorably won.

Some string-pulling was still needed, however, and Sarah was handed the task: She was again to approach Squire Dwight Loomis, this time to ask his influence in getting Ben and Joe both transferred to a hospital in New Haven. It would not be Rockville, but much, much closer to it.

Ben's October narrative revealed some shifts in attitudes and behavior from his earlier heroic accounts. The pivotal cause of these was the fact of victory itself, both for the regiment and for Ben. The portrayal of fear had changed. In the earlier narratives, Ben always attributed fear to others and never called it by its name. Instead, he used euphemisms then popular among soldiers and civilians alike. Those with fear had "blanched faces," "pale faces," "tight faces." In his October account, Ben came closer—as close as he would come—to describing his own terror: "I felt a little timid about walking erect"; "It makes my Blood Tingle in my veins now to think of"; and "how we did Hug the ground expecting every moment was to be our last." In his 5 July note—intended for a smaller group of readers—he wrote, "I thought it was all up with me, for a minuet or two, until I opened my eyes to look at the Hole and it wernt there," and, "with a yell I thought I was gone for sure." Yet, Ben mostly continued to characterize fear as something others, not necessarily he himself, experienced. His use of virtually all but the first person singular in his constructions made fear a more generalized, less focused presence. He remained a photographer whose own face was invisible to readers at home.[16]

The change, however slight, suggests that in Ben's view his honorable behavior and wounding at Gettysburg had not only restored but enhanced his manly social image at home. Thus, he had the right to claim—fleetingly—personal emotions that might have compromised that image earlier. Soldiers had special dispensation to growl; soldiers with honorable wounds had dispensation to sidle up more closely to admissions of fear. In such instances, the ideal of manliness could absorb another of its polar opposites, and the manliness was made stronger by doing so (just as brave Captain Fiske's funeral eulogy invoked his childlike qualities as testimony to his manly conduct).

His Gettysburg narratives compared to those of Chancellorsville were even less concerned about shirks who lacked the requisite measure of courage. In his October narrative, he showed signs of this earlier contempt for "Skulkers, Shirks, and Camp followers" but concluded they were more ridiculous than threatening. Evidently, they were not from his company or regiment, and besides, this time they could not be portrayed as contributors to a major defeat. In both the July and October narratives, there was only bravery in his regiment and his 2d Corps. He referred to both Company D and the 14th with the same sort of endearment he used toward Sarah in one of his earlier letters: "My own little wife" and "our own little regiment." (The regiment had in fact become "little" by 3 July. Only about 180 of the original 1,015 who left Hartford less than a year before were on the line.)

Brave victory washed clean the reputation of officers. In Ben's October narrative, he turned an apparent criticism of Gen. Winfield S. Hancock, his corps commander, into a blast against Rebeldom. His company and regimental officers once again behaved courageously under fire. He mentioned the requisite calm, reassuring comments from Gens. John Gibbon and Alexander Hays. Almost certainly, Hays did more than give them "a few . . . words" as the Confederate battle lines approached. Hays's colorful language, stentorian voice, and high-dudgeoned physical excitement in combat were to become well known to the men in the regiment. (They would also come to despise him for his brash foolishness at the battle of Morton's Ford, where his drunken orders may have needlessly killed or wounded some of them.)[17] There were no more suggestions that McClellan was still without peer.

Linderman notes a close connection between courage and godliness in the soldiers' world view.[18] Ben, however, mostly left God or explicit reference to religious tenets out of his earlier correspondence to Sarah, including the important events genre. In his October letter, he alluded to God and religious conviction only once. He had faith, and he strove to avoid profanity in even his routine correspondence. "[I]lebe Damd" was as coarse as he got, and then only to add unusual emphasis. In many soldiers' world views, there was a distinct parallel between religious faith and the conduct of the war.[19]

In marked contrast to these other soldiers, including some in Ben's own regiment, there is nothing to indicate that he saw God's work in the outcome of battles. More specifically, he did not portray the Gettysburg victory as proof positive that God was on the side of the Union.

Ben's restraint on profanity was most noticeable in his characterization of the "Oaths and imprecations" that rose to a roar as the two sides drew closer and the men loaded and fired as quickly as they could. (At about this time in the assault, the men's roars could be heard above the din of musketry.)[20] "Give them Hell x x x"? Surely with adrenaline pumping and mortality in the balance, some men would have been coarser than that despite prevailing sentiments—especially at home—against swearing. It was, of course, ungodly to swear. But it was also indicative of an unseemly loss of manly control, another crucial component of the social image Ben was striving to maintain. Even though Ben was ostensibly committed to "truth" in his Gettysburg narratives, the more powerful allegiance to his social image dictated that he use the enigmatic "x x x" to indicate the profanity was heavy, yet to leave the specifics to readers' imaginations.

In this passage, he succeeded in communicating something of the emotional pitch of combat and the pervasive sense that the 14th Connecticut and the 2d Corps were not simply whipping the attacking Confederates, but were paying them back for past humiliation inflicted—most profoundly at Fredericksburg. This last battle was also much on the minds of other Federal units during Longstreet's assault. The men of 20th Massachusetts just south of the Angle were shouting "Fredericksburg!" while blasting the attackers to their front.[21] Like Ben's portrayals of prebattle anxiety, there is no clear statement of what he himself was doing. Was Sgt. Benjamin Hirst yelling invective as he pumped bullets into the onrushing gray lines? Was "Never mind who is Hit" something *he* shouted? And, if so, was it an order to distracted privates or an exultant public notice that the Fredericksburg incident was now behind him?

Ben's October characterization of the Confederate enemy was unusual for him. Before, he had always referred to them simply as "the enemy" or "Rebels" or "Grey Backs." In his October letter, he labored at unflattering descriptors: "that Rebellious Crew" with "Polluting footsteps"; Cursed Rebels; Blasted Rebels; the second line sent "howling" back after the first one. Why this shift? Linderman discusses the need to create a conceptual distance between one's righteous own and the enemy others. Mitchell describes a series of fundamental alienations experienced by Federal soldiers from their communities, their surroundings, and the enemy. This last was bolstered by the pattern of characterizing the enemy as "savage"— that is, unmanly, uncontrolled.[22] To see opponents as such was to strengthen the soldier's conviction that he was fighting for a righteous cause, and to ease the qualms about killing fellow human beings. To portray the enemy thus for readers was to bolster *their* conceptions that the soldier was doing his manly, patriotic duty. While Ben was unquestionably concerned about this last, it is not clear why he did not use the same literary technique in his earlier narratives, when his image was somewhat less secure. It seems unnecessary to strengthen alienation if he was never returning to combat. Although his brother John never was caught up with the important events prose to the extent Ben was, John continued to refer simply to "the enemy," "Johnnies," or "Rebs" for the remainder of the war. Ben may have been simply imitating prose that he admired in other accounts of the Gettysburg battle. Or it may have been alienation working in an opposite fashion to that characterized by Mitchell: Ben felt a measure of identity with enemy infantrymen as long as he was sharing the front with them and they were a constant presence.[23] Once he was removed from that landscape, their humanness became less palpable to him—hence more easily questioned in heroic hyperbole. Unquestionably, Ben resented the Confederates' trespass on the soil of his adopted home state.

In none of Ben's narratives did he report killing an enemy soldier—whether or not he could be sure he had done so in the swirl of combat. Like countless other heroic accounts of Longstreet's assault, Ben's reflected his respectful awe at the Confederate steadfastness and discipline in their moving lines of battle. He even used the same phrase found in countless other accounts: the enemy marched "as though upon Parade." The literary distancing was not unqualified or total.

The comrades and others out there on the skirmish line and back behind the wall with Ben are anonymous. We are not told, for example, whether his brother

John was among the skirmishers. Lying hidden in the wheat, did Ben and John call back and forth to one another to be sure each was still all right? Others on that same line did, as they recalled in the regimental history. Ben described what he himself did and felt—or he shifted to the editorial and less personal "we" to portray more inclusive reactions. Why he left his brother almost entirely out of the October narrative is not clear. Neither John nor Joe was mentioned in his Antietam important events accounts (as distinct from his hasty notes to Sarah letting her know they were safe), and Joe's wounding at Fredericksburg was not in the important events narrative of that battle. Ben knew the dead corporal on the picket line at Gettysburg, but his name was not given, nor were those of his own company who were killed or wounded. This was deliberate. But why? Were the details considered too personal, too laden with selfish emotion? If so, then why the detailed discussion of himself on the skirmish line? In his view, was heroic prose to be elevated beyond the first person singular because it was heroic, larger than one man, or two, or three? In this same perspective, was the "Date no matter" another way of saying the events described were too important to be burdened with the specific dates of the description itself? Or to be dragged down by descriptions of the blood and bustle in a field hospital after the fight? Were these, in short, largely stylistic decisions, or were they another example of emotional distancing, concealing one's innermost self from readers through a series of more anonymous constructions?

Ben was also concerned to spare Sarah and others the goriest details of combat. The location and severity of wounds to his Rockville chums—whom Sarah knew—were described, but without vivid details. He did not work at portraying the effects of canister or shell on massed ranks of attackers or the bloody wounds among those brought into the hospital. Once again, he seemed to feel that graphic detail of the effects of battle would simply add gratuitous misery. Yet he certainly preserved such detail in his memory.

There were two tactical concerns in Ben's Gettysburg narratives that cannot be traced to his prewar world view. One is the preoccupation with the number of enemy flags captured. In stressing this, he was typical of the soldiers of his time, for whom a regimental battle flag was the embodiment of the regiment's lifestuff and that of the home communities.[24] The 14th Connecticut officially captured five of them. Four men risked their lives to take them, one was wounded in the effort, and three received Medals of Honor. (There were persistent rumors that a sixth flag, a "beautiful silk one," was stuffed inside an officer's coat and never turned over to higher authorities.)[25] It was an achievement of unprecedented glory, not equaled by the regiment before or afterward. In a particularly unchivalrous but personally consistent act of combat euphoria, Gen. Alexander Hays and two aides gathered a clutch of captured Confederate flags and dragged them in the dust along his division line from the backs of their cantering horses. This was observed by a Confederate artillery officer, Maj. W. T. Poague, standing beside the distraught General Pickett as the surviving attackers withdrew.[26]

The other tactical concern was the lack of Federal pursuit of the repulsed Rebels. The October narrative was armed with hindsight, honed by the abundant newspaper and army palaver about Gen. George G. Meade's cautious pursuit of the retreating Confederates.[27] "Oh, for a thousand or two fresh men to charge upon the discomfited Foe, and push them Home," wrote Ben. Despite the hindsight, he refused to join the critics of General Meade. His lament suggests he considered the Army of the Potomac too played out to counterattack. (In any case, one or two thousand men would not have been sufficient.) His 5 July observation was fresher and different: "[I]f our Artillery could have helped us but very few would have got away." (Just as the Confederates began to fall back, a fresh battery reportedly unlimbered just to the 14th Connecticut's left, in the position earlier vacated by Arnold's Battery, and opened fire on the retreating clusters.)[28] Both portrayals have a common theme: *Something* should have been done immediately following the repulse of Longstreet's men.

The next day, 4 July, and on 7 July when they pulled out in pursuit of Lee's army, only nine of the Rockville boys were present for duty in Company D.

Epilogue

On 7 July, Ben left the field hospital with other walking wounded for a nine-mile march to Hanover and the train to Baltimore. The collection of Ben's original narratives ends with the important events description of Gettysburg. At the military hospital in Chestnut Hill, Pennsylvania, he shared a ward with his brother Joe, enjoyed frequent visits from Sarah, and took furloughs in Rockville. Sarah rented their home in Rockville so that she could be located close to Ben for several months. Letters from John repeatedly urged him to be in no hurry to return to the regiment.[1] Once his broken shoulder healed, he was transferred to the 2d Battalion of the Veterans' Reserve Corps for the duration.

The Gettysburg battle also effectively ended Company D's Rockville heritage: *"From this time forward Company D was never the company it had been."*[2] The regiment's losses at Gettysburg were replaced by conscripts and substitutes— "cons" and "subs" in John's lean prose—who robbed him and the other remaining Rockville boys, deserted in droves, and earned his perennial contempt. The Rockville knot of veterans present for duty hovered at between six and ten men from then on, its members' continuing deaths made up by comrades returning from sickness or wounds.

John fought on for two more years in all of the regiment's battles except Reams's Station (25 August 1864). During the second day of the Wilderness battle the following spring, he took up the regiment's national flag and carried it for the rest of the war. Courage, he assured home folks several times, had little to do with shouldering his hazardous responsibility. He merely wanted to enjoy the color guard's exemption from all the picket and guard details. His only close call in combat came in a skirmish along the Boydton Plank Road in 1864, when a Confederate bullet parted his knapsack shoulder strap.

He wrote regularly, but poorly and mostly without emotion; yet at times his labored style conveyed more feeling through understatement than did Ben's eloquent important events. He and one of his few remaining Rockville chums, John Billson (also a textile operative from England), marched happily from Appomattox to Washington when it was over. In his last ebullient letter to Rockville, he asked

Sarah to get his "good . . . white shirts ready again" because he expected to need them soon.[3]

On World View

Ben's world view can be portrayed as a system that included several basic facets: manliness, respectability/esteem, authority, hierarchy, gender, religiosity, and ethnicity. All facets were closely and dynamically intertwined, so that qualities and tenets of each incorporated those of the others. Together, as a system, they were the basic resources Ben drew upon in portraying his various social identities in various specific contexts. (Of course, much of his daily behavior was not premeditated; but the portion we can still observe—his narratives—most certainly was.) For all their diversity, his identities—army sergeant, brother, household head, citizen of Rockville, and others—shared a singular emphasis on manly respectability.

He entered the war with a world view derived largely from his labor experience as broadly conceived, but also from his education and religious convictions—themselves influenced by his and his family's economic production.[4] To conclude simply that Ben was a product of his working class background is unhelpfully general. Rather, I have suggested that specific features of his class experience preadapted him to some—but not all—features of army culture and social structure. I have further assumed that because textile mills formed Rockville's prewar economic axis, others in Company D had a labor experience similar to Ben's and, therefore, held a world view similarly preadapted to army life. This assumption must not be overworked: The mills were class-stratified on the basis of who owned and who labored. The "laboring class" was itself ranked internally on the basis of skill and wages. Surely diverse world views were at work in a single factory setting.

Ben's concern with manly respectability carried facets of his world view well beyond the weaving department and linked them to more broadly shared features of world view among middle-class Victorians, many from a more wealthy and leisured background than Ben's. His narratives were designed in part to lay claim to a higher socioeconomic station than that of common laborer. We will see that his postwar decisions confirm what was largely implicit in his narratives. He did not regard factory work as a fulfilling career endowed with spiritual grace. It was a job, a means to a more satisfying end.[5]

His attitudes about womanhood and behavior toward Sarah also suggest some social distancing between him and common labor. Respectable women did not work in mills unless it became absolutely necessary. It was unhealthy and degrading.[6]

Specific behaviors among the Hirst household in wartime were obviously different from those of peacetime factory life, but the household remained a crucial adaptive unit. The economic necessity of Sarah's wartime efforts was probably established before the war. She was the men's accountant and banker.[7] There were other wartime adjustments to what must have been earlier themes, including her various efforts to sustain Ben's public image while he was away and her important contributions to making the army life of all three brothers more endurable. But deeper than all this lay the emotional bond between man and wife. Ben and Sarah obviously yearned to be together.

This became a major subplot of Ben's narratives, woven through the persistent finagling to get a furlough, Sarah's peremptory arrival at Falmouth, and the vicarious bittersweet pleasures of the boxes from home. For Sarah and Ben, as for other Victorians, family relations were central to a sense of well-being.[8] Ben's rank—both military and social—kept them apart, while others—those officers whose wives were not as burdened with home-front logistics—used the army camp as a locale for family togetherness. Victorian world view, among other incentives, imbued economically prosperous officers with a demanding need to bring wives into camp. These leisured wives were typically excluded from "business," in keeping with prevailing views about respectable womanhood.[9] Yet, prevailing views about respectable womanhood forced Ben to control his yearning and warn Sarah to stay away from him. The army camp of the enlisted men was no place for a respectable woman. Many enlisted men were frustrated by a lack of means to house and care for their wives and children in camp.

The Hirsts' marriage was probably strengthened by the war.[10] Unlike those of well-to-do officers, it was through separation rather than setting up house in esoteric surroundings. Ben implicitly conveyed renewed respect for Sarah's organizational efforts and her dogged determination to fulfill her part of the wartime household's maintenance. He acknowledged her greater autonomy during his absence—to take work in the mill, for example.[11] We cannot know if the autonomy shift carried over into their relationship after the war. Among more advantaged Victorians, wartime strains evidently produced no lasting power shifts in postwar marriage relations.[12]

Beyond Sarah and Ben's relationship, the Hirst brothers as a basic household unit of social and economic adaptation simply moved from the factory to the army. The brothers ate, slept, marched, and fought together and relied upon each other in crises. (Ironically, it was John, the most sickly of the three in the first months, who each time carried the other two brothers to safety after they were hit.) Joe and John used Ben to convey their wishes to Sarah, and evidently expected her to fulfill most of them.[13] Presumably this was a pattern set in their household relations before the war. In one major sense, there was no need to re-create a family relationship with others in Company D—in the first few months at least—because the Hirsts arrived with a family almost intact.[14]

Ben's feelings about ethnicity and his own ethnic identity were scarcely articulated. Possibly, he was trying to ignore his English birth, being very much aware of the strong nativist element in New England's respectable elite. (He probably retained traces of his English accent whether he wanted to or not.) But Rockville, like Rockdale, was—as Ben later mentioned—an ethnically diverse setting. In

Rockdale, English and Irish immigrants had managed to move upward in the social hierarchy through the "respectable" and into the "elite" strata. Some of Ben's close friends in the army were Irish or English, as he also noted. Rather than trying to conceal his ethnicity as part of his respectable aspirations, it is more likely that he simply took it for granted and considered it not worth mentioning in his narratives. Most of his readers, including Sarah, were probably not native born, so the topic or theme would have been unremarkable to them. When war broke out, Ben seemed to see himself mostly as an American.

Ben's views on authority and hierarchy in the army persisted from his prewar experience and soon became a constant theme. Overseers and factory managers were not inherently superior to those they managed; officers were not inherently superior to those they commanded. Factory and army hierarchy with gradations of authority was necessary, but ideally (in the laborers' or enlisted men's view) it did not extend to life outside either of these institutions.[15] This perspective was particularly important for those with middle-class aspirations.

In both the factory and the army, Ben's best interests could be served by the hierarchy. The trick was to make it work effectively to one's advantage. For Ben, this often took the form of circumventing immediate superiors to get action: Squire Loomis to get him a furlough, General Sumner to punish drunken officers, the people of Rockville to call attention to the plight of the soldiers.[16] Of course, the strategy worked only part of the time—just enough to keep it alive as an option.

The mill's social structure of unitary cooperation as a means for earning corporate profits involved a strong element of collaborative competition within task groups. To outdo one's peers was a way to get ahead. But, getting ahead involved learning some strategy, developing a kind of savoir-faire that was as much social as manual. Typically, getting ahead entailed creating a series of alliances with owners and fellow workers without alienating superiors (by effrontery) or peers (by either pretentiousness or bootlicking).[17] There was almost always an angle to getting something accomplished. Some were better at it than others, of course; but it was a vital body of strategic social wisdom, something to be learned through experience.

In the army one also needed social alliances: the tent group, the mess group, the true comrades to share victuals from home or to help when hit in combat. Officers could sign furloughs or offer temporary lodging in their headquarters. Possibly Ben's conclusion that army promotion was based more on social ties than competence was partly due to a frustrated upward mobility that he could not, respectably, express openly in his narratives. His repeated allegations, however, clearly reveal his conviction that there was a strategy to getting ahead. To be sure, merely to exist as a person requires social knowledge. Here, the focus is on the particular sort of social knowledge required and the similarity of factory and army contexts within which it accumulated.

The need for social alliances coexisted uneasily with the manly ideal of self-reliance. In a speech before the House in 1832, U.S. Representative John Davis of

Massachusetts idealized the proud autonomy of the respectable worker: "[He] leans not on the rich for bread, nor does he look to the poor-house as his ultimate home; but carries forth to his daily toil a proud consciousness that he can depend safely on his own hands; that the dependence between him and the rich is mutual, and as necessary to one as to the other."[18] The tension is expressed implicitly here, if perhaps inadvertently. A mutual dependence between the mill workers and the rich owners, necessary as it was, was not inherently amicable; nor was that existing between officers and enlisted men. Carl Siracusa argues that the respectable worker ideal as portrayed by politicians and others in the mid-nineteenth century was a myth that—by ignorance or deceit—served to hide the actual conditions of factory labor.[19]

His complaining about the conduct of those above and below him was actually a reaffirmation of the hierarchical ideal. Complaining—individual or collective— was decidedly not the special prerogative of soldiers, despite Captain Fiske's declaration. In both the mills and the army, the fundamental source of the rank-and-file's complaint was much the same: the gap between the ideal and the real behavior of those whose conduct governed conditions of their labor and their lives. Good workers (and good soldiers) were steadfast, conscientious, loyal, uncomplaining, with "sober, methodical, industrious habits"—doing a day's work for a day's wages.[20] In return, a measure of benevolent concern for subordinates' welfare distinguished gentlemen from the merely privileged in higher statuses of authority. Mr. Barrows was a gentleman who promised to continue the mill wages and hold open the jobs of married soldiers who enlisted. General Sumner was an esteemed officer whose ideal behavior set him apart from the gaggle of shoulder-strapped incompetents.

Ben's politics, like his perspectives on authority, were probably linked to his mill experience. His affinity for the Democratic party might well have stemmed from the party's proclaimed support for labor as against capitalists and for the immigrant vote.[21] In 1849, Massachusetts Democrats took pains to set themselves apart from Whig-Republican owner capitalists. In so doing, they offered what can well serve as an articulate summary of Ben's social position and perspective. Democrats, they proclaimed, were "the pure, *clarified*, wholesome, *middle* portion of the people. They are mostly persons of some little property, and expecting to earn and lay up more. They are industrious, economical, prudent, independent in their feelings and opinions, and generally heads of families. . . . This class . . . includes the great body of the farmers and country mechanics, with many of the city mechanics and laboring persons."[22] We cannot be certain of Ben's purity, and we can be curious as to what "clarified" means in this context. Still, myth or not, the description seems to fit. Whatever their earlier laborers' existence may have been like, Ben and Sarah in the 1860s clearly were guided by the ideal.

It seems safe to conclude that Ben's patriotism and his decision to volunteer were influenced by both his mill existence and prevailing ideals of respectable manhood held by his social network in Rockville. He did not clearly reveal what motivated him to volunteer, or his broader perspective on the major issues involved in the war. He nowhere articulated his views on slavery or states' rights, for instance.[23] Possibly, he had already discussed the war issues with family and friends and he simply saw no need to insert them into his narratives. He may have felt a special obligation as an immigrant to proclaim his patriotism by volunteering. At least two passing comments in his letters hint at this.[24] (Again, however, ethnicity was scarcely mentioned.) And, he may have needed the money.

John Niven calculated that many mill workers in Connecticut joined up because civilian life was hard, and they could earn as much or more money in the army than in the mills at that time.[25] A private earned $13 per month; Ben was mustered in as sergeant. He and his three brothers each received a state bounty of $25 for volunteering. Assuming Ben worked in the American Mill, Agent Barrows' gentlemanly and patriotic offer to continue the wages of married volunteers would have constituted a respectable economic incentive to enlist.[26] (Presumably, Barrows, like Ben, was convinced the war could not last long.) However, hope for economic gain alone cannot explain why Ben joined the militia soon after hostilities opened.

Respectable manliness was strongly linked to self-control. Honesty, the faith-to-contract, was a measure of both. An honest man was a man in control of himself, unswayed by beckonings of mendacity or frivolity. A Victorian man in control of himself relied on his grit to see him through adversity, never giving in to defeat or despair.[27] There could be no greater test of self-control than war.

Those who survived to reflect upon it tended to portray their actions as demonstrations of their cool ability to overcome duress.[28] Ben certainly portrayed his war in these terms. For him, as for other Victorians, war was a context for demonstrating that one could control his destiny by action. Yet, obviously, this was a retrospective view self-substantiated by the fact of one's survival of uncontrollable mortal chaos. It begged the question: If survival was a matter of Providence, why bother with control?[29]

The religious facet of Ben's world view was more a series of general tenets about fate and relationships between humans and divine powers than a tutored theology linked to a specific denomination. In this, he differed dramatically from the Reverend Captain Fiske and probably from some others in his company and regiment. For example, his emotional control and restraint were consistent with approved Anglican Protestant public behavior; but they were also qualities of manliness in general. What emerges more clearly is Ben's faith in Providence: a conviction that once the individual had done everything possible to ensure the best outcome, what happened ultimately was God's will.[30]

This was decidedly not a do-nothing fatalism; humans could improve their lot through effort, and thereby might favorably influence the workings of Providence. This faith carried well beyond "religion" in the narrow sense.[31] "What must come will come, and you and me are as nothing to it," he wrote Sarah in the depths of her depression on 26 April 1863.[32] This is the most specific expression of providential faith in any of his original narratives. It was meant to be inspirational. And if we use it as a template to help analyze his important events commentaries, it adds "religion" to the reasons why he felt personal details and emotions mostly should be left out of such lofty epics. Furthermore, it was implicit in his and others' continual preoccupation with health. Salves and "Number Nine" pills along with good water and nutrition could help keep dreaded disease at bay, but Providence ultimately determined who was struck down.

Nonetheless, it was control that prevailed in Ben's accounts. Although a basic belief in Providence may have been working on his omission of personal emotional details, a concern with conveying manly control, mastery over emotion, was probably more immediate. Unseemly emotion was controlled by leaving it out.[33]

Still, the prewar world views of Ben and most others could not have preadapted them to combat and its bare-knuckled confrontation between the ideals and the reality of courageous behavior.[34] Some general tenets of courage were very firmly in Ben's and others' minds before Antietam. So were the generally expected behaviors cued by the ideals. Before Antietam, every soldier in Company D could agree that skedaddling, for example, was singularly uncourageous behavior. Actually being under fire created a series of new, specific contexts for applying courageous ideals and weighing the implications of particular behavior. Courage— and the more inclusive tenets of manliness—had to be continually recontextualized as the war went on. Ben's letters revealed some of the shifts, but they became more pronounced for Company D after Gettysburg.[35]

Oppositions were tools for constructing manly courage: it was not cowardice; it was not womanliness (although Ben and others recognized that women left to manage wartime households displayed real courage). Hardness as a consequence of manly confrontation of death was juxtaposed to nurturance; cool control to recklessness and unseemly emotion. But as Linderman observes, extraordinary manifestations of courage softened the oppositions in soldiers' minds. Particularly courageous men could come to embody its opposites.[36] Seeing a comrade fall wounded confronted the courageous soldier with one of the sharpest personal dilemmas of war precisely because it blurred the most powerful oppositions guiding behavior.

Helping a wounded friend back to the doctors was a manly act, called by some the supreme expression of manly courage. It was the ultimate act of loyalty among men who had come to depend on one another as a consequence of the army system. Yet, it was a real threat to the essence of that system—the tactical effectiveness of the company and regiment. It was also a personal threat to the soldier's courageous image if he did not return quickly to the line.[37] How quickly to return created another dilemma, for if the wounded were simply dropped off at a chaotic aid station—or left along a fence line—with nobody to get the attention of the medics, they might die from neglect. Staying to care for wounded, however, not only invited the moniker of coward, but also embodied the nurturing opposite of veteran hardness—nurturing itself being a quality typically associated with womanliness.[38]

Mutual vows to take wounded friends to the rear helped sustain men in battle.

There was the relative security of knowing that if they were hit, someone would haul them out of harm's way. Only the hardest or most alienated could ignore a wounded comrade; yet to do otherwise violated standing orders. What behavior, then, would be the more courageous? "Never mind who is hit!" was a vexing impossibility in the first two years of the war; virtually *everybody* minded who was hit—including the folks at home in Rockville.

Courage was repeatedly constructed for those readers to ponder. Along with one's fellow soldiers, they were the jury. It was important to continue to offer them evidence of it and the more general ideal of manly respectability. Ben's portrayals of steadfast courage quickly became a principal means of maintaining his respectable position in his social networks in Rockville. If few of the readers had experienced combat themselves, they nonetheless could learn from him and others how respectable men ought to behave in this unfamiliar and altogether unrespectable context.

As the war went on, courageous qualities became ramified beyond the context of combat, spreading to mingle with other qualities of manliness, respectability, and authority, and expanding to dominate preexisting ones. For example, courage became entwined with steadfastness and emotional control. Manly respectability could not abide lengthy evidence of one's own fear in combat, nor could it now tolerate extensive outpourings of one's homesickness or physical longing for one's wife. Discussing these topics risked questions about self-control and steadfastness under adversity—now including combat—and it verged upon the excessive emotionality thought to rule women's behavior. In the doldrums following Fredericksburg, Ben wanted the war to end and he wanted a furlough. He did not, however, want to surrender or desert. He would steadfastly and courageously fulfill his commitment—even if others did not. This came to replace the bright anticipation of quick victory he carried from Rockville. It was a substantially overhauled patriotism.[39]

To be ruled by emotions was womanly. To spare women the experience of excessive unhappy emotion was manly. For this reason in part, Ben did not go very far into the details of combat and its aftermath that might unduly alarm and disgust Sarah and other readers.[40] He may have been tempted to do so, given his concerns about courage. Gory details would have enhanced his own reputation for resolute fortitude. But compassion and empathy for loved ones must have been a key consideration as well. Ideally, no respectable man could wish to inflict such scenes on those he loved, just as no loving absentee husband could expect his wife to squander her health on gardening chores or labor in the mills.

The actual time Ben and the Rockville boys spent actively engaged in combat was quite brief in that stage of the war: roughly sixty hours of their first ten and a half months.[41] Yet, that feature of the army culture had the most fundamental impact on Ben's prewar world view. The tenets of courage under fire became a prism for viewing his own conduct and evaluating that of others. It was not that the combat experience contradicted or even called into serious question his preexisting world view any more than did the other conditions of the army life he experienced. Rather, it became a different yet extremely important context for portraying the basic facets of that world view. Except for this new context—more an intrusion than a replacement—Ben's respectable skilled factory-worker Protestant perspective remained fundamentally unchanged during his months in the army and the four epic battles. The primary reason for this persistence was the cultural congruence between the mill system and the army system as he experienced them.

Postwar Rockville and the Respectable Merchant

During the gloomy days in Falmouth camp, Ben evidently considered his social roots still to be in Delaware County, Pennsylvania; this, he supposed, was where

Benjamin Hirst in the late 1860s or early 1870s, probably while he commanded Burpee Post #5, GAR, in Rockville. Photo courtesy of Alden Skinner Camp #45, Sons of Union Veterans of the Civil War.

he would like to be buried if killed in the war. After the war, he left the mills, possibly because of his war injury. Rockville had become home, however. By 1869, he and Sarah opened a small business on Market Street in Rockville:

BENJAMIN HIRST

Whose full line of dry, fancy and millinery goods should receive attention. Mrs. Hirst gives personal attention to the millinery department with which she is fully conversant.[42]

He actively continued his veteranizing. In 1869, he helped organize Burpee Post No. 5, Grand Army of the Republic (GAR), and was elected its commander. His brother John joined as well and became an officer on the post staff. By 1879, the post (named after Company D's first commander, Thomas Burpee) folded and was succeeded by the Veterans' Association. Ben served as its secretary, with George Brigham as treasurer. He also joined a GAR post in nearby Manchester, Connecticut. His army comrade and fellow Englishman John Billson was the commander there at the time.

The Burpee Post in Rockville was reborn in April 1884. Twenty-two charter members assembled to elect George Brigham as their new commander. Ben transferred his GAR membership back to Rockville in May 1887, midway through the serialization of his war papers.[43] In fact, the timing of the newspaper articles was probably part of a major push by veterans and prominent citizens to drum up support for a "suitable" new GAR Memorial Hall and town office building.[44]

Four years later, Ben had given up his Rockville business and was living in Springfield, Massachusetts. From there, he helped organize the Society of the Fourteenth Connecticut Regiment's gala battlefields excursion and reunion at Antietam in 1891.[45] He died in Springfield in 1909, of gangrenous complications of arteriosclerosis in his legs. Sarah by then was an inmate in the Massachusetts State Hospital for the Insane in Northampton, where she lived for another nine years.[46] Ben, Sarah, and Ben's brothers were all buried in Grove Cemetery in Rockville, among the graves of other men of Company D.

Ben's Newspaper Accounts

Prevailing world views tend to be incorporated fairly early in an individual's life and tend to resist fundamental change. Given this, and my general conclusion about the persistence of his factory world view during the war, we should expect Ben's newspaper accounts of 1887–88 to reflect the same facets as his originals. However, world view certainly can be transformed as a result of dramatic conditions such as war.[47]

Comparing his newspaper narratives to his originals allows us to know what twenty-five years' worth of rumination and veteranizing with comrades can produce. We can safely assume that, like his originals, the newspaper narratives were deliberately constructed to portray a particular series of behaviors as responses to a set of prevailing ideals. Furthermore, they were very public narratives. Rockville in the 1880s was full of veterans. Some, like his brothers, were former members of Company D. Ben's accounts would be closely scanned for lapses in historical detail, certainly; but they would also be read through filters of world view.

I could find no angry letters to the editor or other published criticism of his accounts in the newspaper, and, later on, his accounts were incorporated directly into the published regimental history. Ben's published recollections thus evidently appealed to an audience poised to be critical. More to the point, they evidently resonated well with prevailing world views of the time.

Linderman detects a period immediately after the war's end when most veterans seemed reluctant to say much about their exploits.[48] They were evidently trying to get on with their lives while holding their memories in reserve, now and then retrieving bits to ruminate upon and perhaps to fasten to a growing mental collage of the war's place in their experience. Within a decade, however, war narratives became a major theme of personal memoirs—the leisured Victorians' favorite mode of expression.[49] Mundane postwar jobs probably helped to create an enthusiasm for reconstructing the heady experience of combat. For some who wrote—particularly well-off Victorians who enmeshed themselves in struggles of self-image—the experience of war took on a greater importance after it was over.[50] Ben was not of this social rank, but he aspired to some of its social qualities and shared some of its prevailing world view. This permits us to set his newspaper narratives in a larger context.

Anne C. Rose argues eloquently that middle-class Victorians' "pressing need . . . [to] turn the Civil War into a tool of self-validation made them emphasize mastery of self and circumstance in tales of dogged optimism."[51] The characterization is apt for Ben's efforts as well. However, it implies a willingness to trifle with truth for the sake of one's image. That, too, was a recurrent tension for leisured Victorian war narrators, and it must have been an issue for Ben. His social image, he implied several times, was riding as much on the truth of what he reported as on the style and themes he selected. Given Rose's generalization, Ben, like other Victorians, probably concluded that the war needed no fictionalized embellishment to serve its teller's purposes.[52]

The Victorians described by Rose used their memoirs not only to portray self-images, but also as means of sorting out for themselves just who they were and the significance of their lives. This last preoccupation was a facet of the general world view shared by their socioeconomic class, as well as a result of their literary skills. Given Ben's upward social aspirations and his years of postwar occasions to reflect and revise, we might expect more of this writing-as-personal-quest-for-fulfillment emphasis in his published narratives. On the other hand, nothing in his original letters hints that he was preoccupied with the spiritual or moral dilemmas that confronted these other Victorians before, during, and after the war.

How far did Ben's published recollections deviate from his originals, and what does this tell us about world view? As a respectable businessman, Ben was of course careful not to offend potential patrons. He reworked some of the criticism written in his original letters, and he cut most of the angry fulminations against Col. Dwight Morris ("Old Bunch 'Em"). He omitted the gallant Lieutenant Colonel Perkins's name in connection with forcing the men to pay for "missing" cartridge box belts. And the allegations of particular officers' cowardice or shirking became more opaque. A. Park Hammond, his former company commander who was born into Rockville's elite, received only complimentary copy, shorn of the original suggestion that he had shirked his obligations after Antietam. Although the names were now mostly deleted, the recurrent "us against them" posture was left intact toward officer arrogance, incompetence, and shirking. It was even accentuated by new anecdotes such as this recalled from 11 December 1862 near Fredericksburg:

> At this time it was snowing, and as we were reclining on the ground in little groups waiting for the cups and cans to boil, two officers crazy with drink came stumbling along, and after knocking down several stacks of arms, lurched into our little fire and scattered our tins in all directions. We swore some. Then one of the officers drew his sword and said he would kill the — —— that talked to him in that manner, then stepping back said he would do it anyway. The other officer drew him away in time to save Co. D and the regiment from more disgraceful scenes.
>
> NOTE—Perhaps this officer never knew it, but I know that another move on his part and he would have been shot in his tracks. This incident for a time quenched all ambition for promotion out of our company, which seemed to us to be isolated from the regiment, we having no commissioned officer to take up our cause, and we were more to each other on that account.[53]

Ben still bristled at misused authority. Some officers' later acts of courage under fire earned them anonymity in Ben's reworked criticisms, but the criticisms themselves were considered important enough to leave intact and embellish.

Even with considered revisions due to retrospection and a wider audience, Ben remained singularly focused on courage and cowardice. Names of cowards were allowed to remain in the published versions. In fact, he saw fit to add at least one name that had not appeared in his originals.[54] On the other hand, he inserted fairly lengthy testimonials to the bravery of those who died in combat.

Conceivably, the postwar manly image could have been fulfilled by simply ignoring these cowards. They were beneath any real man's further consideration. In combat, however, Ben the sergeant could not ignore them, nor could the other men in Company D. During the war, this became righteous anger. Evidently it ran deep and long.

Ben's helping of the wounded men at Fredericksburg was not mentioned. Instead, he quoted a statement by John McPherson, a soldier of Company D, that bears on Ben's own conduct:

> *Two days before the battle, [Edward W.] Mann told me he thought he should get hit, and if he was, I must take him off the field, and he in like manner would do the same for me. I laughed at him, but seeing he was in earnest in the matter, I made the promise. On the afternoon of the 13th [of December], while the regiment was in its most advanced position, Mann was shot in the left breast and as he staggered to his feet I took hold of him to assist him off the field. We had gone but a few steps when a solid shot passed through Mann's body and he fell at my feet a corpse. [Mann, an English immigrant, left a wife and child in Rockville.]*[55]

In this passage, Ben implicitly declared that leaving the battle line to carry back wounded was not only popular, but also still honorable among comrades—should any of his readers recall the grief-stricken allegations of Albert Towne's father.[56]

His important events portrayals of his own brave actions remained unchanged. He added more examples for the newspaper. He also recalled a vignette about his brother John's bravery that, like other personal asides about his brothers, was not in the originals:

> *Jack [John] came near starting a battle on his own hook the other day [late February 1862, near Falmouth camp]. There is a dam just above Fredericksburg and a kind of a ford just below the dam where the boys from both armies sometimes go a fishing. Jack went a fishing and got so far into the river as to be throwing his line into the same pool of water that some Johnnies [were] monopolizing. Jack hooked a fish and the Johnnies began to beat his line with their fish rods. This made Jack mad so he dropped his fishing tackle for some stones lying in the water and swore he would crack the skull of any gray back that touched his line again. They didn't like Jack's looks and both sides backed off, Jack bringing his fish with him.*[57]

In another recollection, Ben reported his and John's brave and righteous confrontation of some Yank cavalry. The brothers had left their hut intact when they marched out to Chancellorsville:

> *Upon our return we kept a bright lookout . . . until we came within a half mile of where it ought to be. There was smoke coming out of a chimney that looked like ours, and Jack and I . . . took a bee line across lots for that chimney. It was our chimney and we entered the hut without ceremony, where we found two cavalry men taking things easy and homelike. They had gath-*

ered up quite a lot of blankets for the bunks, plenty of tin pans and iron kettles for the kitchen and a lot of firewood for the cook. "Who are you" says one of the men to me. "Who are you," said I "and what are you doing in my house?" "Yes," says Jack, "wasting our firewood, are you, get out." "Get out," said I, "we don't allow anybody to use our beds and dishes, so be lively and get." The way those cavalry men stuck out their eyes would make you laugh, but Jack and I were in no laughing humor just then. We made them get up, and charged them four good blankets, six iron pans, one lot of tin ware and all the firewood for rent. They seemed glad enough to get away without having a fight. I have somewhere read that charity begins at home. Jack and I were home again.

Directly after we got rid of the cavalry men, Jack bethought himself of having dumped a lot of beans in the little run just before we broke up camp, and started double quick for the place which he speedily found, and a lot of the beans pretty well soaked during our absence. We had hot bean soup in less than 30 minutes, while lots of officers and men had to go a mile before they could get wood enough to boil a cup of coffee.[58]

Plenty of righteous anger here, plus some soldierly savoir-faire (and luck) in getting grub. Ben added another example involving his own righteous takedown of a greedy Pennsylvania farmer during the march from Gettysburg to a hospital train in Hanover:

Once we had a good laugh and something to eat, which happened in this way: A big native Pennsylvania dutchman came along with a big loaf of bread under his arm which several of the boys coveted and tried to beg, but it was no use begging. "Me sell him for a quarter" was all the english he could speak, so I made believe I was feeling for a quarter with my good arm, when I pulled out a little Smith & Wesson and told him to drop that loaf, and the way that fellow got over the fence (minus the loaf) and ran, would have done credit to the champion copperhead north, on his way to Canada.[59]

The retrospective ideals and themes in these added portions were identical to those in his important events originals. The difference was that John was now significantly included; the originals had featured either Ben himself or the generalized "we" and "others."

In his newspaper accounts, Ben continued a trend first appearing during his important events narrative of Gettysburg. He detailed more of his feelings, particularly prebattle anxiety. These details were added to his original description of the anxious wait for orders to charge against Marye's Heights:

How slowly the time moves; we can think of a hundred things we have not thought of for years. Why don't we move? This job should have been done

three hours ago. We can hardly stand the strain much longer. We must do
something, so Frank Stoughton, Brigham and myself took down the names
of every man of Company D who left camp with us for Fredericksburg. [List
of names included.] . . . we have just twenty-five men and muskets in Co. D
waiting. Waiting for what, but the unknown future. Why don't you move?
says a rebel shell, as it crashes through the building at our backs. No response
is given, but the boys are unloading all superfluous articles that were picked
up in the city. How intense is our sight and hearing.[60]

It was still just short of an in-depth personal revelation; it was another of Ben's
group portraits, even if he was clearly part of the picture. The controlled, reserved,
emotional distance was still there despite his having earned the right to discuss
fear more openly.

True to the controlled respectable manly image, Ben excised all personal endear-
ments to Sarah, sparse as they were in the originals. (These had been entirely absent from his original important events narratives as well.) He cut out the difficulty with Sarah's mother. But he left intact his concerns about Sarah's health as
proper expressions of a loving husband.

In essence, Ben's newspaper accounts were his important events narratives as
originally written, augmented by specific details about events and vignettes of
bravery and tailored to fit the prevailing ideals of respectable and courageous
manhood. Given Ben's sensitivity to his social image, the consistency between the
two versions suggests those prevailing ideals—his and others'—had not changed
much in the intervening decades. What is more, they served him as well in 1887–
88 as they had in 1862–63.[61]

My interpretive commentary is an effort to understand how a soldier's world view
affected his portrayal of military service and combat. I have not tapped his world
view in its entirety, surely. Nor have I intended to demonstrate that Ben shared the
views of all soldiers. To do so convincingly would involve a general comparison,
placing Ben's narratives in a pool with hundreds of others. Historians have already
plowed that ground to offer ably drawn generalizations. Yet something is inevitably lost in such generalized comparisons: a sense of the specific human being operating through time according to a specific set of preconceptions as well as immediate conditions. Scholars such as Linderman and Mitchell have eloquently described
the pervasive role of the ideals of courage and manhood in soldiers' behavior. That
these same general ideals molded Ben's narratives is to be expected. The issue is to
determine how their influence operated on what he wrote, and, further, what the
sources of his specific ideas about the nature of manliness might have been.

Ben remained the dedicated common soldier and the proud, respectable laborer
in his outlook. He should have the last word. His most considered and eloquent
conclusion about his greatest battle is perhaps his most concise statement of world
view:

I have often been asked to what superior generalship or strategy displayed at Gettysburg we owe this great victory. My answer after a careful study of the battle and the battle field is, none. I have visited it several times since then and gone all over the field in company with Col Batchelder and the Gettysburg guide, Holdworth, until I know it as well as I do the streets of Rockville, and my answer is still the same, none. . . . The claims set up by various generals that our victory was owing to the brilliancy of their movements cannot be sustained. To what then did we owe our success? The only true answer is, under the providence of God, to the grit and courage of the rank and file of the grand old Army of the Potomac, stripped for the fight as it never was before, and still smarting under the useless sacrifice at Fredericksburg, and our humiliating defeat at Chancellorsville. Look at us when we broke camp in front of Fredericksburg in pursuit of Lee, with the long and dreary marches under a burning sun by day, and the drenching storms by night, which taxed the strength of the bravest and the best, while it culled out the sick and those who were physically incapable of standing the strain, and at the same time giving all those who had no heart in the cause or were cowards by nature ample opportunities of sneaking away under various pretexts of which they availed themselves. The man, from the humblest drummer boy or hospital nurse who reached Gettysburg in time to do his duty in the hour of need, is entitled to as much credit for the victory as was the grandest general on the field.[62]

Appendix

Names

The following are persons given more than passing mention in Ben's account. Not included are those political and military figures outside of the 14th Connecticut Volunteers who were well known during the Civil War. Some of these have been described in endnotes at appropriate junctures.[1]

Abby, John Private, Co. D, from Rockville. A native of Ireland. Died of wounds received at Antietam on 17 September 1862.

Allen, Edward P. From Rockville; mustered as private in Co. D and detailed as musician (a bass drummer, according to Ben) after resigning as Captain, Co. F., 5th Connecticut Volunteer Infantry, on 25 October 1861. Later returned to company duty and was mustered out with Co. D on 31 May 1865. Later in the war earned John Hirst's wrath for overstaying his furlough and keeping John from going home. In rare written profanity to his brother Ben, John referred to Allen as "a shit ass."

Barrows, Samuel From Rockville; mustered as private; discharged for disability on 21 July 1863. Evidently not closely related to the kind-hearted American Mills agent, Thomas Barrows.

Billson, John H. ["Bilson"] From Rockville; an English immigrant; mustered as private in Co. D and promoted to corporal on 22 October 1863. Wounded at Petersburg on 22 June 1864. Mustered out with the company on 31 May 1865. Along with John Whiting and Harry Owen, became an especially close friend of John Hirst's after Gettysburg.

Bottomly or Bottomley There is no record of a person by this name in Rockville at the time. The narratives indicate the man addressed as "Friend Bottomly" by Ben evidently lived in the Dedham, Massachusetts, area and may have worked with Ben in the mills there in the late 1850s. He had at least one daughter and a son named John. John Bottomley was evidently a favorite of both Ben and John Hirst; both occasionally sent him small mementos.

Brigham, George N. From Rockville; mustered into Co. D as sergeant; wounded at Gettysburg on 3 July 1863, Morton's Ford on 6 February 1864, and Reams's

Station on 25 August 1864. Promoted to lieutenant on 16 November 1863 and captain on 26 June 1864. Discharged on 8 December 1864. After the war, became Rockville's postmaster and commander of the local GAR post.

Burpee, Thomas F. From Rockville; led the local company of state militia, which included Ben Hirst and George Brigham. Mustered in as captain, but soon thereafter resigned to become a major in the 21st Connecticut Volunteers then being formed. He was a lieutenant colonel commanding that regiment at the time of his heroic death at Cold Harbor on 9 June 1864. Both GAR posts in Rockville were named in his honor.

Butterworth, Thomas Private, Co. D, from Rockville. Mustered into Federal service with the rest of the company on 20 August 1862, but became ill and finally was discharged for disability on 5 November 1863. A close friend of the Hirst brothers.

Crombie, David B. Private, from Rockville. Deserted from Co. D on 19 September 1862.

Dart, Charles E. Sergeant, from Rockville. Volunteered as one of the regiment's color sergeants before Fredericksburg. Wounded at Fredericksburg and died of wounds on 6 January 1863.

Dart, Oliver, Jr. From South Windsor, a private in Co. D and brother-in-law of Corp. John Symonds. Both men were seriously wounded at Fredericksburg on 13 December 1863. Ben helped carry Dart from the field. Dart was discharged for disability on 8 February 1863.

Davis, Samuel H. Captain, Co. H, from New London. After serving for a time as acting commander of the 14th regiment, he returned to his company and was dishonorably discharged 17 September 1863.

Ellis, Theodore G. Major commanding the 14th at Chancellorsville and Gettysburg. From Hartford, he was mustered in as regimental adjutant and promoted to major 3 April 1863. Promoted to lieutenant colonel on 22 September 1863, then quickly to colonel on 11 October 1863. He was mustered out with the regiment on 31 May 1865, after being brevetted to brigadier general 13 March 1865.

Emery, Ira First Lieutenant, Co. D, from Rockville. Fought at Antietam, then resigned his commission on 23 January 1863. He never recovered completely from his debility and died eight years later.

Fay, Michael Private, Co. D, from Ellington. Served through the entire war with the company. A member of the GAR along with the Hirst brothers after the war. Received a reprimand from the post for intemperance.

Fiske, Samuel ("Dunn Browne") Captain, Co. G, from Madison, Connecticut. Mustered as second lieutenant, Co. I. Wrote a series of war narratives for the Springfield, Massachusetts, *Republican* under the pen name of "Dunn Browne." Wounded in the Wilderness on 6 May 1864; died of wounds on 23 May 1864. He is described more fully in the introduction.

Frink, Christopher L. [?] As in the case of their friend Bottomly, neither Hirst brother mentioned Frink's first name. There were two Frinks living in Rockville in 1860: Adam, a twenty-six-year-old weaver from Germany, and Christopher L., a thirty-two-year-old native-born machinist. Ben's comments (e.g., Frink evidently was working at "the gass works" rather than in the mills) suggest it was Christopher.

Goodell, William W. Corporal, Co. D, from Rockville; mustered in as private with the company on 20 August 1862. Killed at Gettysburg 3 July 1863.

Hammond, A. Park Captain, Co. D. Oddly, Captain Hammond's name is not listed in the official roster of the company, probably because he was never properly mustered into Federal service. A son of Capt. Allen Hammond, one of the antebellum magnates of the Rockville area, Park Hammond became a major investor in local commercial enterprises and served for a time in the state legislature after the war.

Hirst, Benjamin, Jr. Private, 124th Pennsylvania Vols. ("Captain Barton's Company"). Sgt. Ben Hirst's father's brother's son from Chester/Ridley Township, Delaware County, Pennsylvania. Ben Jr.'s father operated a machine shop for weaving equipment in Chester until going bankrupt in 1854. He was three years younger than his brother John (Sgt. Ben Hirst's father) and evidently did not immigrate at the same time. The names cause confusion because two generations of Hirsts each contained a pair of brothers named Benjamin and John. At one time in the 1850s, at least three Benjamin Hirsts were living in the vicinity of Chester.

Hirst, William Ben Hirst's oldest brother, married and living in Leiperville, Delaware County, Pennsylvania during the war. He was thirty-six years old in 1862, two years older than Ben.

Hodspodsky, Henry Corporal, Co. D, from Rockville. Mustered into Federal service with the rest of the company as private. Wounded at Antietam and at Deer Creek, Virginia. Mustered out with the company on 31 May 1865.

Hyde, Elbert First sergeant, Co. D, from Ellington (adjacent to Rockville). Mustered in with the rest of the company as corporal. Promoted to first sergeant on 22 October 1863. Wounded in the Wilderness on 6 May 1864 and again at Petersburg on 17 June 1864; discharged 8 June 1865.

Jackson, Patrick Private, Co. D, from Rockville. Wounded at Chancellorsville 3 May 1863; died 4 June 1863.

Loomis, Dwight Prominent attorney in Rockville. Born nearby in 1821. Graduated from Yale Law School. When he became Rockville's first lawyer in 1847, "[It] ... was a staid, typical New England town, plethoric with pure blood and unvexed by the workers of iniquity."[2] He was thus unsure of his welcome there. Evidently, the workers of iniquity were sufficiently vexing to generate a thriving practice. Served in state legislature beginning in 1851. Beginning in 1859, served two terms in Congress as a Republican. In 1864, began to rise through state judicial ranks to become an associate justice of the state's supreme court in 1875. In extolling Loomis's qualities, Cole sketches the archetypal Victorian man: "[Judge Loomis had ideal] mental and temperamental qualities [for the bench] . . . with acute perceptive and analytic faculties, a good memory, rare powers of discrimination, a full measure of forbearance, patience and courtesy, with suitable firmness and dignity and no pretension or pride of opinion, and withal a granite sub-stratum of sterling honesty and integrity, and a conscientious and inflexible fidelity to the duties of his position. . . . In these days of self-seeking, when only those who hunger and thirst after public honors, and whose insatiate cravings move them to active, self-serving effort, are likely to be recognized and honored, it is refreshing to witness an instance of one who has reached the highest honors through the force of his personal merits alone."[3]

Lucas, Walter M. Captain of Co. D from 15 June 1863 to 14 March 1864. From Middletown, he had earlier served as a private in Co. A, 2d Connecticut Volunteers. Promoted from first lieutenant, Co. A of the 14th. Wounded at Gettysburg and at Morton's Ford (6 February 1864); resigned 14 March 1864.

Lyman, Charles Corporal, Co. D., from Bolton. Promoted to second lieutenant, Co. K, on 3 March 1863. Lyman was credited with firing the shot that fatally wounded Confederate Brig. Gen. Thomas Reade Rootes Cobb while the latter was standing in the front yard of Mrs. Stephens's house at Fredericksburg.[4] (Cobb was commanding a brigade under McLaws at the time.) Discharged 31 May 1863 under conditions that Ben Hirst felt were unfair. After the war, rose through bureaucratic ranks in Washington, D.C., to become chief clerk of the U.S. Treasury in 1883, then a commissioner on the Civil Service Commission in 1886.

Metcalf, Martin V. B. Private, Co. D., from Rockville. Wounded 13 December at Fredericksburg; died of wounds 3 January 1863.

Morris, Dwight Colonel, commanding the 14th Connecticut when it was mustered into Federal service. From Bridgeport. Promoted to command of a brigade in French's division (3d), Sumner's corps (2d), before Antietam. He became "Old Bunch 'Em" to the men after he evidently got the regiment lost on a simple march from Falmouth to Belle Plain, Virginia, on 18 November 1862. Discharged for disability on 14 August 1863.

Morse, Luther T. A good friend and possibly a coworker of Ben's in Rockville. His household was not included in the 1860 census, although his name appears in the town property tax records of 1860 and again in 1862 and 1863. He and his family may have moved from Rockville after 1863. The tax records evaluate his property at $75. He did not own a home, land, or livestock, or have other investments shown in the records.

Morton, George W. Private from Rockville in Co. D. Served as cook for various officers. Captured at Chancellorsville, later mentioned as a helpful provider by John Hirst, although the two evidently never became close friends. Mustered out with the company on 31 May 1865.

Murray, Joseph Private, then corporal and sergeant in Co. D; from Rockville. Captured at Reams's Station on 25 August 1864. Escaped from Salisbury, North Carolina, on 1 February 1865 and was mustered out with the rest of the company on 31 May 1865.

Orcutt, Henry W. Corporal, Co. D, from Rockville. Mustered in with company as private. Wounded at Antietam, and again at Morton's Ford on 6 February 1864. Died of wounds on 7 February 1864.

Owen, Henry ("Harry") Sergeant, Co. D, from Rockville. Did not join the company until 23 September 1863, having earlier resigned as a lieutenant in Co. F, 5th Connecticut Volunteers. Mustered in as private and quickly promoted. He became a close friend of John Hirst's. Wounded at Morton's Ford on 6 February 1863; died of wounds on 25 February 1863.

Penfield, Margaret ("Maggie") A teenage girl living with the Hirsts in Rockville. Possibly a relative of Sarah's or Ben's. She was about fifteen years old in 1862.

Perkins, Sanford Lieutenant colonel from Torrington, Connecticut, commanded the 14th Connecticut at Antietam (Col. Dwight Morris being appointed brigade commander) and during the Fredericksburg battle. Wounded at Fredericksburg and discharged for disability on 20 April 1863.

Quinn, Anthony Sarah's brother, a soldier in the 72d Pennsylvania Volunteers.

Quinn, Thomas Sarah's brother, a soldier most likely serving with his brother Anthony in the 72d Pennsylvania Volunteers.

Simpson, James F. First lieutenant, Co. D; promoted from second lieutenant, Co. C. From Waterbury. At Chancellorsville, went off into the woods to camp with Pvt. George Morton as his cook and both were captured when the Confederates overran their isolated position. Both were soon paroled, and Simpson went on to become captain of Co. C in October 1863. His return to his old company with a promotion was evidently permitted because he had not earlier been an enlisted man among them.

Smiley, Joe Husband of Sarah's sister Kate. Evidently joined a Pennsylvania regiment during the Civil War. A letter from John Hirst to Sarah on 6 September 1864 notes: "i did not think Joe smiley would have gone for a soldier but i suppose he was afraid of they draft. i hope he will come out all right."

Smiley, Kate Sarah Quinn Hirst's sister, married to Joe Smiley. Died in February 1865 after a lingering illness.

Stafford, Thomas Private, Co. D, from Rockville. Wounded, missing in action, and presumed to have died of wounds at Chancellorsville on 3 May 1863.

Stoughton, Frank E. ["Stoughten"] First sergeant (or orderly sergeant), Co. D, before his promotions to lieutenant in Cos. H and G and finally to captain commanding Co. G on 29 July 1864. From Rockville, mustered in with Co. D on 20 August 1862. Severely wounded at Gettysburg and discharged for disability on 1 January 1865.

Symonds, John Corporal, Co. D, from Rockville; mustered in with company on 20 August 1862. Wounded at Fredericksburg on 13 December 1862; discharged for disability on 7 February 1863.

Towne, Albert H., Jr. Private, Co. D, from Rockville. Mustered in with the company on 20 August 1862. Missing and presumed killed in action at Fredericksburg on 13 December 1862.

Vinton, Chelsea C. Second lieutenant, Co. D, from Rockville; discharged 26 December 1862.

Wadhams, Henry W. Second lieutenant, Co. D at Chancellorsville; from Waterbury. Mustered as sergeant in Company C. Wounded at Fredericksburg. Promoted to 2d lieutenant, Co. D, on 3 March 1863; became first lieutenant, Co. K, on 13 November 1863. Killed 26 May 1864, North Anna River, Virginia.

Watslong, John A Rockville acquaintance of the Hirsts. Possibly a rival of John Hirst's for the attentions of a local lady. Enlisted in Co. H, 15th Connecticut Volunteer Infantry, 26 December 1862. Discharged for disability on 6 May 1865.[5]

Whiting, David W. Corporal, Co. D., from Rockville. Mustered in with company on 20 August 1862. Killed at Reams's Station on 25 August 1865. He and John Billson became particularly close friends of John Hirst's later in the war.

Wilkie, Thomas Private, Co. D, from Tolland, adjacent to Rockville (Rockville is in Tolland County). Mustered with company on 20 August 1862. One of Ben's tentmates before the battle of Antietam. A native of England, veteran of the Crimean War, and close friend of the Hirsts and Tom Butterworth. Died 23 October 1862 of wounds received at Antietam.

Williams, John Private, Co. D., from Rockville. Mustered with company on 20 August 1862. Captured at Chancellorsville on 3 May 1863 when left to guard Co. D's knapsacks. Paroled 15 May 1863; mustered out with company on 31 May 1865.

Winans, Augustus W. Private, Co. D, from Rockville. Probably a native of Germany. Mustered in with company on 20 August 1862. Discharged for disability 15 January 1863.

Notes

~~~~~~~~~~~

Introduction

1. The originals of the Hirst letters are located in the historical collection of Alden Skinner Camp #45, Sons of Union Veterans of the Civil War, in the GAR Hall rooms of the Town Hall, Rockville, Conn. The collection is hereafter cited as ASCC.

2. Reid Mitchell describes the correspondence between a Connecticut lieutenant and his wife: "Lieutenant Kies's preoccupation with his domestic life in the midst of war warns us of the danger of neglecting the personal when seeking the meaning of the Civil War experience. . . . [The] nexus of personal communication was a context in which men experienced the more purely military aspects of the war. Furthermore, it provided much of the motivation that kept men in the service of their country and their homes." Reid Mitchell, "The Northern Soldier and His Community," in *Toward a Social History of the American Civil War,* ed. Maris A. Vinovskis (New York: Cambridge Univ. Press, 1990), 79–80.

3. In his introduction to *The Great Cat Massacre and Other Episodes in French Cultural History* (New York: Basic Books, 1984), 3, historian Robert Darnton declares: "This book investigates ways of thinking in eighteenth-century France. It attempts to show not merely what people thought but how they thought—how they construed the world, invested it with meaning, and infused it with emotion. . . . [I]t might simply be called cultural history; for it treats our own civilization in the same way that anthropologists study alien cultures. It is history in the ethnographic grain." Darnton's book, Gerald F. Linderman's *Embattled Courage: The Experience of Combat in the American Civil War* (New York: Free Press, 1987), and Reid Mitchell's *Civil War Soldiers: Their Expectations and Their Experiences* (New York: Simon & Schuster, 1988) and *The Vacant Chair: The Northern Soldier Leaves Home* (New York and Oxford: Oxford Univ. Press, 1993) have been especially helpful in orienting my analytical commentary.

4. See, for example, James I. Robertson Jr., *Soldiers Blue and Gray* (Columbia: Univ. of South Carolina Press, 1988), 124, and John Niven, *Connecticut for the Union* (New Haven: Yale Univ. Press, 1965), 114.

5. Cf. Darnton, *Cat Massacre,* 261–62:

> I should confess some of my own methodological shortcomings. I worry especially about two: my failure to resolve the problem of proof and the problem of representativeness. . . . I would . . . argue that this kind of culture history should not be subjected

to the same standards of evidence that rule in the history of international relations or politics. World views cannot be pinned down with "proof." They are bound to be fuzzy around the edges, and they will slip through the fingers if one grabs at them as if they were pages from the *Congressional Record*.

 . . . I confess that I do not see a clear way of distinguishing idiom from individuality. I can only testify to the importance of working back and forth between texts and contexts. That may not be much of a methodology, but it has advantages. It does not flatten out the idiosyncratic element in history, and it allows for a consideration of the common ground of experience.

6. Samuel Fiske ("Dunn Browne"), *Mr. Dunn Browne's Experiences in the Army* (Boston: Nichols and Noyes, 1866).

7. Charles D. Page, *History of the Fourteenth Regiment, Connecticut Vol. Infantry* (Meriden, Conn.: Horton, 1906).

8. John Billings, *Hardtack and Coffee* (Boston: George M. Smith and Co., 1887; rpt. Alexandria, Va.: Time-Life Books, 1982); Carlton McCarthy, *Detailed Minutiae of Soldier Life in the Army of Northern Virginia, 1861–1865* (Richmond, 1882; rpt. Alexandria, Va.: Time-Life Books, 1982); Sam R. Watkins, *"Co. Aytch," Maury Grays, First Tennessee Regiment; Or, A Side Show of the Big Show* (Nashville: Cumberland Presbyterian Publ. House, 1882; rpt. Wilmington, N.C.: Broadfoot, 1987); Bell Irvin Wiley, *The Life of Billy Yank: The Common Soldier of the Union* (Baton Rouge: Louisiana State Univ. Press, 1952; rpt. 1978) and *The Life of Johnny Reb: The Common Soldier of the Confederacy* (Baton Rouge: Louisiana State Univ. Press, 1943; rpt. 1978); Linderman, *Embattled Courage*; Mitchell, *Civil War Soldiers* and *Vacant Chair*; Robertson, *Soldiers Blue and Gray*; Michael Barton, *Goodmen: The Character of Civil War Soldiers* (University Park: Pennsylvania State Univ. Press, 1981). For a very comprehensive, if dated, bibliography on firsthand accounts of the Civil War, see Garold L. Cole, *Civil War Eyewitnesses: An Annotated Bibliography of Books and Articles, 1955–1986* (Columbia: Univ. of South Carolina Press, 1988).

9. Mitchell, "The Northern Soldier," 79–80, 85. Mitchell notes that the soldier in combat had other preoccupations as well.

10. For an extensive discussion of the world view concept, see Robert Redfield, "The Primitive World View," *Proceedings of the American Philosophical Society* 96 (1952): 30–36, and Anthony F. C. Wallace, *Culture and Personality* (New York: Random House, 1961), 99–101.

11. Anthony F. C. Wallace coined the term "mazeway" to refer to what is here termed the individual world view. He characterized a group's world view as an "organization of diversity" rather than a single seamless set of doctrines shared by every member. Wallace, *Culture and Personality*, 27. In a classic article that informed some of his later work he explored revitalization movements as particular contexts for rather sudden and radical reformulation of individual world views. Anthony F. C. Wallace, "Revitalization Movements," *American Anthropologist* 58 (1956): 264–81.

12. The family analogy has long been a popular theme of historical treatment of both factories and army regiments or companies. For examples of the factories, see Robert Glen, *Urban Workers in the Early Industrial Revolution* (New York: St. Martin's Press, 1984), 281; Anthony F. C. Wallace, *Rockdale* (New York: Knopf, 1978), 21; and David A. Zonderman, *Aspirations and Anxieties: New England Workers and the Mechanized Factory System, 1815–1850* (New York: Oxford Univ. Press, 1992), 104, 109, 131. For ex-

amples of regiments or companies, see Mitchell, *Civil War Soldiers,* 17, and Robertson, *Soldiers Blue and Gray,* 21.

13. This sketch is based on the following studies of English textile workers: Duncan Bythell, *The Handloom Weavers: A Study in the English Cotton Industry During the Industrial Revolution* (Cambridge: Cambridge Univ. Press, 1969); Glen, *Urban Workers*; Charlotte Erickson, *Invisible Immigrants: The Adaptation of English and Scottish Immigrants in Nineteenth-Century America* (Coral Gables, Fla.: Univ. of Miami Press, 1972); Charlotte Erickson, *Leaving England: Essays on British Emigration in the Nineteenth Century* (Ithaca: Cornell Univ. Press, 1994); and James Phillips Kay Shuttleworth, *The Moral and Physical Condition of the Working Classes Employed in the Cotton Manufacture in Manchester,* 2d ed. (London: James Ridgway, 1832; rpt. New York: August M. Kelley Publishers, 1970). It is also informed by accounts of English textile workers in America, found in Cynthia J. Shelton, *The Mills of Manayunk: Industrialization and Social Conflict in the Philadelphia Region, 1787–1837* (Baltimore: Johns Hopkins Univ. Press, 1986), and Wallace, *Rockdale.* In another publication, the Hirsts' place of birth was mistakenly given as "Southport," a result of my faulty proofreading. Robert Bee, "Fredericksburg on the Other Leg," in *The Third Day at Gettysburg and Beyond,* ed. Gary Gallagher (Chapel Hill: Univ. of North Carolina Press, 1994), 133.

14. The father, Joseph, was born in Yorkshire in 1804. Mary's birth year is unknown. Their son William was born in 1826, Ben in 1828, and Joseph Jr. in 1833. Dates of Joseph Sr.'s, William's, and Ben's births are in Anton Henry Haas, "Abstracts from the *Naturalization Records of Delaware County, Pennsylvania, 1795–1860,"* an unpublished manuscript on file in the Delaware County Historical Society, Broomall, Pa. Mary's, Joseph Jr.'s, and John's names do not appear in these records. Joseph Jr.'s birth year is from Joseph Hirst Pension File SC 52015, National Archives Military Service Branch, Washington, D.C.

15. The baptism certificate was critically important to John's later efforts to obtain a disability pension for his Civil War service, because he could not produce a certificate of birth and, he declared, he may have given an incorrect birth date to the recruitment officer "owing to the *Enthusiasm* created at the time." An affidavit by Ben established the month and year of John's birth. John Hirst Pension File WC 666-960, National Archives Military Service Branch, Washington, D.C.

16. Both quotations found in Glen, *Urban Workers,* 1.

17. Bythell, *Handloom Weavers,* 13, 16; Shuttleworth, *Working Classes,* 100, 104.

18. Bythell, *Handloom Weavers,* 89

19. Yarn spun in factories in nearby Manchester was distributed to the weavers' households by a middleman, or putter-out, who then collected the finished cloth from the households.

20. Bythell, *Handloom Weavers,* 43, 47, 61, 260–61, 270. Fancy weaving required more skill; wool weaving was heavier work requiring more strength.

21. Bythell, *Handloom Weavers,* 9–10, 13–14, 37–38. Actually, the families were scattered wage laborers, subject to the capricious textile market and unable to control either the cost of the yarn or the price received for their finished cloth.

22. Glen in *Urban Workers* centers his extensive analysis on the dynamics of Stockport's textile workers' (principally weavers') efforts to organize in the 1790–1820 period.

23. Stockport's workers had earlier been a major component (1,400 to 1,500 people) in the infamous Peterloo Massacre near Manchester on 16 August 1819. Fifty-four of

them became casualties of the clash between angry workers from the area and militia and constabulary units. Glen, *Urban Workers,* 217–53.

24. Bythell, *Handloom Weavers,* 86. Bythell adds, however, that powerloom operations required several types of attendants besides weavers themselves, which reduced somewhat—but not altogether—the labor savings of powerlooms over handlooms.

25. Bythell cautions that weavers' radical postures and personal involvement in labor action were individually variable and apt to be most active only during major economic crises. For this, as well as other discussion of weavers in the labor unit, see Bythell, *Handloom Weavers,* ch. 9.

26. Quote is from Richard Guest in Glen, *Urban Workers,* 144.

27. Conceivably, the senior Hirst was still a handloom weaver when his son John was baptized in 1836. If so, he was decidedly in the minority. In the 1830s, handloom weavers were scarce in the region. Only about 400 to 1,000 of them were left in Stockport. By 1836, a burst in factory building had created a textile labor demand that easily would have absorbed all the unemployed handloom weavers.

28. Bythell, *Handloom Weavers,* 92.

29. Shuttleworth, *Working Classes,* 100, 104.

30. Bythell, *Handloom Weavers,* 147.

31. Ibid., 11, 13–14, 37, 61. For details on child workers in Rockdale, Pennsylvania, mills, see Wallace, *Rockdale,* 41, 63, 67, 182–83, 305, 328, 381. These tasks must have been similar to those performed by children in English weaving and spinning operations. Shelton quotes Pennsylvania labor organizers in 1833 who declared that factory abuses of child labor had been corrected in England. Shelton, *Manayunk,* 138. The date of the Hirst family's emigration is from Haas, "Abstracts," (no page numbers; Joseph Sr. is #744; Ben is #745; William is #765.)

32. Glen, *Urban Workers,* 256. Glen discusses this household economic strategy, noting that in 1823, with a man and wife working the handlooms at home and sending their sons (ages ten and fifteen) to work in the factories, the family could make a weekly income of 22 shillings 6 pence—well above subsistence level at that time.

33. All preceding information on textile market dynamics taken from Bythell, *Handloom Weavers.*

34. Even to those sympathetic to the plight of laborers in teeming Manchester, the Irish collectively were little better than animals. In *Working Classes,* for example, Shuttleworth seldom missed an opportunity to remind readers of the "pernicious" and "debased" influence of Irish laborers imported to the Manchester area during labor shortages. His elite paternalism, although intended to be benevolent, led him to similar descriptors of English laborers as well. In good times, urban weavers' wages were generally higher than those in the countryside. Bythell, *Handloom Weavers,* 12. England's poor laws had been established much earlier to offer emergency compensation—often in the form of food or other provisions—for indigent workers. Typically, the idle poor were put to work at outdoor public works projects at low wages. In 1834, Parliament passed an amendment to the poor laws that drastically curtailed the compensation. This contributed to a major labor action that developed into the chartist movement of the early 1840s. For discussion of the operation of the poor laws, see Bythell, *Handloom Weavers,* ch. 10, and Shuttleworth, *Working Classes.*

35. Glen notes that Irish immigration into Stockport picked up in the 1830s. By 1851, the Irish were about a quarter of Stockport's total population. "At the end of the century

certain Stockport public houses still contained wooden partitions to keep English and Irish patrons separated." Glen, *Urban Workers,* 280.

36. Bythell, *Handloom Weavers,* 16; Glen, *Urban Workers,* 256–57.

37. Erickson, *Invisible Immigrants,* pt. 2; Erickson, *Leaving England,* 15, 24–25.

38. Mill workers who had begun their toil as children, noted one New England observer, were "pretty quick to observe, . . . with a good deal of inward rebellion and outward submission." George E. McNeill, deputy state constable of Massachusetts, in an 1875 report on schooling and hours of child labor in Massachusetts. Quoted in Carl Siracusa, *A Mechanical People: Perceptions of the Industrial Order in Massachusetts, 1815–1880* (Middletown, Conn.: Wesleyan Univ. Press, 1979), 194.

39. There is nothing in Ben's narratives or in what can be reconstructed of his pre- and postwar behavior to suggest that he saw factory labor as spiritually uplifting—a calling rather than simply a job.

40. This portion of the sketch relies heavily on the studies by Wallace's *Rockdale* and Zonderman's *Aspirations and Anxieties.*

41. The Callaghan mill was small, and he had leased it in 1848. "It housed four mules, eighteen power looms and hand looms, and worked both cotton and wool. . . . Callaghan was making fancy goods and his mill required older, highly skilled male operatives." Wallace, *Rockdale,* 44.

42. *The Upland Union,* 2 January 1850.

43. Wallace, *Rockdale,* 41.

44. *Delaware County Republican,* 20 October 1854.

45. This cousin's mother, Mary Hirst, served as a wartime nurse in an army hospital in Washington, D.C., as Ben's narratives will note. Members of the uncle's household are listed in the 1850 U.S. Census, Ridley Township, Delaware County, Pennsylvania. An Episcopalian rector named Marmaduke Hirst lived in the Chester/Rockdale vicinity in the 1830s, but it is not known whether he was also a relative of Ben's. Wallace, *Rockdale,* 300–304.

46. For a detailed and illustrated discussion of the various mill machines, see Wallace, *Rockdale,* ch. 4.

47. Zonderman, *Aspirations and Anxieties,* 37.

48. Pennsylvania passed a ten-hour workday maximum law in 1848, but Delaware County factory managers ignored it until 1853. Wallace, *Rockdale,* 394. For physiological effects of the labor, see Zonderman, *Aspirations and Anxieties,* 42.

49. In one (fictionalized) account, an enterprising female weaver sought relief by tying a cloth "rag baby" to the looms. When the looms were in motion, the "baby" broke into a frenetic dance. Eliza Jane Cate quoted in Zonderman, *Aspirations and Anxieties,* 28. Others mentally composed poetry to be transcribed after work.

50. Wallace, *Rockdale,* 327.

51. Ibid. Wallace notes that most machines were equipped with a clutch that could disengage them from the central shaft, pulley, and belt system if something went wrong, but this could still cause disruption for the entire mill.

52. Wallace, *Rockdale,* 179. The winter work hours were based on briefer daylight and the need to avoid "lighting up" (i.e., lighting oil lamps for illumination) twice in the same day. Workers generally detested the winter working conditions and often staged literal "blowout" parties to mark the transition to summer hours. See Zonderman, *Aspirations and Anxieties,* 78–80, for attitudes about "lighting up" and the "blowout."

53. Some prominent owners' wives in the county worked hard to create operatives' schools that taught the three Rs embedded within evangelical Protestant theology. See Wallace, *Rockdale,* especially ch. 7.
54. Wallace, *Rockdale,* 20.
55. See Zonderman, *Aspirations and Anxieties,* 108, for a discussion of the premium system.
56. Wallace, *Rockdale,* 387.
57. Women weavers outnumbered men two to one on the factory pay lists in one Rockdale mill in the 1840s. Apparently, many of these women were part-time workers, so that the numbers of females and males in the weaving room on any given day were probably about equal. Wallace, *Rockdale,* 147.
58. Zonderman, *Aspirations and Anxieties,* 111.
59. For examples, see Zonderman, *Aspirations and Anxieties,* 107; Shelton, *Manayunk,* 171, describes the misuse of laborers.
60. Quoted in Zonderman, *Aspirations and Anxieties,* 150. Zonderman's description of rules prevailing in New England factories is more specific than Wallace's. Zonderman, like Wallace, also emphasizes factory management's efforts to control both the factory work itself and the conduct of operatives away from the factory.
61. Zonderman, *Aspirations and Anxieties,* 28.
62. Eliza Jane Cate, recalling conditions in Lowell, Massachusetts, in 1840; quoted in Zonderman, *Aspirations and Anxieties,* 104–5. This is meant to be suggestive of a general workers' attitude in the Mid-Atlantic factories as well—at least before the labor strife of the 1840s. The writer, however, was native born, not an immigrant, writing with a female's retrospection.
63. Zonderman, *Aspirations and Anxieties,* 123.
64. Ibid., 17.
65. Ibid., 134.
66. Rockdale remained relatively quiet in the late 1820s and early 1830s during the strikes and marches in Manayunk. During the early stages of the national panic of 1834, Rockdale workers remained generally peaceful while Manayunk workers again struck. For an account of labor unrest in Manayunk, see Shelton's *Manayunk.* Part of the differences in these two Pennsylvania districts as portrayed may be due to different agendas of the authors. Shelton is primarily focused on the developing class consciousness of oppressed laborers. Wallace's concern is a more general interplay of Protestant evangelism and class interests in Rockdale.
67. The characterization is Wallace's. Wallace, *Rockdale,* 402 and elsewhere.
68. Workers' action also helped kill Pennsylvania's militia law in 1849. The law required all adult males between eighteen and forty-five years old to assemble (under elected officers) annually on the first and second Mondays of May. This was particularly burdensome to factory operatives because they received no wages for the time spent at the muster. The wealthy could pay a small fee in lieu of service. Ben may briefly have served in the quasi-military system. See Wallace, *Rockdale,* 383, 385–86.
69. Wallace, *Rockdale,* 369–70.
70. Ibid., 369.
71. Ibid.
72. They tended to follow the example set by Alonzo Potter, Episcopal bishop of Pennsyl-

vania after 1841, who staunchly opposed labor organizations and Masonic orders. Wallace, *Rockdale*, 335.

73. Wallace, *Rockdale*, 372.

74. Ibid., 63, 387, 360. In January 1844, powerloom weavers in one of the Rockdale mills earned an average of just over $11 by the piecework system. Their overseer received about $97, calculated at the rate of 25 percent of the weavers' total monthly earnings. This was during the "calm prosperity."

75. The point is emphasized throughout Shelton's *Manayunk*. Her analytical focus and theoretical underpinnings are different from Wallace's. Her discussion emphasizes workers' class consciousness and collective efforts to organize against owners' oppression.

76. For reference to Bill's worry about mill closings, see Ben Hirst's letter to Sarah on 16 May 1863 in chapter 8. His fears evidently were justified, as noted in John Hirst's letter to Ben on 3 September 1863 (Letter File 80, Hirst Letters, ASCC). John briefly mentioned the farm purchase and Bill's resulting need for money in letters to his brother Joe on 10 April 1864 and to Ben on 18 October 1864 (Letter Files 111 and 134, Hirst Letters, ASCC).

77. Zonderman discusses the importance of the kinship cluster for individual adjustment in *Aspirations and Anxieties*, 130. As expected, he focuses on clusters of sisters in his New England study. Wallace notes the importance of brothers in *Rockdale*, 65.

78. The 1850 census indicated between one-quarter and one-half of all the mill workers' households included boarders. For both the education and boarding estimates, see Wallace, *Rockdale*, 67.

79. Wallace, *Rockdale*, 64.

80. In *Rockdale*, Wallace reports Irish and English immigrants tended to settle in hamlets where their countrymen were already numerous. Both Irish and English belonged to the same church congregations, however. Besides the fact that many of the mill owners were English or Irish, this may have been a partial result of parallel chronology of immigration and growth of the mills in Rockdale. In both old England and New England, factories grew by using largely native labor. Immigrants were imported later, often to break strikes but generally to flood the labor market with workers willing to work for lower wages than the established natives. Ethnic hostility was inevitable under those conditions.

81. "Declaration for Widow's Pension," 2 August 1909, in Benjamin Hirst Pension File WC 688-730, National Archives Military Service Branch, Washington, D.C.

82. Wallace, *Rockdale*, 347. Wallace sees this as part of a growing conservatism in America at the time, manifested in evangelical Protestantism, machine politics, and both anti-union and anti-Mason ideology.

83. Wallace, *Rockdale*, 349.

84. Ibid., 368–69. Here Wallace is referring specifically to a professional labor organizer active in the Rockdale area, an Irishman named Hiram McConnell.

85. "General Affidavit," 22 Jan. 1906. John Hirst, Pension File.

86. *Delaware County Republican*, 2 Nov. 1855 and 8 Oct. 1858.

87. Rockville's population from Cole, *History of Tolland County, Connecticut* (New York: W. W. Preston & Co., 1888), 837; Rockdale's from Wallace, *Rockdale*, 35.

88. The 1860 census lists Ben and his household as living in a single dwelling. His real property was valued at $1,000, his personal property at $100. The Rockville property

tax lists for October 1862 appraised his real property value at $600. The home-owning friends he mentioned in his narratives evidently lived in dwellings of comparable value. In contrast, Congressman Dwight Loomis, a prominent citizen of Rockville mentioned by Ben intermittently, owned a house valued at $3,500 in 1863.

89. The 1860 census lists Ben's occupation as "spinner." This is almost certainly an error. Ben's own statements in his surviving army papers declare he was a weaver at the time of his enlistment. At least one aside in his narratives locates his job in the factory weaving department. Spinners were occupationally distinct from weavers—typically more skilled and better paid.

90. Benjamin Hirst, Pension File; John Hirst, Pension File; and Joseph Hirst, Pension File.

Chapter 1

1. All three of Company D's original officers and all but two of the original thirteen noncommissioned officers were from Rockville. The two exceptions were from the nearby towns of Bolton and Ellington. Page, *History*, 416–20. The company was mustered into Federal service with one captain, one first lieutenant, one second lieutenant, one first sergeant, four sergeants, eight corporals, and ninety-three privates—some of whom were detailed as musicians or wagoners. Rockville is technically a borough of the town of Vernon in Tolland County, Connecticut. Thus, the men from Rockville who joined the 14th are listed as residents of the town of Vernon in the regimental history's roster. Page, *History*, 416–30.

2. In 1861, Abraham Lincoln issued a call for 500,000 troops. This was Connecticut's share of the total, organized into thirteen regiments.

3. Page, *History*, 14.

4. Ibid., 16.

5. Ibid., 23.

6. Ibid., 25.

7. Ibid., 28.

8. Ibid., 43.

9. Ibid., 39.

10. Ibid., 58.

11. Ibid., 64–65.

12. Ibid., 70.

13. Ibid., 72.

Chapter 2

1. Armsmaker Samuel Colt had agreed to outfit a company of men, all of whom were to be at least five feet seven inches tall, to be known as "Colt's Rifles." But then he began to ruffle political feathers within the state by making demands for special regular army status and five-year enlistments for the men. Gov. William Buckingham finally dismissed Colt and disbanded the regiment. More than half the men went home, but the remainder joined the 5th Connecticut Volunteer Infantry. Niven, *Connecticut for the Union* (New Haven: Yale Univ. Press, 1965), 56–57.

2. In addition to native born, the company included contingents of Irish, English, and German immigrants.

3. Benjamin Hirst, "War Papers: History of Co. D, 14th Regt., Conn. Vols.," 1. *Rockville Journal,* 3 Feb. 1887.

4. Maj. Gen. Edwin Vose Sumner commanded the 2d Corps, Army of the Potomac under Gen. George B. McClellan. These troops had been sent to reinforce the Federal Army of Virginia under Gen. John Pope, then entangled with Gen. Robert E. Lee's Confederates on the battleground of the first Bull Run. The second day of the battle was on 30 August, the date of Ben's letter. He was reporting the retreat of Pope's troops toward Washington. For a thorough study of the second Bull Run campaign, see John J. Hennessy, *Return to Bull Run: The Campaign and Battle of Second Manassas* (New York: Simon and Schuster, 1993).

5. This letter is written in pencil and is difficult to read in spots. It is evidently missing some material, although it begins on one side of the page and continues on the reverse of that same page. Also, in later letters Hirst invariably signed off with a statement such as "Your affectionate Husband B. Hirst." There is no such closing in this letter, but then there is no space for it on the second page.

6. This was the second battle of Bull Run, 29–30 August 1862, pitting Gen. Robert E. Lee's Army of Northern Virginia against Gen. John Pope's newly formed Army of Virginia and components of Gen. George B. McClellan's Army of the Potomac.

7. This was the movement of McClellan's Army of the Potomac to reinforce Pope's Army of Virginia during the second Bull Run campaign.

8. Generals Irvin McDowell and Fitz-John Porter were blamed by General Pope for the defeat at the second Bull Run. Both were relieved of their commands. McDowell was soon exonerated and given a series of noncombat assignments. Porter was cashiered from the service, not to be reinstated until 1886 (with the rank of colonel). The merits of the case against Porter are still debated. According to Hennessy, the troops tended to blame the hated McDowell (as did Ben), while the high command and government tended to blame the politically indiscreet Porter. Hennessy and others have demonstrated that the ultimate blame should lie with Pope and the dilatory McClellan. Hennessy, *Return to Bull Run,* 463–72.

9. Maj. Gen. Nathaniel Prentiss Banks, Maj. Gen Irvin McDowell, and Maj. Gen. Franz Sigel were corps commanders in Gen. John Pope's Army of Virginia. Along with those troops in the battle were those of Maj. Gen. Fitz-John Porter, 5th Corps, Army of the Potomac.

10. Henry "Harry" Owen was commissioned a lieutenant in the 5th Connecticut Volunteers. He later resigned, then reenlisted as a private in the 14th Connecticut and was quickly promoted to sergeant in October 1863. He died of a wound received at Morton's Ford on 6 February 1863. Page, *History,* 418.

11. Hirst, "War Papers," 2, 10 Feb. 1887.

12. Maj. Gen. George B. McClellan commanded the Army of the Potomac at that time. Maj. Gen. Ambrose Everett Burnside had commanded the 9th Corps, Army of the Potomac, until 3 September 1862. At Antietam he commanded McClellan's left wing.

13. Col. Dwight Morris, who also commanded the 14th Connecticut.

14. The battle of South Mountain. Union troops under Burnside (1st and 9th Corps) attacked Confederates under Gen. D. H. Hill and seized the high ground around Turner's Gap that night (14 September). Mark M. Boatner III, *Civil War Dictionary* (New York: David McKay Co., 1959), 20.

15. Hirst, "War Papers," 2, 10 Feb. 1887.

16. Ibid., 3, 17 Feb. 1887.

17. Ibid.

18. Federal troops under Col. Dixon S. Miles at Harpers Ferry found themselves trapped and surrendered to Maj. Gen. Thomas J. Jackson's Confederates on 15 September 1862—all except 1,300 cavalrymen under Col. Benjamin F. Davis and Lt. Col. Hasbrouck Davis. These cavalrymen fought their way out of Jackson's encirclement and went on to capture ninety-seven wagons of Longstreet's reserve ammunition train before reaching Union lines at Greencastle, Pennsylvania. Boatner, *Civil War Dictionary*, 227.

19. As noted in the introduction, the Hirsts were not exactly sure of John's birth date. Evidently, they simply agreed among themselves about when to celebrate it.

20. Hirst, "War Papers," 4, 3 Mar. 1887.

21. Ibid., 5, 10 Mar. 1887.

22. This passage suggests that John Watslong and John Hirst may once have competed for the attentions of the same lady in Rockville.

23. Hirst, "War Papers," 5, 10 Mar. 1887.

24. The troops were moving out in the opening stages of what was to become the Fredericksburg campaign.

25. Hirst, "War Papers," 5, 10 Mar. 1887.

26. Major General Burnside was named to replace McClellan as Commander, Army of the Potomac, on 7 November 1862. This was the third time he had been offered command of that army. He accepted reluctantly and at the urging of fellow generals who did not want Gen. Joseph Hooker to be named to the command. Boatner, *Civil War Dictionary*, 107.

27. Hirst, "War Papers," 5, 10 Mar. 1887.

28. In his newspaper narratives, Ben changed this passage to read: "You say Cahoon, Tracy and Edwards are home. I think it must be on furlough as they exchanged into the regulars at Harper's Ferry. It is either that, or a dodge to get out of the service." Hirst, "War Papers," 6, 17 Mar. 1887. According to the regimental history, Cahoon deserted in December 1862, and the other two who were corporals in the 14th Connecticut were discharged for disability two weeks after they transferred to the regulars. Page, *History*, 419–21.

29. Hirst, "War Papers," 6, 17 Mar. 1887.

30. Ibid.

Chapter 3

1. A point made by Wiley, *Billy Yank*, 183, and Robertson, *Soldiers Blue and Gray*, 105.

2. Mitchell, *Vacant Chair*, 82.

3. Page, *History*, 65.

4. For instance, the following from Pvt. Newton Scott, Co. A, 36th Iowa Volunteers, to a girl back home on 9 April 1863: "But I will Have to close for I Have my sheet filled & nothing writen[.]" Newton Scott, Letters from an Iowa Soldier in the Civil War, compiled by William Scott Proudfoot, 1994, rev. 1997; Internet website: http://www.ucsc.edu/civil-war-letters/home.html.

5. Mitchell, *Civil War Soldiers*, 13. Mitchell describes the correlation between the growth of the industrial factory in the North and the decline of personal independence. Many soldiers resisted this. In a particularly apt passage he gives an example: "In peacetime

[Caleb] Blanchard had been a mill hand in Connecticut. He was uneasy about his place in society back home, but was determined not to let himself or his family feel inferior to anyone. He wanted his family to feel 'as good as enybody and to be independant.' His fight to protect republican freedom began not at the front but at home."

6. Cf. Linderman, *Embattled Courage*, 27, 31.
7. Linderman, *Embattled Courage*, ch. 1.
8. Page, *History*, 21.
9. In addition to Linderman and Mitchell, see Wiley, *Billy Yank*, 68–69, and Robertson, *Soldiers Blue and Gray*, 217.
10. Fiske, *Dunn Browne*, 57.
11. Some examples: "Fault-finding is the easiest kind of writing to which one can turn his hand." And, "The few men who came from a mere sense of patriotic, Christian duty stand their ground, and bear every thing without much murmuring; and doubtless half the grumblers don't mean all that they say, and would come up to the mark in a battle manfully. But I should do injustice to my honest belief if I said otherwise than that the spirit of the army is going down and backward every day." (This last was written as his company chopped down trees to clear fields of fire for artillery near Bolivar Heights in October 1862.) Fiske, *Dunn Browne*, 54, 86.
12. W. S. Tyler, "Biographical Notice," in Fiske, *Dunn Browne*, 32. This is an example of a juxtaposition similar to that described by Linderman in *Embattled Courage*, 27. By having displayed the ultimate in adult manliness, Fiske was entitled to be praised in death by invoking his childlike qualities.
13. Barton, *Goodmen*, 79–81; Linderman, *Embattled Courage*, 76–77.
14. After the disaster at Morton's Ford, John wrote the details of arrangements to ship a color bearer's body home and to purchase a beautiful painted casket for another chum. For discussion of the importance of proper mourning ritual, see Mitchell, *Vacant Chair*, ch. 8.
15. Page, *History*, 43–44.
16. Cf. Mitchell, *Civil War Soldiers*, 13.
17. Cf. Wiley, *Billy Yank*, 24; Linderman, *Embattled Courage*, 169–70.
18. Fiske, *Dunn Browne*, 64. To the extent that McClellan's political ambitions and party affiliations were clear at that time, part of Fiske's ire moved along party lines. The captain was an outspoken, hidebound Republican. His specific charges against the general commanding, however, focused on McClellan's evident lack of enthusiasm for the bold offensive.
19. Mitchell, *Vacant Chair*, 17.
20. Fiske, *Dunn Browne*, 40, 42.
21. Linderman, *Embattled Courage*, 113.
22. Mitchell, *Vacant Chair*, 22.
23. Fiske, *Dunn Browne*, 67.
24. Ibid., 85–86.
25. Ibid., 101–5.
26. Linderman, *Embattled Courage*, 84–86; Linderman suggests why this was true of other soldiers' accounts: drunkenness was considered impure and unmanly. Still, Ben did not conceal his taste for liquor. Its medicinal properties were extolled with tongue in cheek.

27. Fiske, *Dunn Browne,* 89.
28. Ibid., 70.
29. Ibid., 96.
30. Ibid., 98.
31. Ibid., 45–46.
32. Cf. Linderman, *Embattled Courage,* 98.
33. Fiske, *Dunn Browne,* 49–50.
34. The state adjutant general later set the regiment's total loss at 137, including 28 missing. Page, *History,* 49.
35. Fiske, *Dunn Brown,* 58.
36. Randall C. Jimerson describes the motivations for keeping Civil War diaries in *The Private Civil War: Popular Thought During the Sectional Conflict* (Baton Rouge: Louisiana State Univ. Press, 1988), 4. Jimerson quotes Col. Charles Wainwright of New York, whose own perspective seems close to Ben's: Wainwright wished "to so fix the events of my soldiering in time and place, that I may easily recall them in years to come, should my life be spared."
37. The muting was even more pronounced in his newspaper accounts, as discussed in the epilogue.
38. Fiske, *Dunn Browne,* 46–48.
39. See, for example, John William DeForest, *A Volunteer's Adventures: A Union Captain's Record of the Civil War,* ed. James H. Croushore (New Haven: Yale University Press, 1946), 65, 182; Henry M. Stanley, "Henry Stanley Fights with the Dixie Grays at Shiloh," in *The Blue and the Gray,* ed. Henry Steele Commager (Indianapolis: Bobbs-Merrill, 1950; rpt. New York: Fairfax Press, 1982), 354, 355; Wiley, *Billy Yank,* 77–78.
40. Ben's style and content can be compared to that of Sullivan Ballou, a major in the 1st Rhode Island Volunteers, whose articulate, passionate last letter to his wife had such an emotional impact on viewers of Ken Burns's PBS television series on the Civil War. He was evidently of a higher social class than Ben. But others, evidently beneath Ben's socioeconomic status, judging from grammar and spelling, were considerably more forthcoming and erotically explicit about their passions. See Robertson, *Soldiers Blue and Gray,* 113. For a more extensive discussion of sex in the Civil War, see Thomas P. Lowry, *The Story the Soldiers Wouldn't Tell: Sex in the Civil War* (Mechanicsburg, Pa.: Stackpole Books, 1994).
41. Thanks to Prof. Frank Byrne for independently detecting the double entendre in this letter and thus convincing me that it was less ambiguous than I originally thought.
42. Billings, *Hardtack and Coffee,* 217–24.
43. Robertson, *Soldiers Blue and Gray,* 98.
44. Linderman, *Embattled Courage,* 27.
45. See Mitchell, *Vacant Chair,* 128, for a discussion of nineteenth-century views of women's qualities that prompted his concluding characterization: "As children of nature, women can have loyalties, but not ideologies."

Chapter 4

1. H. S. Stevens, *Souvenir of Excursion to Battlefields by the Society of the Fourteenth Connecticut Regiment and Reunion at Antietam, September 1891; With History and Remi-*

niscences of Battles and Campaigns of the Regiment on the Fields Revisited (Washington, D.C.: Gibson Brothers, 1893), 78.

2. Ibid., 82.
3. Page, *History,* 84.
4. Ibid., 86–87.
5. Ibid., 88.
6. Ibid., 92.
7. Fiske, *Dunn Browne,* 108.
8. Ibid., 136.
9. Page, *History,* 110. Evidently, Uncas was either Black or Native American. The original bearer of that name was a famous Mohegan tribal leader in colonial Connecticut.
10. Fiske, *Dunn Browne,* 130–31.

Chapter 5

1. Hirst, "War Papers," 6, 17 Mar. 1887.
2. Secretary of War Edwin M. Stanton.
3. Maj. Gen. Edwin Vose Sumner commanded the Right Grand Division of the Army of the Potomac at the time. He later asked to be relieved of that command and died on 21 March 1863. Boatner, *Civil War Dictionary,* 818.
4. Capt. Samuel Storrow Sumner, serving as aide-de-camp to his father at the time.
5. The officers were drunk. Ben's retrospective account of this incident is quoted in the epilogue.
6. Hirst, "War Papers," 9, 7 Apr. 1887.
7. Ibid., 7, 24 Mar. 1887.
8. Ibid.
9. Maj. Gen. Winfield Scott Hancock then commanded the 1st Division, 2d Corps. The Irish Brigade (2d Bde.) of that division was led by Brig. Gen. Thomas Francis Meagher. The 3d Division, French's, led the attack in column by brigades, Kimball's (1st), then Andrews's (3d), then Palmer's (2d, including the 14th Connecticut). When it was stopped, Hancock's division attacked and was also stopped by the Confederate artillery and musket fire. Howard's 2d Division then moved out to attack to the right of the 1st and 3d Divisions, but was stopped and pinned down. *Official Records,* ser. 1, vol. 21:286–87. U.S. Dept. of War, *The War of the Rebellion: A Compilation of the Official Records of the Union and Confederate Armies,* ser. 1, vol. 21 (Washington, D.C.: Govt. Printing Office, 1888), 286–87.
10. Men became disoriented on the field after the assault was stopped. Two 14th Connecticut men looking for their regiment encountered their brigade commander, Colonel Palmer, who could not tell them the location of either the regiment or his brigade. He did, however, point to a flag lying untended on the ground nearby and said he believed it belonged to the 14th. It was, in fact, the regiment's state flag and was carried off to safety by the two soldiers. Page, *History,* 86.
11. Lt. Chelsea Vinton.
12. Hirst, "War Papers," 7, 24 Mar. 1887.
13. Ibid.
14. Ibid., 8, 31 Mar. 1887.

15. Ibid.

16. The regimental roster does not include Jesting's name, even with consideration of Ben's possible misspelling. The context suggests Jesting was considered absent without leave by his fellow soldiers.

17. Letters from John Hirst later in the war indicate John Bottomly was the elder Bottomly's son. Although "Bottomly" was obviously a caring friend to both Hirst brothers, I could find no reference to his first name in any of their narratives.

18. Mr. Towne was the father of Albert H. Towne Jr., who was killed at Fredericksburg. "Simons" was Cpl. John Symonds, discharged for disability on 7 February 1863. Oliver Dart was discharged for disability on 8 February 1863. Color Sgt. Charles E. "Charlie" Dart died on 6 January 1863 from wounds received at Fredericksburg. George N. Brigham, a sergeant at the time, was later promoted to second lieutenant of Co. I. Elbert F. Hyde, a corporal at the time, eventually became first sergeant of Co. D. Kilbourn E. Newell was a private at Fredericksburg, but was later promoted to second lieutenant of Co. H. Thus, two sergeants and one corporal left the company while it was engaged in combat to help one corporal and one private to the aid station. If the incident involved questionable conduct at the time, it evidently did not affect the later promotions of those involved.

19. Maj. Gen. William Buel Franklin commanded the Left Grand Division at Fredericksburg and was blamed by Maj. Gen. Ambrose Everett Burnside and the Committee on the Conduct of the War for the disaster at Fredericksburg, although Burnside himself also accepted blame. Both were reassigned to lesser commands. Maj. Gen. Edwin Vose Sumner was relieved of his command at his request after the battle and died about three months later. Boatner, *Civil War Dictionary,* 107, 304–5, 818.

20. Hirst, "War Papers," 10, 14 Apr. 1887.

21. Based on what follows, I have assumed the person referred to in this letter as "x x x" was Ben's mother-in-law. Ben's own mother died before the war. If his mother-in-law's behavior was deviant enough to earn her a reprimand, it was unlike Ben to convey his respects to her.

22. The entire letter is in pencil except for this inserted statement in ink. The insert is crossed out in pencil. The letter itself is actually page 4 of his first recopied installment of his journal.

23. The reference here may well be to the children of the William Henry Porter family, African Americans who lived close to Ben and Sarah in Rockville. In 1860, the Porter household included ten children, one of whom, Joseph Porter, was killed in action in 1864 while serving with the 29th Connecticut Volunteers. Another son, Charles Ethan Porter, became a noted artist. Interviews, Ardis Abbott and Myrtle Loftus, Vernon Historical Society, Sept. 1995 (notes in possession of the author). Ben's comment in this letter was deleted from his newspaper narratives.

24. Maj. Gen. Darius Nash Couch was appointed to command the 2d Corps, Army of the Potomac, on 7 October 1862, when Major General Sumner was elevated to command of the Right Grand Division. Boatner, *Civil War Dictionary,* 204.

25. Soldiers' boxes from home were being opened and searched for liquor. See Billings, *Hardtack and Coffee,* 219, and the following chapter for more discussion of this.

26. Hirst, "War Papers," 10, 14 Apr. 1887.

27. The reference here is unclear. It might refer to Lincoln's Emancipation Proclamation, which took effect on 1 January 1863 and displeased Democrats. Or, it might refer to

Lincoln's 10 March proclamation of temporary amnesty for deserters: those absent without leave from their units who returned for duty by 1 April would not be punished. This was done in hopes of slowing the increasing desertion rates in the army. Ben's statement immediately following this one (and his unremitting hostility toward shirks) make the latter reference more likely.

28. This is a rare instruction to Sarah about privacy. Presumably, she would show this particular letter only to her most trusted circle of readers.

29. Maj. Gen. Joseph Hooker took command of the Army of the Potomac on 26 January 1863. He took effective action to improve the logistical system—particularly the rations—of that army.

30. Thomas Seymour, a Democrat, was running against the incumbent Republican governor, William Buckingham.

31. Hirst, "War Papers," 11, 21 Apr. 1887.

32. A play on the name of Leiperville, Delaware County, Pennsylvania, where Kate Smiley, Sarah's sister, as well as Ben's older brother William and wife were living at the time.

33. Lincoln decided to visit the Army of the Potomac in camp and confer directly with General Hooker about the latter's strategic plans. The president reviewed the troops on Friday, 10 April.

34. Hirst, "War Papers," 11, 21 Apr. 1887.

35. Ibid., 11, 21 Apr. 1887.

36. Possibly a reference to one of the mills owned by the prominent developer John P. Crozer in Delaware County, Pennsylvania.

37. These two sentences were not in his original correspondence, so the instructions for privacy were decidedly not private. Hirst, "War Papers," 11, 21 Apr. 1887.

38. Dwight Loomis was by then just finishing his second congressional term and did not seek reelection.

Chapter 6

1. For a discussion on soldiers' views about Providence, see Mitchell, *Vacant Chair*, 138. See this book's epilogue for some concluding observations on this feature of Ben's world view.

2. One of the officers Ben singled out as a shirk, Lt. Ira Emery, never recovered; he lingered on in worsening health and despondency until his death eight years later. Henry P. Goddard, *Memorial of Deceased Officers of the Fourteenth Regiment, Connecticut Volunteers* (Hartford: Case, Lockwood & Brainard, 1872), 38–39. Lieutenant Emery is listed in Ben's pension records as the officer who "recruited" Ben in Rockville.

3. In *Embattled Courage*, 129, Gerald Linderman aptly summarizes Ben's quandary at Fredericksburg: "One of the few standing orders more heeded than ignored was the one forbidding soldiers to drop out of the charge in order to aid wounded companions. It was observed because courage was at issue, and to help another might easily be construed as a cowardly attempt to escape combat." Yet, Ben's and others' testimony indicates it *was* frequently ignored in the 14th's early battles.

4. Despite Ben's opaque comment about his conduct, George N. Brigham distinguished himself by being wounded while attempting to capture an enemy flag at Gettysburg and was promoted to lieutenant several months later. He was wounded again in the Reams's Station debacle in August 1864. Whatever his feelings toward Ben at the time,

he remained friendly and helpful to Ben's brother John through the rest of the war. In the 1880s, he was a prominent citizen of Rockville and commander of the local GAR post. He listed "Segts Benj & John Hirst" among his "most intimate comrades in service" on his GAR membership application form. (Forms are in ASCC.)

5. Mitchell, "The Northern Soldier," 84.
6. As noted in chapter 4, Charles Lyman, another NCO in Company D, also reported helping wounded. He was lying directly beside Symonds and Dart when they were hit; but instead of helping them he held his position (perhaps because his two comrades were already receiving help), then rose up and charged with the others. He stopped to give aid to the wounded as the whole regiment was withdrawing. Page, *History*, 89–91. He was promoted to lieutenant soon after the battle and fought at Chancellorsville. He was later dismissed from the service on what Ben felt were trumped-up charges. After the war he became a respected civil servant in Washington.
7. Fiske, *Dunn Browne*, 112.
8. Ibid., 119.
9. For a discussion of Connecticut's wartime politics, see Niven, *Connecticut for the Union*, especially ch. 11.
10. Michael Barton in *Goodmen* discusses the centrality of emotional control in the world views of mid-nineteenth-century Northerners. See also Mitchell, *Vacant Chair*, 7.
11. Lt. Col. Thomas F. Burpee died a hero's death leading a charge of his 21st Connecticut men at Cold Harbor on 9 June 1864. The GAR post in Rockville was later named in his honor.
12. Mitchell, "The Northern Soldier," 84. Mitchell writes: "Soldiers demanded courage of their officers in a way they rarely did of their fellow soldiers. Soldiers who had enlisted under their company commanders had a right to feel particularly betrayed if their captains proved cowardly." The observation summarizes Ben's earlier feelings toward Company D's officers and the keen interest in the newcomers' previous behavior under fire.
13. Ben's tendency to complain about his company and regimental officers was more typical of common soldiers during the war's first years. By mid-1863, many of the original company and field-grade officers were gone. The survivors were joined in command by newly commissioned veteran common soldiers. Later in the war, then, "[o]ften those most critical of officers exempted their own lieutenants and captains." Linderman, *Embattled Courage*, 233. In this context, however, Linderman describes a growing social chasm between officers and enlisted men as the war continued.
14. Fiske, *Dunn Browne*, 130–31.
15. See James M. McPherson, *What They Fought For, 1861–1865* (Baton Rouge and London: Louisiana State Univ. Press, 1994), 61–63.
16. Linderman, *Embattled Courage*, 246.
17. See Mitchell, *Vacant Chair*, 144–50. However, there was intense interest in the details of the dying as well, particularly in marking the last words of the dying and the courageous way they confronted their fate.
18. Soon after the battle, Captain Fiske declared that the singular tactical blunder of the regiment was to lie down and seek scanty shelter just beneath the wall, rather than to keep going under the withering fire to get in among the defenders.
19. Fiske's comment referred to the importance of mail from home for soldiers' morale.

At mail call, he reported, "[I]t would have done your . . . heart good . . . to have seen the eye light up, and the hand stretch forth to grasp the missive of affection (very likely ill-spelled, and directed in crooked lines, with no capital letters, down into one corner of the envelope)." Fiske, *Dunn Browne,* 59.

20. Page, *History,* 107.
21. Fiske, *Dunn Browne,* 137–38.
22. Ibid., 141.

Chapter 7

For extensive coverage of the Chancellorsville campaign, see Ernest B. Furgurson, *Chancellorsville 1863: The Souls of the Brave* (New York: Alfred A. Knopf, 1992). Harry W. Pfanz has produced two important general studies of the Gettysburg battle: *Gettysburg: The Second Day* (Chapel Hill: Univ. of North Carolina Press, 1987), and *Gettysburg: Culp's Hill and Cemetery Hill* (Chapel Hill: Univ. of North Carolina Press, 1993). George R. Stewart offers a detailed popular study in *Pickett's Charge: A Microhistory of the Final Attack at Gettysburg, July 3, 1863* (Boston: Houghton Mifflin, 1959; rpt. New York: Fawcett, 1963). In addition to *The Third Day at Gettysburg and Beyond* (Chapel Hill: Univ. of North Carolina Press, 1994), Gary W. Gallagher has edited two volumes on Union and Confederate leadership on the first and second day's battles: *The First Day at Gettysburg* (Kent, Ohio: Kent State Univ. Press, 1992) and *The Second Day at Gettysburg* (Kent, Ohio: Kent State Univ. Press, 1993). For the actions of Connecticut units at Gettysburg, see Charles P. Hamblen's articulate *Connecticut Yankees at Gettysburg,* ed. Walter L. Powell (Kent, Ohio: Kent State Univ. Press, 1993). Excellent comprehensive first-person narratives by Confederate Col. William C. Oates and Union Lt. Frank A. Haskell are bound together in Glenn LaFantasie, ed., *Gettysburg: The Narratives of Lt. Frank Haskell, U.S.A., and Col. William C. Oates, C.S.A* (New York: Bantam Books, 1992).

1. Page, *History,* 121–22.
2. Major Ellis's official report declares the regiment went south to the road junction, and "from this position moved along the plank road leading to Spottsylvania Court House and formed a line of battle facing to the southwest on the right of the road." Quoted in Page, *History,* 128. The plank road referred to in this passage was surely the Orange Plank Road running west from the Chancellor house. For details of troop movements on 2 and 3 May, see the excellent series of maps prepared by the National Park Service under the supervision of historian Edwin C. Bearss in 1962.
3. Page, *History,* 121–22.
4. Ibid., 122.
5. Ibid., 123.
6. An NCO from Company B, Elnathan B. Tyler, declared forty-three years later that the knapsacks were in fact recovered. As they were falling back from the Rebel flank attack, they happened to pass by the clearing where they had grounded their knapsacks the night before. "Any other regiment than the Fourteenth might not have stopped to get their knapsacks under the circumstances, but we had experience in losing knapsacks and in absence of positive orders not to resume them, we hunted up our own as quickly as possible, and then leisurely and in perfect order still, went back and took up a new position some distance to the rear." Page, *History,* 122. Possibly both men were correct, and Ben's Company D for some reason could not stop to pick up their

gear as Company B had done. Ben reconfirms his loss by referring to "our new knap-sacks" in his letter of 5 June 1863.

7. Johnsville was "Johnsonville" in the regimental history. Uniontown must also have been known as "Union Mills" at that time. Page, *History,* 133. See also Ben Hirst's letters of 30 June and 9 October ("Date no matter") in the next chapter.

8. Page, *History,* 134.

9. Ibid., 142.

10. Ibid., 144–47. Ben Hirst described the ride in his newspaper account of 9 June 1887: "[A] man on horse back left our lines and dashed across the fields until he reached the buildings; gave some orders and rode back again unharmed." There are several accounts of the fight for the Bliss farm. The most extensive is Elwood W. Christ, *"Over a Wide, Hot, . . . Crimson Plain": The Struggle for the Bliss Farm at Gettysburg, July 2nd and 3rd, 1863* (Baltimore: Butternut and Blue, 1993). See also Hamblen, *Connecticut Yankees at Gettysburg,* ch. 6, and John M. Archer, "Remembering the 14th Connecti-cut Volunteers," *Gettysburg: Historical Articles of Lasting Interest* 9 (July 1993): 61–79.

11. Page, *History,* 153. The withdrawal of Arnold's Battery will be discussed further in chapter 9.

Chapter 8

1. Brig. Gen. William Hays was a West Point graduate and Mexican War veteran. He was wounded and captured at Chancellorsville. He survived the war and died on duty as a major in the 5th U.S. Artillery. Boatner, *Civil War Dictionary,* 390.

2. This refers to the breaking of Maj. Gen. Otis O. Howard's 11th Corps by Lt. Gen. Thomas J. "Stonewall" Jackson's Confederates during the evening of 2 May.

3. Ben is referring here to a renewed attack by Jackson against the troops of the Union's 12th Corps, deployed just to the south of Plank Road.

4. Hirst, "War Papers," 13, 5 May 1887.

5. Capt. Samuel Davis from New London commanded Co. H of the 14th at Chan-cellorsville. He was dishonorably discharged on 17 September 1863.

6. This refers to the assault on Lee's right at Fredericksburg by the Union's 6th Corps under Maj. Gen. John Sedgwick. Sedgwick's troops penetrated the dreaded sunken road defenses on 3 May, halted to regroup, then resumed a westward push to join Hook-er's troops at Chancellorsville. Lee's Confederates under McLaws, Anderson, and Early counterattacked at Salem Church on 4 May and stopped Sedgwick's advance. The 6th Corps withdrew back across the Rappahannock in a thick fog that night.

7. This was a false rumor. Capt. Samuel Fiske ("Dunn Browne") was captured. He was paroled on 22 May 1863. See Fiske, *Dunn Browne,* 146–69.

8. According to the official roster, Co. D's second lieutenant at that time was Henry W. Wadhams. The reason for his arrest is unknown.

9. Gibbon's 1st Division, 2d Corps, had been left at Falmouth to cross over into Fred-ericksburg along with Sedgwick's 6th Corps on 3 May 1862. During Sedgwick's west-ward push on 3 and 4 May 1863, Gibbon's division remained behind to protect the Falmouth camp. Hancock's 1st Division, 2d Corps, and French's 3d Division, 2d Corps had earlier moved into the Chancellorsville battle.

10. This was probably the engraved identification tag that Kelly gave Ben on 13 April 1863 (see Ben's letter to "Sallie" [Sarah], 14 April 1863, in ch. 5).

11. Evidently a relative of Sarah's; the nickname makes positive identification impossible.

12. Hooker had received information that Lee was preparing to move out from his Fredericksburg position. He needed to verify this. On 5 June 1863, three Union regiments of the 6th Corps, with artillery support, probed Lee's defenses at Franklin's Crossing, then withdrew back across the Rappahannock after a brief skirmish. This was followed by a probe by Union cavalry that became the battle of Brandy Station on 9 June. Boatner, *Civil War Dictionary,* 309.

13. Capt. Isaac R. Bronson, Co. I, died on 3 June 1863 of wounds received at Chancellorsville on 3 May. He was from New Haven.

14. Hirst, "War Papers," 14, 12 May 1887. The reference is opaque. Ben may have been referring to a flurry of negotiations and preoccupation following the arrest of Ohio's "Copperhead" former congressman, Clement Vallandigham (5 May 1863), and his subsequent banishment to the Confederacy (25 May 1863). On 3 June, Lincoln revoked Maj. Gen. Ambrose Burnside's orders to shut down the pro-Democrat *Chicago Times,* which had opposed the government's handling of the Vallandigham affair.

15. This possibly refers to Hooker's efforts to move parallel to Lee's army in its northward push, remaining between the Confederates and Washington. However, there is no way to know whether Ben himself was aware of this intent. Most likely, it was simply a doubt that anything much would come of all the marching and early-morning alerts.

16. Hirst, "War Papers," 15, 19 May 1887.

17. Ibid.

18. Maj. Gen. Winfield Scott Hancock succeeded Maj. Gen. Darius Couch as commander of the 2d Corps on 22 May 1863. Couch had asked to be relieved after Chancellorsville in protest against Hooker's inept handling of that battle. Boatner, *Civil War Dictionary,* 204, 372.

19. This was probably the fighting around Upperville, Virginia, as Confederate Gen. J. E. B. Stuart withdrew to Ashby's Gap, back toward Gen. Robert E. Lee's main body of troops, after clashes with Union infantry and cavalry at Aldie (17 June) and Middleburg (17 and 19 June). Boatner, *Civil War Dictionary,* 6, 548, 861–62.

20. The second battle of Bull Run.

21. Four days later (28 June), French was succeeded by Brig. Gen. Alexander Hays as commander of the 3d Division, 2d Corps.

22. Hooker was relieved on 28 June by Maj. Gen. George Gordon Meade.

23. Ben's newspaper account notes this letter was received in Rockville on 3 July 1863. Hirst, "War Papers," 16, 26 May 1887.

24. This must have been an understatement! After the heat and combat during Longstreet's assault, John helped Ben back to the hospital, saw to it that he was properly attended to, then after dark went back to the battlefield where he remained awake all night distributing canteens from the dead to wounded Confederates still lying in front of the 14th's position. Hirst, "War Papers," 19, 23 June 1887.

25. Hirst, "War Papers," 16, 26 May 1887.

26. Ibid., 17, 2 June 1887.

27. A runaway horse crashed into Capt. J. B. Coit and knocked him cold. Hirst, "War Papers," 18, 9 June 1887.

28. Hirst, "War Papers," 18, 9 June 1887. Gen. Alexander Stewart Webb commanded the 2d Brigade, 2d Division, 2d Corps, on Gen. Alexander Hays's left.

29. Hirst, "War Papers," 18, 9 June 1887.

30. Ibid.
31. Ibid., 18, pt. 2, 16 June 1887.
32. Gen. John Gibbon assumed temporary command of the 2d Corps during the battle (until he was wounded), succeeding Gen. Winfield S. Hancock, who directed the several army corps defending Cemetery Ridge.
33. Hirst, "War Papers," 18, pt. 2, 16 June 1887.
34. Other accounts declare that it was Gen. Alexander Hays who trailed captured Confederate flags behind his horse along the line. See Stewart, *Pickett's Charge*, 224–25. Conceivably both officers did so.
35. Hirst, "War Papers," 18, pt. 2, 16 June 1887.

Chapter 9

Portions of this chapter were compiled as "'Fredericksburg on the Other Leg': Sergeant Ben Hirst's Narrative of Important Events, Gettysburg, July 3, 1863" in Gary W. Gallagher, ed., *The Third Day at Gettysburg and Beyond* (Chapel Hill, 1994), 132–60.

1. Linderman argues that courage was the central value for all Civil War soldiers. He draws a distinction between courage and manliness, but sees them as closely related in soldiers' "constellations of values," stating, "A failure of courage in war was a failure of manhood." *Embattled Courage*, 8. Mitchell also describes the centrality of courage as a value for soldiers struggling to live up to their home folks' expectations. Mitchell, "Northern Soldier," 85.
2. Fiske, *Dunn Browne*, 154–55.
3. Page's account of the Wilderness noted that the officers of Cos. C and I "had each man take a tree and fight Indian fashion" against a Confederate charge. Page, *History*, 237. DeForest declared that during combat at Opequon, the Confederates "fought more like redskins, or like hunters, than we. The result was that they lost fewer men, though they were far inferior in numbers." DeForest, *A Volunteer's Adventures*, 190.
4. Mitchell, *Civil War Soldiers*, 84.
5. Fiske, *Dunn Browne*, 178.
6. Ibid., 180.
7. Not all veteran regiments had the same horrified reaction. Some made jokes, conceivably to ease their uneasiness, about protruding skeletal hands with pointing fingers indicating the route of march. See Bruce Catton, *Glory Road*, vol. 2, *The Army of the Potomac* (Garden City, N.Y.: Doubleday & Co., 1952), 251, and Charles A. Fuller, *Personal Recollections of the War of 1861* (Hamilton, N.Y.: Edmonston Publishing Co., 1990), 90. On a march near Ashby's Gap at about the same time, a soldier discovered an amputated arm, hand still attached, lying in the dust along the road: "The temptation proved too much. He gave it a slight kick with his toe, probably to see what it was, but that was enough. It became a football for every one, and had to run the gauntlet, from the head of the brigade to the rear along the road to Upperville. Such was the blunting, hardening influence of grim, diabolical war." Robert Goldthwaite Carter, *Four Brothers in Blue* (1913; reprint, Austin: Univ. of Texas Press, 1978), 290. Whether hardened or not, soldiers typically could not let marches through half-buried dead go unmentioned.
8. Fiske, *Dunn Browne*, 175–76.

9. Ibid., 183.
10. Quoted in Page, *History*, 142; emphasis added.
11. Stevens, *Souvenir*, 16.
12. Soldiers armed with Sharps teamed up, one firing and the other loading. This made for a significantly higher rate of defensive fire, but also made the rifles' barrels very hot. Men used precious canteen water to cool them periodically. Page declared, "Accounts seem to agree that the Confederate line broke quicker in the immediate front of the Fourteenth than any where else." Page, *History*, 152–53, 155. If so, the Sharps may have been a major factor. The regimental history praised the effectiveness of these breechloaders several times in later battles.
13. William B. Hincks (who received the Medal of Honor for gallantry that day and was later promoted to major), quoted in Page, *History*, 149.
14. Page, *History*, 151; Stewart, *Pickett's Charge*, 183, 187.
15. Linderman, *Embattled Courage*, 32.
16. Compare this to Linderman's general observation: "Often the most powerful fear was that one's fear would be revealed—and that meant a prohibition on discussion . . . . Fear was not an anxiety to be shared but a weakness to be stifled." Linderman, *Embattled Courage*, 23.
17. Stewart declares General Hays's enthusiasm in battle was "an almost sexual excitement." Stewart, *Pickett's Charge*, 134–35, 71. For discussions of the Morton's Ford battle, see Page, *History*, ch. 12, and Bruce Trinque, "Rebels Across the River," *America's Civil War*, Sept. 1994, 38–45, 88.
18. Linderman, *Embattled Courage*, 103–10.
19. Mitchell, *Civil War Soldiers*, 88–89.
20. Stewart, *Pickett's Charge*, 201.
21. Ibid., 186.
22. Mitchell, *Civil War Soldiers*, 26.
23. Linderman notes that frontline soldiers "seemed to denounce all parties to the war except the enemy in combat." Linderman, *Embattled Courage*, 236.
24. Mitchell, *Civil War Soldiers*, 25.
25. Page, *History*, 155–56. The roster of captured colors gives some impression of the bunching and mingling of Confederate units as they approached the 14th Connecticut's narrow front. It included those of the 14th Virginia of Armistead's Brigade, Pickett's Division, Longstreet's Corps; the 52d North Carolina of Pettigrew's (then Marshall's) Brigade, Heth's (then Pettigrew's) Division, Hill's Corps; the 1st Tennessee and the 14th Tennessee, both of Archer's (then Fry's) Brigade, Heth's (then Pettigrew's) Division, Hill's Corps; and the 16th North Carolina of Scales's Brigade, Pender's (then Trimble's) Division, Hill's Corps. Portions of Hill's Corps had been placed under Longstreet's command for the assault. The 14th Tennessee hailed mostly from Clarksville. Of the 960 of them who left home for the seat of war, 365 were present for the battle of Gettysburg. After the first day's battle, 60 remained; after the third day's assault, only 3 were left. Their colors were captured by the 14th Connecticut's sergeant major, William B. Hincks, who had been firing two Sharps rifles during the assault while a lieutenant loaded them for him. To the left front of the 14th Connecticut position today is a small monument to the 26th North Carolina. Bruce Trinque argues effectively that that unit was in fact well to the right of the 14th Connecticut

position at the climax of the assault. See Bruce Trinque, "Arnold's Battery and the 26th North Carolina," *America's Civil War*, Jan. 1995, 61–67.

26. Stewart, *Pickett's Charge*, 224–25. As noted in chapter 7, Ben recalled in 1887 that soon after it was captured, General Gibbon dragged the 14th Tennessee's flag behind his horse.

27. For a discussion of Meade's options in pursuing Lee's army, see A. Wilson Greene, "From Gettysburg to Falling Waters," in *The Third Day at Gettysburg*, ed. Gary W. Gallagher (Chapel Hill: Univ. of North Carolina Press, 1994), 161–201.

28. Stewart's account of the battle declares Arnold's Battery remained in position along the wall and delivered a final volley of double-shotted canister just as the "North Carolinians of the 26th" were about to reach the defensive line. Stewart, *Pickett's Charge*, 201. See also Thomas M. Aldrich, *The History of Battery A, First Regiment Rhode Island Light Artillery in the War to Preserve the Union, 1861–1865* (Providence: Snow and Farnham, 1904), 216. The 14th's regimental history, however, insists that Arnold's battery withdrew immediately after the afternoon barrage, leaving one gun which had rolled forward down the slope. Page, *History*, 150, 153, 165. At stake in the discrepancy is the importance of the 14th in repulsing the charge. Federal artillery commander Henry J. Hunt's postwar recollection supports the 14th Connecticut's version. See Hunt, "The Third Day at Gettysburg," in *Battles and Leaders of the Civil War*, ed. Robert Underwood Johnson and Clarence C. Buel (New York: Century, 1887–88), 3:374. Reportedly, no battery replaced Arnold's until after the assault had been beaten back. Allegedly, the replacement battery immediately opened with canister and managed to kill one 14th man and wound others who by then were dashing down the slope in front of the wall, chasing retreating Confederates. Stevens, *Souvenir*, 33. For some reason, the replacement battery's action was not reported in the later and more considered regimental history. See also Trinque, "Arnold's Battery" for the action of Arnold's Battery.

Epilogue

1. An example written on 25 August 1863: "hyde [Sgt. Elbert F. Hyde] as is fingers full Just now. he wishes you or some of they other was here he is so down hearted as to talk about trying to get transferred into some other reg so dont you be in no hurry about coming back untill things get better. if i was you and could get out of it i would do it." Letter File 79, Hirst Letters, ASCC.

2. Hirst, "War Papers," 20, 30 June 1887.

3. John Hirst to Sarah, Letter File 147, 2 May 1865. Letter File 152, Hirst Letters, ASCC.

4. This linkage was described in the introduction.

5. Anne C. Rose provides an extensive analysis of middle-class Victorians' views of the war in her *Victorian America and the Civil War* (New York: Cambridge Univ. Press, 1992). Rose's conclusions are based on detailed study of the writings and lives of seventy-five individuals born between 1815 and 1837. "All were middle class in the sense that they pursued white-collar occupations. More specifically, they were sufficiently wealthy, educated, and prominent to be considered community leaders, whether the community composed a town, city, or the nation" (p. 3.). Ulysses S. Grant, James A. Garfield, and William Tecumseh Sherman are included in this group. Clearly, these

middle-class Victorians were above Ben's station. Moreover, they felt compelled to derive a sense of satisfaction and fulfillment from their *careers*—as distinct physically and semantically from *jobs* held by respectable laborers (see p. 67).

6. A laborer who had "lived in twenty different factory towns" observed in 1871 that "young women who work in the factories are many of them ruined in morals and nearly all in health. A rosy-cheeked girl put in a mill will begin to fade in three months. They make poor housekeepers." Quoted from a Massachusetts Bureau of Statistics of Labor Report in Henry F. Bedford, ed., *Their Lives and Numbers: The Condition of Working People in Massachusetts, 1870–1900* (Ithaca: Cornell Univ. Press, 1995), 27.

7. The wife typically collected family paychecks and worked out the family budget in Rockdale laboring families. This was a major distinction between laboring class and well-to-do managers' families. Wallace, *Rockdale*, 67–68.

8. This point is extensively developed by Rose in *Victorian America*, 184–85.

9. Wallace, *Rockdale*, 69. The author discusses the role of women in prosperous managerial families of the Delaware County region: "[T]heir own primary work was neither heavy housework nor factory production but rather the administration of servants, church activity, and the cultivation of artistic and literary interests." See also Rose, *Victorian America*, 70, for a similar comment on women's efforts to seek self-definition. Clearly not all officers or their wives were of this leisured social stratum. This perspective on women's ideal social roles was not restricted to the elites.

10. Rose discusses the sources of strain and strengthening in wartime families in *Victorian America*, 187, 191.

11. Rose describes Gen. William Tecumseh Sherman's reaction to his wife's agreeing to sell memorabilia at a Sanitary Commission fair in 1865: it was "unbecoming"; but he supposed she could "do as she pleased." She did. Rose, *Victorian America*, 186.

12. Rose, *Victorian America*, 188.

13. John continued to ask Sarah to send him things in boxes, but it was evidently at her urging. He was courteous when he did so, thanked her profusely, and did not want to inconvenience her. See, especially, John Hirst to Sarah, 30 Oct. 1863, and John Hirst to Ben, 11 Jan. 1865. Letter Files 88 and 143, Hirst Letters, ASCC.

14. Rose, *Victorian America*, 189, offers an extensive discussion of enlisted men's efforts to re-create fictive family bonds in army camps.

15. In fact, some factory owners in both England and America succeeded in controlling their operative's lives at home as well as in the factory. For examples, see Glen, *Urban Workers*, 281; Shuttleworth, *Working Classes*, 100; and Zonderman, *Aspirations and Anxieties*, 150. More broadly, much of the labor struggle of the antebellum period was generated by the issue of managers' efforts to control the lives of operatives. Shelton in *Manayunk* and Wallace in *Rockdale*, for example, explore these larger issues in a geographical and temporal context most relevant to Ben Hirst's labor experience.

16. See especially his letter to Sarah of 1 Oct. 1862.

17. In a speech before the House, U.S. Representative Charles Upham in 1855 articulated the ideal—and situated it geographically: "[T]here is no part of the world where men rise, without patrimony or patronage, by the inherent force of merit and talent, to high positions in society, more surely or more generally than in Massachusetts." Quoted in Carl Siracusa, *A Mechanical People*, 94.

18. In Siracusa, *A Mechanical People*, 91.

19. Siracusa, *A Mechanical People*, 108. See also Shelton, *Manayunk*.

20. The quote is from U.S. Representative John Palfrey of Massachusetts in the mid-nineteenth century, in Siracusa, *A Mechanical People*, 107.

21. For prewar Democratic political ideology in Massachusetts, see Carl Siracusa, *A Mechanical People*, 122–24; in Pennsylvania, see Wallace, *Rockdale*, 369, 389.

22. From an address by the Democratic State Central Committee in Massachusetts for 1849. Quoted in Siracusa, *A Mechanical People*, 129–30.

23. Ben's occasional use of racist epithets was fairly common among Union soldiers. See David Blight, "A Union Soldier's Experience," in *Divided Houses*, ed. Catherine Clinton and Nina Silber (New York: Oxford Univ. Press, 1992), 68. When he used the epithets to express hostility, they were aimed at a specific group in Rockville rather than an entire population.

24. Siracusa writes that English and Germans—compared to Irish—were fairly well received by native Yankee workers in Massachusetts, where Ben worked for awhile. "As they found their appropriate niches and demonstrated their economic value, they fulfilled the prophecies of the politicians [i.e., as "respectable workers"]. Most important, the [Civil] war had certified their worthiness." Siracusa, *A Mechanical People*, 175.

25. Niven, *Connecticut for the Union* (New Haven: Yale Univ. Press, 1965), 111–19.

26. Niven writes that "during the depression of 1857, . . . Connecticut mill workers received drastic cuts in wages, but commodity prices were not reduced proportionally until a year later. Even in prosperous years like 1851, a highly paid skilled worker with a family of five made about $10 a week, slightly less per week than what his family needed for food, shelter, and clothing. . . . In the mill towns of Connecticut the average wage was $5 per week." Niven, *Connecticut for the Union*, 115–16. The Hirst brothers' mill wages when they enlisted are not known. Data from Massachusetts in 1860, although possibly unreliable, show cotton mill weavers' weekly wages as follows: overseers of weavers, $17.41; section hands, $7.74; second hands, $7; lowest rate for weavers, $4.50. Cited in Bedford, *Their Lives and Numbers*, 61.

27. Rose, *Victorian America*, 237.

28. See Rose, *Victorian America*, 237–38.

29. Nineteenth-century Protestant faith was typically linked to control, of course, and both were linked to each other and to labor reform via the temperance movement. Ben was almost certainly exposed to temperance dogma, but clearly he decided it was not for him. For an insightful discussion of religion and temperance in labor reform in New England, see Teresa Anne Murphy, *Ten Hours' Labor, Religion, Reform, and Gender in Early New England* (Ithaca: Cornell Univ. Press, 1992).

30. Mitchell, *Vacant Chair*, 140. Mitchell discusses the "providential" American view of life.

31. This is similar to the world view described in Max Weber's *Protestant Ethic and the Spirit of Capitalism*, trans. Talcott Parsons (New York: Scribner, 1958). One important difference: Ben nowhere hinted that good works would lead him into a state of grace.

32. This statement is strikingly similar to that uttered by a Delaware County self-made mill owner of English-Hugenot extraction. Contemplating the devastation to his mill caused by the flood in 1843, he stated: "I trust and believe I meet it with the resignation of a Christian and firmness of a man somewhat accustomed to vicissitudes." Quoted in Wallace, *Rockdale*, 379. Unlike Ben, however, this mill owner had become a devout Baptist.

33. Rose makes this point in referring to Gen. Ulysses S. Grant's tendency to distance

himself from war's horror in his personal memoirs. Quoting his dispassionate, third-person description of the fighting in the Wilderness, she observes: "A commander's need for dispassion, his personal immunity from harm, and the distance in time of two decades must have worked to restrict Grant's acknowledgement of the grief caused by the devastation. Yet his measured portrayal arose, too, from the preeminent importance in his biography of another theme, the possibility of controlling one's circumstances." Rose, *Victorian America,* 241.

34. At least one of the men in Company D, Thomas Wilkie, had prior combat experience in the Crimean War. See chapter 2.

35. In different ways, three combat incidents later revealed shifts in the prevailing ideals of courageous behavior. The first was the cancellation of what the men felt was a suicidal assault at Mine Run in late November 1863; the second was the failure to respond to Grant's orders for yet another assault at Cold Harbor the following spring; and the third was the humiliating collapse of Hancock's troops at Reams's Station, Virginia, on 25 August 1864. These are implied in Page, *History,* ch. 11, 13, 14.

36. One of Gen. Joshua Chamberlain's regimental commanders once remarked to him: "General, you have the soul of the lion and the heart of the woman." Linderman, *Embattled Courage,* 27. In his funeral oration, Captain Fiske was not only characterized as childlike, but (because he had spent part of his adolescence caring for a paralytic) as having "almost the tact and tenderness of a Florence Nightingale." W. S. Tyler, "Biographical Notice," in Fiske, *Dunn Browne,* 12, 32.

37. See Linderman, *Embattled Courage,* 27.

38. Mitchell notes the "feminine responsibility of nurturing their soldiers physically" that fell to officers. Mitchell, *Vacant Chair,* 82.

39. For a discussion of whether there was a late-war "decline in positive expressions of ideological and patriotic commitment" among soldiers who joined up in 1861–62, see James McPherson, *What They Fought For,* 41–46.

40. For a similar tendency, see David Blight, "A Union Soldier's Experience," 66. This persisted in typical postwar memoirs; see Rose, *Victorian America,* 245. Soldiers' letters evidently differed on this score. See Robertson, *Soldiers Blue and Gray,* for a sampling of graphic vignettes some wrote home to loved ones.

41. This, of course, changed to long weeks of almost continuous combat beginning with Grant's spring campaign in 1864.

42. Advertisement, *Tolland County Journal,* 21 September 1877.

43. The revived unit was officially designated as Burpee Post #71, Grand Army of the Republic. Membership data are from GAR records, ASCC.

44. On 14 April 1888, a corner lot was purchased for the building site. In September 1890, GAR members convened for the first time in a handsome new red-brick building to house the GAR Memorial Hall and town offices. George S. Brookes, *Cascades and Courage: The History of the Town of Vernon and the City of Rockville* (Rockville, Conn.: T. F. Rady & Co., 1955), 353–55.

45. See Stevens, *Souvenir.*

46. Benjamin Hirst, Pension File, includes Ben's death certificate and the references to Sarah's institutionalization.

47. See, for example, Wallace, "Revitalization Movements."

48. Linderman, *Embattled Courage,* 266–97. Grand Army of the Republic posts did not see much growth until about 1880.

49. Rose, *Victorian America,* 245.
50. Rose, *Victorian America,* 245, 247.
51. Rose, *Victorian America,* 237. This passage ends with the phrase: "that pertained to whites only." Ben's attitudes on race have already been explored. This need for validation arose in part from a restlessness over conflicting tenets of antebellum world view: a declining religious spirituality set against an emerging secular self-gratification. There is no evidence that Ben experienced such restlessness.
52. "In the war, . . . [Victorians] found a cause of their own making so monumental that they needed simply to tell a straightforward story to convey its importance. . . . [F]inding one's own words to tell the story was essential, too, because the critical problem of this generation was identity. . . .[T]he personal perspective not only presented itself as a tool for ordering experience, but gained credibility by successful and repeated use." Rose, *Victorian America,* 252.
53. Hirst, "War Papers," 7, 24 Mar. 1887. The context of the anecdote implied that the officers were members of the 14th Connecticut.
54. In addition to David D. Crombie, Ben mentioned that "Frank D" (Frank D. Maine) skedaddled from Antietam. "We have not seen him since, and hear he is at home and at work [in Rockville] already." Hirst, "War Papers," 4, 3 Mar. 1887. The regimental history listed Maine as discharged for disability in October 1862.
55. Hirst, "War Papers," 8, 31 Mar. 1887.
56. Ben wrote that "Col. Chamberlain of Maine" found young Towne's body in front of Chamberlain's brigade and took from it a testament bearing Towne's name and hometown, which he sent to Rockville later in the war. Hirst, "War Papers," 8, 31 Mar. 1887.
57. Hirst, "War Papers," 10, 14 Apr. 1887.
58. Ibid., 13, 5 May 1887.
59. Ibid., 19, 23 June 1887.
60. Ibid., 7, 24 Mar. 1887.
61. Rose makes a more sweeping comment on persistence in describing her sample of prominent Victorians: "[T]he most decisive social and intellectual trends of the mid-century period were in place before the war and were not transformed fundamentally by the conflict." Rose, *Victorian America,* 13.
62. Hirst, "War Papers," 18, 16 June 1887.

Appendix

1. Unless otherwise noted, all information on members of the 14th Connecticut comes from the official roster in the 1889 report of the Connecticut Adjutant General, checked and reprinted in Page's *History,* 373–509.
2. Cole, *History of Tolland County,* 161.
3. Ibid., 162–63.
4. Ibid., 596.
5. Military data from Connecticut Adjutant General's *Record of Service of Connecticut Men in the Army and Navy of the United States in the War of the Rebellion* (Hartford: State Printer, 1889), 610.

Bibliography

Aldrich, Thomas M. *The History of Battery A, First Regiment Rhode Island Light Artillery, in the War to Preserve the Union, 1861–1865.* Providence: Snow and Farnham, 1904.

Archer, John M. "Remembering the 14th Connecticut Volunteers." *Gettysburg: Historical Articles of Lasting Interest* 9 (1993): 61–79.

Barton, Michael. *Goodmen: The Character of Civil War Soldiers.* University Park: Pennsylvania State Univ. Press, 1981.

Bedford, Henry F., ed. *Their Lives and Numbers: The Condition of Working People in Massachusetts, 1870–1900.* Ithaca: Cornell Univ. Press, 1995.

Bee, Robert L. "Fredericksburg on the Other Leg." In *The Third Day at Gettysburg and Beyond,* edited by Gary W. Gallagher, 132–60. Chapel Hill: Univ. of North Carolina Press, 1994.

Billings, John. *Hardtack and Coffee.* Boston: George M. Smith and Co., 1887. Rpt. Alexandria, Va.: Time-Life Books, 1982.

Blight, David. "A Union Soldier's Experience." In *Divided Houses,* edited by Catherine Clinton and Nina Silber. New York: Oxford Univ. Press, 1992.

Boatner, Mark M., III. *The Civil War Dictionary.* New York: David McKay Co., 1959.

Brookes, George S. *Cascades and Courage: The History of the Town of Vernon and the City of Rockville.* Rockville, Conn: T. F. Rady & Co., 1955.

Bythell, Duncan. *The Handloom Weavers: A Study in the English Cotton Industry During the Industrial Revolution.* Cambridge: Cambridge Univ. Press, 1969.

Carter, Robert Goldthwaite. *Four Brothers in Blue.* 1913. Rpt. Austin: Univ. of Texas Press, 1978.

Catton, Bruce. *Glory Road.* Vol. 2 of *The Army of the Potomac.* Garden City, N.Y.: Doubleday & Co., 1952.

Cole, Garold L. *Civil War Eyewitnesses: An Annotated Bibliography of Books and Articles, 1955–1986.* Columbia: Univ. of South Carolina Press, 1988.

Cole, J. R. *History of Tolland County, Connecticut.* New York: W. W. Preston & Co., 1888.

Connecticut Adjutant General's Office. *Record of Service of Connecticut Men in the Army and Navy of the United States during the War of the Rebellion.* Hartford: State Printer, 1889.

Christ, Elwood W. *"Over a Wide, Hot, . . . Crimson Plain": The Struggle for the Bliss Farm at Gettysburg, July 2nd and 3rd, 1863.* Baltimore: Butternut and Blue, 1993.

Darnton, Robert. *The Great Cat Massacre and Other Episodes in French Cultural History.* New York: Basic Books, 1984.

DeForest, John William. *A Volunteer's Adventures: A Union Captain's Record of the Civil War.* Edited by James H. Croushore. New Haven: Yale University Press, 1946.

Erickson, Charlotte. *Invisible Immigrants: The Adaptation of English and Scottish Immigrants in Nineteenth-Century America.* Coral Gables, Fla.: Univ. of Miami Press, 1972.

———. *Leaving England: Essays on British Emigration in the Nineteenth Century.* Ithaca: Cornell Univ. Press, 1994.

Fiske, Samuel ("Dunn Browne"). *Mr. Dunn Browne's Experiences in the Army.* Boston: Nichols and Noyes, 1866.

Fuller, Charles A. *Personal Recollections of the War of 1861.* Hamilton, N.Y.: Edmonston Publishing Co., 1990.

Furgurson, Ernest B. *Chancellorsville 1863: The Souls of the Brave.* New York: Alfred A. Knopf, 1992.

Gallagher, Gary W., ed. *The First Day at Gettysburg: Essays on Confederate and Union Leadership.* Kent, Ohio: Kent State Univ. Press, 1992.

———. *The Second Day at Gettysburg: Essays on Confederate and Union Leadership.* Kent, Ohio: Kent State Univ. Press, 1993.

———. *The Third Day at Gettysburg and Beyond.* Chapel Hill: Univ. of North Carolina Press, 1994.

Glen, Robert. *Urban Workers in the Early Industrial Revolution.* New York: St. Martin's Press, 1984.

Goddard, Henry P. *Memorial of Deceased Officers of the Fourteenth Regiment, Connecticut Volunteers.* Hartford: Case, Lockwood & Brainard, 1872.

Greene, A. Wilson. "From Gettysburg to Falling Waters." In *The Third Day at Gettysburg,* edited by Gary W. Gallagher, 161–201. Chapel Hill: Univ. of North Carolina Press, 1994.

Haas, Anton Henry. "Abstracts from the *Naturalization Records of Delaware County, Pennsylvania, 1795–1860.*" Unpublished manuscript on file at the Delaware County Historical Society, Broomall, Pa. No date.

Hamblen, Charles P. *Connecticut Yankees at Gettysburg.* Edited by Walter L. Powell. Kent, Ohio: Kent State Univ. Press, 1993.

Hennessy, John J. *Return to Bull Run: The Campaign and Battle of Second Manassas.* New York: Simon and Schuster, 1993.

Hirst, Benjamin. Pension File WC 688-730, National Archives Military Service Branch, Washington, D.C.

———. "War Papers: History of Co. D, 14th Regt., Conn. Vols." Nos. 1–44. *Rockville* [Conn.] *Journal,* 3 Feb. 1887–9 Feb. 1888.

Hirst, John. Pension File WC 666-960. National Archives Military Service Branch, Washington, D.C.

Hirst, Joseph. Pension File SC 52015. National Archives Military Service Branch, Washington, D.C.

Hirst Letters. Historical Collection. Alden Skinner Camp #45, Sons of Union Veterans of the Civil War, Rockville, Conn.

Hunt, Henry J. "The Third Day at Gettysburg." In *Battles and Leaders of the Civil War.* Vol 3. Edited by Robert Underwood Johnson and Clarence C. Buel. New York: Century, 1887–88.

Jimerson, Randall C. *The Private Civil War: Popular Thought During the Sectional Conflict.* Baton Rouge: Louisiana State Univ. Press, 1988.

LaFantasie, Glenn, ed. *Gettysburg: The Narratives of Lt. Frank Haskell, U.S.A., and Col. William C. Oates, C.S.A.* New York: Bantam Books, 1992.

Linderman, Gerald F. *Embattled Courage: The Experience of Combat in the American Civil War.* New York: Free Press, 1987.

Lowry, Thomas P. *The Story the Soldiers Wouldn't Tell: Sex in the Civil War.* Mechanicsburg, Pa.: Stackpole Books, 1994.

McCarthy, Carlton. *Detailed Minutiae of Soldier Life in the Army of Northern Virginia, 1861–1865.* Richmond, 1882. Rpt. Alexandria, Va.: Time-Life Books, 1982.

McPherson, James M. *What They Fought For, 1861–1865.* Baton Rouge and London: Louisiana State Univ. Press, 1994.

Mitchell, Reid. *Civil War Soldiers: Their Expectations and Their Experiences.* New York: Simon & Schuster, 1988.

———. "The Northern Soldier and His Community." In *Toward a Social History of the American Civil War,* edited by Maris A. Vinovskis, 78–92. New York: Cambridge Univ. Press, 1990.

———. *The Vacant Chair: The Northern Soldier Leaves Home.* New York and Oxford: Oxford Univ. Press, 1993.

Murphy, Teresa Anne. *Ten Hours' Labor, Religion, Reform, and Gender in Early New England.* Ithaca: Cornell Univ. Press, 1992.

Niven, John. *Connecticut for the Union.* New Haven: Yale Univ. Press, 1965.

Page, Charles D. *History of the Fourteenth Regiment, Connecticut Vol. Infantry.* Meriden, Conn.: Horton, 1906.

Pfanz, Harry W. *Gettysburg: The Second Day.* Chapel Hill: Univ. of North Carolina Press, 1987.

———. *Gettysburg: Culp's Hill and Cemetery Hill.* Chapel Hill: Univ. of North Carolina Press, 1993.

Redfield, Robert. "The Primitive World View." *Proceedings of the American Philosophical Society* 96 (1952): 30–36.

Robertson, James I., Jr. *Soldiers Blue and Gray.* Columbia: Univ. of South Carolina Press, 1988.

Rose, Anne C. *Victorian America and the Civil War.* New York: Cambridge Univ. Press, 1992.

Scott, Newton. *Letters from an Iowa Soldier in the Civil War.* Compiled by William Scott Proudfoot. 1994. Rev. 1997. Internet website: http://www.ucsc.edu/civil-war-letters/home.html.

Shelton, Cynthia J. *The Mills of Manayunk: Industrialization and Social Conflict in the Philadelphia Region, 1787–1837.* Baltimore: Johns Hopkins Univ. Press, 1986.

Shuttleworth, James Phillips Kay. *The Moral and Physical Condition of the Working Classes Employed in the Cotton Manufacture in Manchester.* 2d ed. London: James Ridgway, 1832. Rpt. New York: August M. Kelley Publishers, 1970.

Siracusa, Carl. *A Mechanical People: Perceptions of the Industrial Order in Massachusetts, 1815–1880.* Middletown, Conn.: Wesleyan Univ. Press, 1979.

Stanley, Sir Henry M. "Henry Stanley Fights with the Dixie Grays at Shiloh." In *The Blue and the Gray,* edited by Henry Steele Commager, 351–59. Indianapolis: Bobbs-Merrill, 1950. Rpt. New York: Fairfax Press, 1982.

Stevens, H. S. *Souvenir of the Excursion to Battlefields by the Society of the Fourteenth Connecticut Regiment and Reunion at Antietam September 1891; With History and Reminiscences of Battles and Campaigns of the Regiment on the Fields Revisited.* Washington, D.C.: Gibson Brothers, 1893.

Stewart, George R. *Pickett's Charge: A Microhistory of the Final Attack at Gettysburg, July 3, 1863.* Boston: Houghton Mifflin, 1959. Rpt. New York: Fawcett, 1963.

Trinque, Bruce A. "Rebels Across the River." *America's Civil War,* Sept. 1994, 38–45, 88.

———. "Arnold's Battery and the 26th North Carolina." *America's Civil War,* Jan. 1995, 61–67.

U.S. War Dept. *The War of the Rebellion: A Compilation of the Official Records of the Union and Confederate Armies.* 128 vols. Washington, D.C.: Govt. Printing Office, 1880–1900.

Wallace, Anthony F. C. "Revitalization Movements." *American Anthropologist* 58 (1956): 264–81.

———. *Culture and Personality.* New York: Random House, 1961.

———. *Rockdale: The Growth of an American Village in the Early Industrial Revolution.* New York: Knopf, 1978.

Watkins, Sam R. *"Co. Aytch," Maury Grays, First Tennessee Regiment; Or, A Side Show of the Big Show.* Nashville: Cumberland Presbyterian Publ. House, 1882. Rpt. Wilmington, N.C.: Broadfoot, 1987.

Weber, Max. *Protestant Ethic and the Spirit of Capitalism,* translated by Talcott Parsons. New York: Scribner, 1958.

Wiley, Bell Irvin. *The Life of Johnny Reb: The Common Soldier of the Confederacy.* Baton Rouge: Louisiana State Univ. Press, 1943. Rpt. 1978.

———. *The Life of Billy Yank: The Common Soldier of the Union.* Baton Rouge: Louisiana State Univ. Press, 1952. Rpt. 1978.

Zonderman, David A. *Aspirations and Anxieties: New England Workers and the Mechanized Factory System, 1815–1850.* New York: Oxford Univ. Press, 1992.

Index

The Boys From Rockville was designed and typeset on a Macintosh computer system using PageMaker software. The text and titles are set in Minion with Arabesque Ornaments. This book was designed by Todd Duren, composed by Angela Stanton, and manufactured by Thomson-Shore, Inc. The recycled paper used in this book is designed for an effective life of at least three hundred years.